THE GOLDEN EGG

BOOKS BY
GERALD CARSON

The Old Country Store
Cornflake Crusade
The Roguish World of Doctor Brinkley
One for a Man, Two for a Horse
The Social History of Bourbon
The Polite Americans
Men, Beasts, and Gods
The Golden Egg: The Personal Income Tax:
Where It Came From, How It Grew

THE GOLDEN EGG

EGG

The Personal Income Tax
Where It Came From,
How It Grew

by

GERALD CARSON

HOUGHTON MIFFLIN COMPANY BOSTON
1977

A portion of this book has
appeared in *American Heritage*.

The quotation from *The People, Yes* by Carl Sandburg,
copyright, 1936, by Harcourt Brace Jovanovich, Inc.,
copyright, 1964, by Carl Sandburg, is reprinted by
permission of the publishers. The quotations from
The Partners by Louis Auchincloss are reprinted by
permission of Houghton Mifflin Company.

Library of Congress Cataloging in Publication Data

Carson, Gerald.
    The golden egg.

    Includes bibliographical references and index.
    1. Income tax — United States — History.   I. Title.
HJ4652.C29   336.2'42'0973   76-30347
ISBN 0-395-25177-X

Printed in the United States of America

c   10   9   8   7   6   5   4   3   2   1

To

The Ways and Means Committee

of the House of Representatives

and

The Senate Committee on Finance

Except as Hereinafter Provided

A certain man had a wonderful goose that always laid golden eggs. But thinking to seize the whole treasure at once, he killed the goose. So, trying to become rich all at once, he lost his steady supply of Gold.
MORAL: Don't be greedy or you will end up with nothing.

— Aesop's Fables

Acknowledgments

MY THANKS go first to Oliver Jensen, who suggested that an article of mine on the history of the personal income tax which appeared in *American Heritage* (December 1973) under his editorship was in effect the outline for a full-length book; and to E. M. Halliday, who urged the idea in persuasive terms.

Libraries and other institutions whose resources and helpful reference staffs made it possible to go forward with the project include the American Institute of Certified Public Accountants; Chamber of Commerce of the United States; the Conference Board; Department of the Treasury; District of Columbia Public Library; the Free Library of Philadelphia; Hennepin County Library, Minneapolis, Minnesota; the Edsel Ford Memorial Library, Hotchkiss School; Mid-Hudson Libraries and its affiliate, the Millerton Free Library; the New-York Historical Society; Library of Congress, Economics Division; the New York Public Library; the New York State Library including the Law Library; Public Interest Economics Foundation; Tax Foundation, Inc.; University of Chicago Library; Vassar College Library; the Will Rogers Memorial, Claremore, Oklahoma. Lee Dalzell of the Williams College Library graciously verified a number of references. I am grateful also to the editorial department of the *Christian Science Monitor,* and to Joseph F. McCarthy, Chief Librarian, New York *Daily News,* and Philip Wisner at the *Wall Street Journal* who were responsive in making materials available from their archives.

Donald C. Alexander, Commissioner of Internal Revenue, reacted positively to the projected work. I am indebted to P. L. Rothchild, Assistant to the Commissioner (Public Affairs), and to Terence F. Gastelle, who arranged interviews, found the answers to varied and sometimes troublesome questions, checked out facts and gave generously of his time, as did Miss Patricia Thomas, Librarian, Chief Counsel's Library. This cooperation does not imply, however, that the imprimatur of the Internal Revenue Service was asked for, or received.

An incomplete list of individuals to whom I wish to express my appreciation for many different kinds of assistance includes Professor Robert Allen; Frederick Anderson, Editor, Mark Twain Papers; Richard A. Baker, Historian, United States Senate; Boris I. Bittker of the Yale Law School; Walter J. Blum, Professor of Law, University of Chicago; William Bonner, Associate Director, National Taxpayers Union; James H. Boren; Louise Brown, Tax Reform Research Group; Debby Covington, who sells books yet gave me a useful book on tax practice; Alfred B. Fitt, General Counsel, Congressional Budget Office; Sara C. Forden, who followed tax news for me in the Washington *Post* and translated an article from the German; Herman A. Gray, former professor of law, New York University; U.S. senators Mark O. Hatfield, Edmund S. Muskie, and William Proxmire; Lawrence J. Horan, Associate Economist, The Equitable Life Assurance Society of the United States; Joanne B. McDermott, Executive Assistant to Dr. Laurence N. Woodworth,

Joint Committee on Internal Revenue Taxation; Richard Morgan and John F. Shelby, *International Herald Tribune*; Professor Margaret G. Myers and Dr. David Weinberg of the Economics Department and Professor Louis Pamplune of the French Department, Vassar College; Richard M. Ketchum; Jerry D. Klepner, Director of Communications, National Treasury Employees Union; Dr. Joseph A. Pechman, Director of Economic Studies, the Brookings Institution; William G. Phillips, Staff Director, Foreign Operations and Government Information Subcommittee of the Committee on Government Operations; Barbara J. Smith, editor, *Imprimis*, Hillsdale College; Mr. and Mrs. Philip Long; Susan A. Stephens, Assistant Professor, Department of Classics, Yale University; Margaret Cox Sullivan, President, Stockholders of America, Inc.

Extraordinary and crucial assistance came from members of the Washington Bar who read the manuscript and made valuable comments, corrections, and clarifications: Clifton E. Curtis and Gail Harmon of Roisman, Kessler & Cashdan and Michael Mulroney of Lee, Toomey & Kent. John T. Koehler of Hudson, Creyke, Koehler, Brown & Tack interpreted the "Cohan rule" for me (see Chapter 12). John P. Manwell of Kirkland, Ellis & Rowe provided historical details of American Bar Association positions on the income tax. Responsibility for any errors which may remain rests solely, of course, upon the author.

Special words of appreciation are due my agent, Henriette Neatrour of Curtis Brown, Ltd., and to my editor, Robert Cowley, for patience, professionalism, and friendship. All of the departments at Houghton Mifflin Company concerned with turning a typescript into a finely crafted volume performed their specialized tasks with high competence. My wife, Lettie Gay Carson, took time from her own crowded schedule, as she has done so many times before, to listen, encourage, read and read again and ask pointed questions, such as "What does this mean?" The completion of this work, then, has been in truth a cooperative enterprise.

G. C.

Preface

THIS BOOK is about human nature and money and Congress, which brings together two, at least, of the world's most interesting topics.

A vast literature on the graduated income tax already exists, written by lawyers, accountants, government officials, angry protesters, pamphleteers, and theorists on public finance. My purpose is quite different; it is to delineate for the nonspecialist reader the historical background of the income tax from its beginnings to the present time and to show its human consequences. This task necessarily entails an examination of the ideology, demonology, and folklore of the tax, including its astonishing expansion from a frankly discriminatory class levy to the mass tax of today, which has made the Internal Revenue Service the biggest business in the United States.

The book deals with clashing social goals, for a tax system is also a philosophical system. You will meet in these pages a scattering of heroes, a fair showing of rogues, and several generations of taxpayers who have labored diligently, ingeniously, and with a deep sense of mission to shift their tax burden onto the shoulders of others. The purpose is neither to praise nor to bury but rather to emulate the French landscapist André Dunoyer de Segonzac, who described his artistic intention thus: *Je n'impose rien; je ne propose même rien; j'expose.*

For over a hundred years the warning has been sounded in and out of Congress: "Don't kill the goose that lays the golden eggs." Regrettably, not all taxpayers or all those who govern us from Washington and invoke Aesop's legendary tale have given sufficient thought to its moral: the greedy who want more lose all. Hence the fable appears in full on the motto page of this book and provides its title.

GERALD CARSON

Carson Road
Millerton, New York

Contents

Contents

PART ONE

PART ONE

1

There Ariseth a Little Cloud

FEW MEN are now alive who had the pleasure or the pain, depending upon the angle of vision, of paying a personal income tax in 1914 under the internal revenue law, which went into effect in October 1913. Trivial by today's standards, the rate was a mere 1 percent on taxable income above $3000 ($4000 for married couples) less substantial deductions and abatements, sloping gently upward to a plateau of 7 percent on incomes above $500,000. Falling upon less than 1 percent of the population, the new exaction was discriminatory, and deliberately so. And it had come to stay. "Never since then," as the *New York Times* observed wistfully forty-three years later, "has the taxpayer had it so good." [1]

Did anyone imagine, one wonders, when the first payment became due on March 1, 1914, that this little cloud, this minor annoyance of the well-to-do, would in one generation become a mass tax, the most golden of the golden eggs? Yet this modest levy shortly became the major support of the federal government and the most powerful economic lever in the hands of our decision-makers for promoting the general welfare as seen from the perspective of Washington. [2] Controversial and often uncertain in its philosophy, ever-changing in its statutory provisions, the individual income tax has, nevertheless, shown its muscle in financing five hot wars and one cold, bringing to justice hoodlums and murderers when all other forms of police power failed, and reshaping the profile of American society. Taxes come in all shapes and sizes, but the income tax stands above and apart from all others because of the size of its bite, its high visibility, and its incidence. Incidence, in case you didn't know, is one of those arcane terms favored by economists and fiscal experts. It is concerned with identifying the person who bears the burden, ordinarily assumed to be the taxpayer himself. There is no escape — except for a few. That is why we read with indignation, perhaps mingled with envy, such a newspaper headline as 276 WITH INCOME OVER $100,000 PAID NO TAX IN 1971, along with the information offered by an Undersecretary of the Treasury that the fortunate 276 "are the barest tip of the iceberg." [3]

A few rare patriots who place a high valuation upon the benefits returned to them in the form of government services believe that they should be paying more than they do, and send voluntary contributions to the U.S. Treasury.[4] Occasionally a celebrity in the entertainment world, guided by an astute publicity man, announces his or her delight at the privilege of paying a stiff tax, and a no less revered figure than the great jurist-philosopher Supreme Court Justice Oliver Wendell Holmes declared, "I like to pay taxes. With them I buy civilization," and for emphasis he said it again in slightly different words: "Taxes are what we pay for civilized society." [5]

The Internal Revenue Service insists that the payment of taxes is voluntary since the taxpayer fills out his own tax return and makes the assessment on himself. This strenuous exercise in citizenship has been hailed by a former Commissioner of Internal Revenue, Johnnie M. Walters, as a "marvel of the world," and another former commissioner, Sheldon S. Cohen, has quoted approvingly the thought of a South Carolina rabbi that "taxes are the rent we pay for the privilege of making our home in a democratic society . . . It is a cheap rent . . . that we pay." [6]

To put a fine point on it, compliance is voluntary but payment is not. Nor is the tax to be regarded as a contribution. The courts have spoken often and clearly on this point. Judge Learned Hand, for example, declared, "Taxes are enforced exactions, not voluntary contributions," and a 1949 decision of the Tax Court of the U.S. by Judge Charles Rogers Arundel included these words: "A tax is a forced charge . . . in no way dependent upon the will . . . of the person taxed . . . The primary purpose of taxation is to obtain money which the sovereign may use in the performance of its many governmental functions." [7]

Every income-tax payer, all the more than eighty millions of us [8] who file our Form 1040s or 1040As each fiscal year, have, when aroused, our own warmly held opinions of what tax policy ought to be and how the Internal Revenue Code should be refined, purified, and Hollanderized, though we may not have, when attempting to describe our fiscal and social outlook, the ready command of such theoretical terms as "ability to pay," "equal sacrifice," or "benefit approach." However, taxation, as the Attorney General of the United States argued in the famous *Pollock* case (see Chapter 5), "is an uncommonly practical affair." [9] Each new development in the tax structure has a ripple effect touching our most intimate lives, our homes, families, recreations, morals, and customs — the whole American scene. First, there are the statutory provisions embodied in the Internal Revenue Code, which, because it's continuously overhauled by Congress, inevitably makes alterations in the social and economic order. The code is supplemented by a vast accumulation of precedents, administrative rulings, and case law, which have added complexities and more than a touch of whimsy to existence since that little cloud appeared on the horizon.

Sooner or later the IRS rules on everything. A policeman can take the cost of his uniform out of his adjusted gross income. A lighter instance occurred in a busy day at the Boston office of H & R Block, Inc., the big tax-preparing firm, when a pretty client asked if she could "take off" her clothes. She was not preparing to streak, however. Just wanted to know if she could deduct the cost of her airline stewardess uniform. The answer: yes. But a fireman is taxed for meals provided by the firehouse because the Tax Court has ruled that that is his "home." Meals eaten by a waitress at her place of employment are taxable unless they are furnished for the convenience of her employer, which is a somewhat unlikely situation. The revenue agent is instructed to question her closely on this point. A commuter cannot deduct the cost of getting to and from his job.[10] But the Congress takes an extraordinarily benevolent view of the business travels of corporate executives, which might, for example, bring a vice president to Louisville, Kentucky, at the time of the running of the Kentucky Derby. In fact, Congress has shown a special solicitude for those engaged in the breeding, training, showing, and racing of horses.[11] This concern may serve well the interests of national defense at some time in the future if the Pentagon should decide that it was necessary to reactivate the cavalry.

We are all subject to the often obscure objectives of the income tax laws — actors who take dancing lessons to increase their skills, farmers, ex-husbands, ex-wives, singles and marrieds, baby sitters, pets (medical expenses not deductible), and Ute Indians owning oil royalties.[12] An undertaker, thinking of future patronage, cannot wine and dine an elderly couple at his country club and charge the festive evening off as a business expense; [13] but clarinet lessons for a toothy boy with severe malocclusion are an acceptable medical deduction if recommended by an orthodontist. On the other hand, when a girl with a 13 percent curvature of the spine took ballet lessons as a regimen of exercise monitored by a doctor, her father was denied medical costs of $8436 for her residence at a ballet academy; the Tax Court decided Leigh had studied ballet before the diagnosis and might have taken the lessons anyway. Similarly, when an assistant projects engineer for a construction company was depressed mentally and had difficulty in standing and walking after surgery for the repair of two hernias, both his personal physician and a psychiatrist recommended that he take up table tennis or dancing lessons for light exercise and a social environment. He chose to dance at an Arthur Murray studio. The cost of the postoperative dancing came to a pretty penny — more than $9000 dollars, which he deducted as a medical expense. But the Tax Court said the Arthur Murray hostesses were not therapists, and the lessons, no matter how beneficial, were a personal expense. Decision: no tax deduction.

Transportation costs incurred in attending meetings of Alcoholics Anonymous are allowable. So are kickbacks to keep a job or an account, provided there has been no breach of public policy. Bribes paid to public officials, however, are not deductible. This is surely a hardship situation since at one stroke it eliminates a large category of possible deductions.[14]

The mix of morals with taxation presents many striking paradoxes to the mind of the puzzled lay observer. Two Minneapolis homosexuals who were married by a Methodist minister filed a joint return. The IRS examining officer refused to accept the declaration, refigured the liability by using the rates for singles, and handed them a refund of $309, which they indignantly spurned. Heterosexual marriages are often postponed or hurried up, depending on the consequences of a tax-timed wedding. Under certain circumstances, two persons who are in love and are both substantial earners find that they will pay dearly for the privilege of marrying, which in effect assesses a financial penalty against their observance of the traditional social code. A divorced couple who became reconciled decided to cohabit without benefit of clergy. Remarriage would have cost them $5460 in income taxes.

The promotion of unwedded bliss seemed to be the objective of the IRS to a two-income couple, Anita and Christopher Murray. They dramatized what they considered discrimination on the part of the law by going through a mock wedding ceremony on the steps of St. Patrick's Cathedral in New York City, she in her wedding dress and veil, he in black tie and escorted by a best man, with Mendelssohn booming out from a tape recorder and a friend officiating in black clerical gown. A placard, prominently displayed, read, "This Wedding Cost $3000 in Taxes." The Murrays have now founded Married Americans for Tax Equality (MATE) to press the government to stop penalizing marriage.[15]

Congress did not, of course, arrange the tax code to favor homosexuals or discourage heterosexual marriage. The awkward situation arose as a mathematical quirk in the hastily drawn Tax Reform Act of 1969, the unintended result of Congress's trying to give singles, and especially the elderly spinster, a better break. But, as Professor Irving Kristol has wryly observed, "The unanticipated consequences of social action are always more important, and usually less agreeable, than the intended consequences." [16] Money obtained even at the point of a gun is subject to federal incomes taxes, though collection may be difficult. The congressional conscience permits, indeed requires, the IRS to tap the gains of embezzlers, swindlers, smugglers, extortionists, and gamblers; and the Supreme Court has ruled that legal fees of a stockbroker found guilty of violating the Securities Act of 1933 were deductible as ordinary and necessary expenses of the securities business.[17]

Educational costs incurred in enhancing a professional specialty are deductible provided the new skills are applied to the same trade or business. For instance, a psychiatrist could study to be a psychoanalyst and the U.S. Treasury would pay its share of the cost in abatement of taxes; but if he wanted to become, say, a tap dancer, the IRS would say no.

Vasectomies are sheltered from the income tax and so are voluntary female sterilizations. The list of permitted deductions could be extended indefinitely — to plywood bedboards, orthopedic shoes, cab fare to the office of an investment counselor — and will constitute a recurring theme in future chapters, where their theoretical underpinning will be presented from several points of view.[18]

Over the years the side effects of income taxation have been ironic, comic, tragic, spectacular, and certainly unanticipated; for many things happen that were not in the minds of Congress or foreseen by the distinguished gentlemen who sit on the powerful Ways and Means Committee of the House of Representatives, mark up the bills, and so produce a superabundance of pistachio nuts, Chinese gooseberries, and catfish farms. Of this more later. (See Chapter 13.) A Detroit man earned one cent too much and found himself in debt to the revenue. His liability: one cent. A Georgia farmer,

subject to a four-cent assessment, paid in one-cent installments to uphold his legal right to make a quarterly remit-
tance. A retired banker who also composed music found that
the instructions to taxpayers began to arrange themselves for
him in the melodic pattern of a five-part choral work, starting
with the portentous phrase "Who Must File," followed by
the incantation "Why You Must File a Return," with a con-
solatory conclusion in madrigal form. In Buffalo, New York,
a woman overcome with worry that the government would
confiscate her grocery store because of reporting errors, went
out of her mind and was committed to the state hospital for
the insane. A happier story came from nearby Dunkirk,
where a navy seaman, aged eighteen, who expected a $23
tax refund received a check for $555,555.[19]

Today one cannot pay a doctor's bill, receive a bonus, win
a prize, buy or sell property, take a customer to see a show,
sign an alimony agreement,[20] draw up a lease, establish a
trust, mingle business and pleasure in foreign travel, or die,
without setting in train certain consequences of professional
interest to the IRS accountants and auditors. Why is it, one
may ask, that the branch of government that touches human
activities at more points than any other gives the citizen such
a rough trip? For one thing, our tax laws resemble an old
inner tube that has survived many a blowout and puncture
and has become a thing of shreds and patches. For another,
the revenue service has to grapple with the accumulated
decisions of the courts and its own complicated rulings. For
still another, the IRS must be armed against the machina-
tions, not of the average citizen, but of the cleverest adversary the best law schools can produce.

Currently, some sixty million income tax returns are being
filled out by somebody other than the taxpayer, thus gen-
erating an estimated $500 million a year for tax preparers

big and little, competent and incompetent.[21] But as long as the income tax law is as complicated as it is, reflecting as it does a balance of political tensions and the complexities of living in an industrialized, high-technology society, the unemployment figures for the tax experts will be zero. As earlier societies have relied for guidance and salvation on philosopher-kings, priests, and medicine men, ours requires the services of well above one hundred thousand tax practitioners to help us arrange our lives as prudently as possible before meeting the fate that surely awaits us each April 15.

The stakes are high. Other industrialized countries pay substantially more in total taxes than we do in the United States. But the distinctive feature of our system is the reliance placed on income taxes. Our personal and corporate levies accounted for over 65 percent of our federal revenue in 1969 and at present make up 58 percent. This is a larger fraction collected from incomes than the revenues of almost any other country.[22] It is difficult to think of government policy decisions in the economic field that are more important than tax decisions. Realistically, they are made under a political system that gives some elements in the community better access than others to the tax-levying process. If individual citizens are to make wise tax choices, measuring public benefit against private sacrifice, we must define our goals and understand the alternatives open to us, deciding whether the rate structure is too progressive or not progressive enough, whether the tax base is too broad or too narrow. Both rates and base must be viewed as parts of a single whole. "Both come from Capitol Hill," Boris I. Bittker, Sterling Professor of Law at Yale University, points out, "which, though less lofty than Mount Sinai, is the only nonsectarian source of revelation in our society." [23]

If the broad objective is the general good, there are also

deep and sincere disagreements among different power centers in their perception of where our best interests lie. There are thorny questions of law, accounting, and economics to be resolved. Social outlook and human nature must be taken into account in determining who should pay and how much. These subjects will be discussed later in more detail. But first, for a historical perspective on the American experience let us turn back to the past to look briefly at some of the ways those who govern have practiced the art of taxation, which Jean-Baptiste Colbert, the renowned finance minister of Louis XIV, described as "in so plucking the goose as to procure the largest quantity of feathers with the least possible amount of squealing." [24]

2

An Idea With a Long History

A TAX ON INCOMES is usually regarded as a modern phenomenon associated with the development of commerce and industry, the emergence of a money economy, and new pools of private wealth.[1] But the rudiments of income taxation may be discerned in primitive societies when public necessities, such as the common defense, began to be felt, and the chief of the clan or tribe was supported by gifts, either of service or property. These voluntary commitments were in time transformed into a legal obligation and their performance was brutally enforced. During the early millennia of recorded history, we encounter taxes on a merchant's profits or the annual increase of a farmer's flocks and herds, as well as the Jewish tithe paid to the Levites, all testifying to the ancient origins of a simple form of income taxation. Even the complex fiscal theory of taxation rising in step-by-step gradations appears in the writings of the Indian sage, Manu, a pre-Christian tax reformer who criticized taxes levied by arithmetical proportion because, he pointed out, the man taxed 10 percent on 100 rupees is actually struck more severely than the man who pays at the same fixed figure on 1000 rupees, and the poor man is rated with prodigious severity in comparison with the man who can touch 10,000 rupees in a year. Fortunately for the Mesopotamian farmer-herder and his adversary, the tax-gatherer, it was not necessary for either to master the vexatious concept of net income. The tax man simply measured the grain on the threshing floor or counted the lambs. But the pressure was there and the consequences of tax evasion thoroughly unpleasant. Furthermore, the occupation of collector was quite lucrative. Thus we have notice of the first taxpayers' revolt known to history, recorded on three clay cones and an oval-shaped plaque excavated by the French in 1878 at the site of the Sumerian city-state in Mesopotamia called Lagash. In the third millennium b.c. the Lagashites threw out the reigning dynasty and installed a new and presumably less expensive ruler.[2]

In Sieburg, Germany, a unique tax museum, housed in an old Benedictine abbey, exhibits a relief piece depicting the Sumerians kneeling to pay their cattle tax. Collection methods were harsh. A bas-relief from an Egyptian pharaoh's tomb shows the tax men beating a taxpayer, one stroke for every day his taxes were in arrears, which makes our present 9 percent interest charge for every day's deficiency seem a minicrisis indeed. For more serious offenses noses and ears were cut off, and again our modern money fines and prison sentences seem to be gentle deterrents. Those without agricultural income were also effectively reached in Graeco-Roman Egypt. The handicrafts and service trades paid capitation, or head taxes, which had some of the characteristics of an income tax, being assessed at different rates on an estimated gross income according to each occupation and with no deductions. Among those rated were weavers, dyers, sellers of linen, tailors, bakers, potters, barbers, vendors of pickled fish, and embalmers of mummies.[3]

Athens, up until the Peloponnesian War, was a low-budget

country with light taxation, a flourishing artistic life and no public debt; small wonder it is remembered as a golden age. Rome gave us the word "tax," from *taxatio*, meaning an estimate or appraisal, and used tithing in the time of the republic. Under the later empire a whole web of crushing indirect taxes made the task of the praetorian praefects (civilian magistrates) so complex that they found it necessary to retain large staffs of accountants, or *scriniarii*, a development that we of the late twentieth century are in a position to appreciate. When substantial amounts of arrears accumulated, and the possibility of collection appeared remote, the sums due were sometimes written off. These occasional general remissions, happy events in themselves, also had beneficial side effects. They prevented "ingenious officials from raking up ancient claims against taxpayers who had failed to keep all their receipts . . ." On the darker side, the Roman tax-gatherers did not hesitate to extract information and enforce payments through applying torture when they deemed it appropriate.[4] The privileges and exemptions enjoyed by the powerful classes, the oppressive burdens laid on the rest of the citizenry, the war-induced collapse of the currency, all weakened the will of the people to resist the barbarian incursions and so contributed significantly to the decline and fall of Rome.

Information on Western European tax practices of the post-Roman era to the end of feudalism is scanty. In the early Middle Ages the rulers enjoyed prerogatives that entitled them to exact personal services, such as road-building and fighting, and levies on agricultural commodities, which were collected by the public officers. Tithe barns for storing the payments made in commodities still stand in Sieburg, and for sheltering the *dime royale* in Angers, France. Later, during the Renaissance, with the expansion of trade and the formation of substantial amounts of private capital, these obligations were commuted into money payments, like the *taille personnelle* in France, which applied to personal property, and the *taille réelle* on the ownership of hearth and land. Rudimentary elements of graduated income taxation have also been identified in the English history of the fifteenth century. In England, as on the continent, there were also numerous roundabout taxes, such as customs duties, market fees, tolls at roads, bridges, ferries, and city gates. All were burdensome indirect taxes on the necessities of life, which were shifted to the lower classes. An exception was the tax system of the city-state of Florence when it was a flourishing democratic and commercial center. A graduated income tax was imposed, reaching at one time 50 percent; it was known as the *graziosa*, or "gracious tax," because it fell lightly on those with marginal incomes. The connection between war and taxation is seen again in a curious episode of the Third Crusade, when both England and France levied an income tax, known as the "Saladin Tithe," to finance the recovery of the Holy Land from the Moslem sultan Saladin.[5]

The modern income tax dates from the time of the Napoleonic Wars. In 1799 the British turned to the income tax to finance the struggle against France when Napoleon I was at large in Europe and a direct menace to England. The rate was 10 percent — proportional, not graduated — with a *graziosa* feature, which excluded from the levy the first £60 of income. Repealed in 1802, the tax was reimposed in 1803 when the war broke out again. The tax was so odious in the eyes of those who were subject to it that in 1816, with the war finally ended, Parliament ordered the destruction of all records.[6]

But the income tax had proved itself. In 1842 Sir Robert Peel's ministry, moving away from heavy indirect taxation and toward free trade, reinstated the tax. For three quarters of a century, the British income tax existed as a "temporary" measure. Gladstone at last, in 1880, conceded that it was permanent. "Temporary" is a risky word to use in connection with taxation.[7]

In the American colonies ruled by the British Crown, government assumed limited responsibilities, consisting chiefly of defense and the protection of commerce; there was no social welfare and only minimal expenditures for public improvements. Taxes collected by the colonies themselves varied by regions, but their impact was light up to the time of the French and Indian Wars. The South, for example, controlled politically by a class of large estate holders, was not hospitable to taxes on land. There the emphasis was placed on export and import duties. The middle colonies employed at various times both the property tax and the poll or head tax, fixed at so much for each adult male, regardless of his circumstances or income. Democratic New England used the general real estate tax and in the eighteenth century collected excise taxes on such luxuries as wines, spirits, carriages and chaises, coffee, snuff, and, of course, tea. To this was added a kind of elementary income tax, or, in the language of the seventeenth century, a "faculty tax," meaning a levy upon the "returns and gains" of the arts, trades, professions, and handicrafts.[8] The tax was not assessed on actual earnings but on assumed earnings estimated at an arbitrary figure according to the occupation — so much for a butcher, any butcher; so much for a baker, or a barber, or an artisan like a blacksmith or shipwright. This tax fell into disuse and disappeared after the Revolution, giving place to the more manageable general property tax. In the 1840s several of the states experimented with the income tax during the boom in state-sponsored internal improvements, such as canals and plank roads, but the taxes were found to be difficult to administer and collections did not bear out the predictions of their proponents.[9]

During the wars against the French, the British colonies in America issued bills of credit and other forms of paper currency to meet the costs. The money was based on anticipated revenue from future taxes, but new issues were piled one on another, the promise of redemption being postponed indefinitely, which brought about the distresses of a depreciated currency and inflation. Then the attempt of the English government to recover the costs incurred in the French wars through new taxes levied on the colonies shifted the emphasis from local concerns to "the great imperial issue of taxation." The result? First, a ragged alignment of resentful and rebellious provinces, each with its own social system and economic interests, all separate entities with little experience in working together, yet finally coming together in mid-1776 under a Continental Congress, which resolved for independence, a decision that still stands as a political marvel.[10]

The Continental Congress could create an army. But it lacked the authority to collect taxes and there was no tangible basis for seeking credit abroad. No other recourse was available than the familiar one, the issue of paper money. Dr. Franklin vigorously opposed it, but the emissions, thirty-seven of them, came faster and faster as values fell, until the squarish bits of yellow paper, worth on their face well over $240 million, slid to a low of $5 million — and that is a liberal estimate. Taxation with representation, the embattled Americans found, was even more expensive than taxation without representation. "'Tis true," as John Locke wrote, "Governments cannot be supported without great Charge . . ." The only consolation for the patriot who was levied on was that this time taxation was, as Locke insisted it should be, "with his own consent, i.e., the Consent of the Majority . . ." [11]

Obviously, to fight a common war, some plan of formal union among the disparate colonies was urgently needed. What came out of Congress was a weak document, viewed as an organic constitution, the hastily improvised Articles of Confederation, reflecting the jealousies of the several states, their fear of central government and a strong executive. The United States, functioning under the Articles from 1781 to 1787, was not the federal nation we know, but rather a loosely drawn league of sovereign states, which withheld essential powers from the Congress, including the power to raise taxes. The national government, therefore, had to rely on loans and requisitions; that is, voluntary contributions from the states, which "came finally," according to the late dean of tax experts, Randolph E. Paul, "to be regarded as a romantically honorable act, or even as a sort of amiable and quixotic manifestation of eccentricity." [12] In summary, the United States could conduct foreign affairs, declare war, make peace, look after the Indians and the postal service, but it could not on its own direct authority pay for anything.

The authority to tax is necessarily coupled with the power to coerce. Reluctant and apprehensive taxpayers often remind us of Chief Justice John Marshall's ominous words on that subject: ". . . The power to tax involves the power to destroy." [13] Yet a government lacking this power, which goes to the heart of sovereignty, cannot long endure. This explains the sense of urgency that spurred the delegates to the Constitutional Convention to produce the framework of a genuine federal union in which the taxing power was central to all other powers. The Federalists, gentlemen of principle and property, could breathe easier after June 21, 1788, when the president of the Continental Congress, Cyrus Griffin, announced that the Constitution had been ratified by the requisite nine states, including the provision that direct taxes were to be proportional to the population of each state, a figure arrived at by counting slaves as three fifths of a person and not counting Indians at all. The meanings of "direct" and "proportional" were not precisely defined and later had to be fought out in two titanic legal battles over the personal income tax.[14] But the principles of a just tax, represented by uniformity and universality, were safely if somewhat ambiguously enshrined in the Constitution, and with the clarification provided by the income tax amendment (the Sixteenth), made possible the financing of American participation in this century's wars, the development of our mixed economy, and the arrival of the welfare state.

It was not easy to lead the turbulent colonists toward the goal of nationalism. "The mass of men are neither wise nor good . . ." John Jay had written to General Washington in June of 1786, when American affairs were in critical disarray. Washington concurred: "We have probably had too good an opinion of human nature in forming our confederation . . . Men will not adopt and carry into execution measures the best calculated for their own good, without the intervention of a coercive power." Soon after the adoption of the Constitution, in 1803, the Supreme Court asserted the supremacy of the judiciary over the legislature; that is, the authority to pass on the constitutionality of the acts of Congress, to nullify them, and therefore to fortify the central government against mobocratic attacks on the rights of property.[15]

When Alexander Hamilton assumed the post of Secretary of the Treasury, he proposed that the United States meet its financial obligations fully and promptly, including the assumption of the debts contracted by the states in the War of Independence. On March 3, 1791, an internal revenue law was enacted placing duties in the form of excise taxes on a wide variety of articles and practices, including sugar, tobacco, snuff mills, mortars and pestles, carriages, auction sales, legal documents, licenses to retail liquors or practice law, slaves, and the distillation of native whiskey. The whiskey excise, especially, revived the bitter memory of impositions by the British Parliament and the unwelcome presence of the excise man. Rioting, stimulated by demagogues, occurred in the back-country settlements of Pennsylvania, a commotion usually remembered as the Whiskey Rebellion. This was an authentic taxpayers' revolt, put down with overwhelming force by President Washington and Hamilton, both well understanding that the authority of the new U.S. Constitution was being challenged.[16]

During the imbroglio with France in 1797–1798 the first *direct* tax was laid by the federal government on houses, land, and slaves as well as any share in an estate, a first step in the evolution of the federal estate tax.[17] These taxes were removed in 1801 during the administration of Thomas Jefferson. There was no further recourse to any form of internal taxation until the second war with Great Britain, known in hostile New England as "Mr. Madison's War," revived and extended the system of domestic taxation.

To fight the War of 1812, Albert Gallatin, then Secretary of the Treasury, attempted a policy of loan financing, issuing irredeemable Treasury notes, which were, in effect, fiat money. Excise taxes appeared again in addition to an extra tax on imported rum because its use by the people was to be discouraged. This tax deserves particular notice as an early instance of the taxing powers being used not only for revenue but also to accomplish a social purpose. Alexander J. Dallas succeeded to the Treasury post in the autumn of 1814, a year of American military reverses that included the capture of Washington by the British and the burning of the

Capitol and the White House. The financial situation was equally precarious. The nation was virtually bankrupt. But a reluctant Congress still resisted the tax measures proposed by Dallas including his historical suggestion, in January 1815, of an income tax. It was assumed at the time that this would not be considered a direct tax within the meaning of the Constitution.[18]

Those citizens who were potentially liable for the tax were saved by the arrival of a welcome dispatch on the evening of February 13, 1815. Secretary Dallas was a dinner guest of J. M. P. Serurier, the French minister, along with the Secretary of the Navy, Benjamin Williams Crowninshield, former Senator William Maclay, John C. Calhoun, and the perennial president *pro tempore* of the Senate, John Gaillard. The company was halfway through its dinner when a servant entered with a note. It conveyed the joyful news that a peace had been signed with England, and the Executive Mansion was illuminated in celebration of the event. During these trying years Dallas, the tall, courtly Philadelphia lawyer, sometimes publicly burst into tears of frustration, and he made this comment upon his struggles with the fisc: "If I was not mad when I came, it is not impossible that I shall become mad before I go away." [19]

The war taxes were allowed to expire in 1817, when customs receipts rose high enough to finance federal expenditures. From that date until the Civil War years, almost half a century, the United States was practically without an internal revenue system. In these decades the government was financed chiefly by tariff duties and the sale of public lands. But the situation regarding revenues was far from satisfactory. The state of the Treasury fluctuated wildly between windfall surpluses and politically embarrassing deficits; and sometimes Congress, being human, went on spending sprees because the money was there.[20] In 1815 the personal income tax was an idea whose hour had not struck. But in 1861–1862 the circumstances were radically different. There was no way for the federal government to avoid such financial burdens as had never been dreamed of.

3

The First Federal Income Tax

THE FINANCIAL POLICY set in early 1861 by Salmon P. Chase, as he took up his duties as Secretary of the Treasury, was based upon the optimistic, not to say fatuous, expectation that the war would be over by midsummer; he proposed, therefore, to borrow rather than choose the hard option of prompt, adequate taxation. The Secretary recommended instead the use of taxes only to meet ordinary expenditures and the interest and sinking fund on loans. Nor did Congress respond energetically to the emergency, though the public pressed eagerly for fiscal measures equal to the crisis.

The borrowing took the form of bonds and $150 million of Treasury notes. The back of the notes was printed in green ink, hence the nickname, often used pejoratively, "greenbacks." They were issued in small denominations under the Legal Tender Act of 1862 and were receivable for all private and public debts except customs duties and interest on the public debt, which had to be paid in specie. But they were not convertible into gold and, in fact, by the end of the year the banks had suspended specie payments. The greenbacks, like the *assignats* of the French Revolution or the currency issued during the American Revolution by the authority of the Continental Congress (Mark Twain: "He didn't give a continental for anybody"), were simply paper money made legal by government fiat. So the Civil War was fought on soft money, with the classical sequelae of inflation, speculation, hoarding, privation for the poor, and a vast increase in the cost of waging the war.[1]

The fiscal package Congress put together in 1861 and 1862 included the restoration of a long and intricate list of internal taxes that had not been seen for forty-six years, the unprecedented novelty of a tax on personal incomes, and sharp increases in the duties levied on imported goods. Whether the lowering of the tariff that had taken place in 1857 caused the commercial and banking panic that came in that year is still a subject of controversy. Certainly the sharp drop in the government's income in 1858 and after could not have come at a more inopportune time. Even before Fort Sumter was fired upon by the Charleston batteries, the Treasury was in a deficit position, or as Representative Justin S. Morrill, Vermont Republican and an influential member of the House Ways and Means Committee, put it, the U.S. Government "was obliged to go to bed without its supper."[2]

The departure from Congress of many low-tariff advocates representing the seceding states made it possible for the overwhelmingly Republican Congress to raise money and provide, not incidentally, generous protection for American manufacturers. The law was known as the Morrill Act because it was largely shaped by Representative Morrill, an authority on public finance and a stalwart protectionist. Another increase in foreign duties came the following year to counterbalance the effects on manufacturing of the income and internal excise taxes. Morrill, then chairman of the Subcommittee on Taxation of the Ways and Means Committee, took up the provisions of the act one by one in a long explanation to the House of Representatives. "The subject," he confessed, "is a dry one, and I have, without exhausting the materials, sufficiently taxed the committee." But he insisted the duty on imports had to go up to strengthen American manufacturers, the "steam giants," who formed the strongest feature of the economy. "Otherwise," he declared, "we shall have destroyed the goose that lays the golden eggs." [3]

The tax on personal incomes, tucked into the Revenue Act of 1861 and of historic importance as a new development in the American federal tax system, was designed to make only a modest contribution to the fisc, suitable for a short war. Many congressmen and senators denounced it even as they voted for it. Morrill, for example, called the tax "one . . . of the least defensible . . . the Committee . . . concluded to retain." The tax consisted of a flat rate of 3 percent on all incomes in excess of $800 a year. It probably could never have passed without the support of western congressmen whose constituents opposed a direct tax on land. Land, after all, was what they had in abundance. Cash income in the range of $800 they did not have. So they cheerfully accepted the tax on dividends and interest, which they would not have to pay. The inadequacy of the 1861 revenue law quickly became apparent. Not due until mid-1862, the tax was never collected. Congress met again, seven months before it was payable, in a more resolute mood.[4]

The policy that guided the second war revenue measure, which was signed by President Lincoln on July 1, 1862, was to tax many objects moderately rather than to lay heavy charges on a few, and Congress searched for taxables with such ingenuity and tenacity that people complained, "Everything is taxed except coffins!" Iron, leather, luxury goods like pianos, yachts, and billiard tables, necessities like drugs, patent medicines, and whiskey were levied on; also railroad tickets, telegrams, dividends and interest, gunpowder and feathers. Thirty-one kinds of documents had to bear internal revenue stamps. Licenses were required for following almost every trade or profession except the ministry.[5] Duties on imported goods went up again. Few forms of property escaped, but the 1862 act did suspend the direct tax on land for two years. An inheritance tax was provided for and the personal income tax was retained in the revised statute, with a lowered exemption and a lift in the rates. The novel doctrine of ability to pay was invoked at this time; it meant a sliding scale on taxable income. This had the effect of shifting a greater proportion of the war's cost from the West and middle South to the eastern part of the United States. The new exemption was fixed at $600 and the rate at 3 percent from that figure up to $10,000 and 5 percent from $10,000 on up, a gentle gradient by modern standards. Deductions were permitted for rental housing, repairs, losses, and other taxes. Securities of the United States were taxed at 1.5 percent, to make their purchase attractive.

There was no determined opposition to this tax statute though some sharp questions were asked in Congress, focusing on the progressivity of the measure. Lines of argument came into view that have maintained their vigor for a hundred years and more. The proponents of graduation argued that it was only right that possessors of large receipts who had at their command discretionary income far beyond what was necessary to maintain a satisfactory standard of living should pay at a higher rate; the other side declared that graduation punished the rich for being rich and would lead to dangerous class divisions. The adjective "communistic" began its long career in the rhetoric of taxation. Yet the personal income tax was only one item in a very complicated revenue law and perhaps it was not remarkable, though it seems so now, that when President Lincoln signed the bill into law a leading Washington newspaper devoted three lines of type to the news, slightly less than the length of the next item, which reported that a law had been passed to prevent the practice of polygamy in the Territory of Utah.[6]

The absence of machinery to mobilize the resources of the nation was a vexing question. The revenue law was drawn so that the Secretary of the Treasury had the power to hire employees to detect fraud and provided for the establishment of a *permanent* tax-collecting agency, the Bureau of Internal Revenue, dating from 1862. The bureau was organized into 185 collection districts, with district collectors, assessors, and assistant assessors as salaried officers. At the grassroots level there were functionaries called revenue collectors, who were paid a percentage of what they collected; this assured their constructive interest in the figures.[7]

George S. Boutwell, Republican politician and lawyer, was the first Commissioner of Internal Revenue, and his oil portrait hangs today in a prominent location in the corridors of the national headquarters building of the Internal Revenue Service in Washington. Notified of the appointment while on duty with the Union Army at Cairo, Illinois, Boutwell took up his duties seventeen days after the President signed the 1862 act. First, he read the law. In a few days he had a clerk, then a secretary, soon a third employee. Within a year the Bureau of Internal Revenue had 149 employees, a modest figure, yet a nice percentage gain for any bureaucracy. The new commissioner looked over the records of the old Excise Bureau, established during the War of 1812, but found no help in them since they were modeled on the system in effect in Great Britain, and in any event Boutwell had no time for leisurely study while setting up collection districts, sifting job applications, preparing forms, instructions, and books of account. Each hurried day brought new crises and the need for novel administrative decisions. Were the male members of the celibate Shaker community at Lebanon, New York. heads of families and so entitled to the $600 deduction? (Yes.) Should a chiropodist have a surgeon's license? (Yes.) Were undertakers manufacturers if they made their own coffins? (Yes.) Were dentists who fit teeth into a plate manufacturers? (No.) Was a boarding house taxable as a hotel? (No.) And so on. Everything had to be done at once without the aid of precedent or experience. Yet the revenue laws were "not merely endured," Boutwell declared, "but welcomed by the people in a manner . . . unparalleled." [8]

Other characteristics of the 1862 income tax law, in addition to higher and graduated rates, were withholding at the source and the opening to inspection of the personal returns to one and all, including the publication of the assessment lists in the newspapers. Each time that Congress shaped a new revenue bill during the war years and after, the two houses hotly debated the principle of the income tax, the case for or against a graduated or a straight proportional levy, and the vexing question of whether to open the personal assessments to the public gaze.

Schuyler Colfax declared early on that he could not go back to Indiana .and say that he had voted for a bill that would excuse the millionaire from assuming his share of the sacrifice while the small farmer paid his. Roscoe Conkling, spokesman for the vested interests of New York, objected to the tax in toto, and Charles Sumner, in the 1864 debate, quoted from Adam Smith and the French economists in a spirited defense of graduation, but by 1870 he was for repeal on the ground that "an income tax is a war tax." James A. Garfield, who entered Congress in December 1863 after a brilliant war record, joined the opposition in denouncing the publicity feature and indeed considered the whole concept both unjust and unconstitutional.

During a debate in May 1866, when members of the House

were looking back at the wartime schedules and forward to the revenue needs of a country at peace, Lewis Winans Ross, a Democratic representative from Illinois, suggested that the income tax ought to go up to 25 percent on incomes above $60,000, which moved Morrill, by then chairman of the House Ways and Means Committee, to reply somewhat warmly that such a requisition could "only be defended on the same ground that the highwayman defends his acts." Morrill had reluctantly supported the income tax as a wartime necessity, including its authority to permit prying, but warned of trouble for the publicity provision as a permanent feature, observing drily that "Americans, like people elsewhere, though not averse to a knowledge of the secrets of others, are quite unwilling to disclose their own." Those opposed to the whole idea of the income tax bore down heavily on the arguments that it was endurable only as a necessity of the war, would be hateful in peacetime, was ever inquisitorial in nature and therefore likely to turn Americans into a nation of liars. And sometimes the debate wandered into such questions as whether millionaires or their sons, or men with $25,000 a year income, went into the field with the army. And if they did, did they go with a musket on their shoulders or with epaulets? [9]

In the summer of 1864 the tax rate went up again, but once more, as in 1861, before the money was collected there was another new revenue act, enacted on March 3, 1865. It moved the bottom bracket up to 5 percent on incomes between $600 and $5000 and to 10 percent on all gains above $10,000. The revenue officer was empowered to raise, on his own motion, the figure of any income he thought was underreported, and penalties running from 25 percent to 200 percent were imposed for various degrees and forms of tax-dodging. The tax was again collected at the source, with no adjustment for the inflation of the currency or exemptions for dependents. This time the income tax made its weight felt at the Treasury as never before, amounting to nearly 25 percent of the revenue internally collected in the postwar year of 1866. The contribution that the income tax made to the war economy during the crucial years 1863–1865 was, by contrast, only 9 percent of the total taxes collected for the period.[10] The reason: congressional reluctance to grasp the nettle.

In the early days of the Civil War public opinion in the North overwhelmingly supported immediate and heavy taxation as the agent of the revenue made his rounds with his complicated forms — each four pages long — and searching questions. But Commissioner Boutwell had a good working knowledge of human nature. Moods of high elevation are hard to maintain, he warned Congress: "Patriotism will do some things, but to tax and to please is not given to man. Whoever taxes the people must provide some way of enforcing the tax." This problem was dealt with minimally in 1863 when Congress authorized the Secretary of the Treasury to appoint not more than three agents to aid in the prevention, detection, and punishment of frauds. Evidently three men were not enough, for as the next commissioner, Joseph J. Lewis of Pennsylvania, acknowledged, "It is certain that immense frauds have been perpetrated, for such have been discovered and prosecuted to judgment or to compromise"; and he called for stronger legislation, noting that "so long as avarice and falsity are a part of humanity, revenue laws, however thoroughly administered, will be sometimes evaded." In a warning that still rings familiar in ears attuned to the vibrations felt annually around April 15, the commissioner gave dour notice that "the duties on incomes will, in general, be assessed more exactly and collected more closely than heretofore. The assessors are armed with powers for investigation and discovery which have not heretofore been conferred . . ." At this time, in 1863 and 1864, the Commissioner of Internal Revenue farmed out delinquent accounts to private contractors, who had every inducement to work like Trojans since they were paid commissions ranging up to 50 percent. And sometimes when their collections had been made they left hurriedly for parts unknown with their own and the government's money. Incidentally, President Lincoln overpaid his income tax by $1250 in 1864. It was refunded to his estate in 1872.[11]

A first-person account by a young housewife describes her encounter with two revenue collectors of Civil War days — a good guy and a bad guy. Kitty lived with her husband, Arthur, a factory foreman, and a small son, Percy, in a neat but modest rented house with a vegetable garden. By good management and strict economy they even kept a servant girl, on a total income of $800 a year. One day a nice-looking and quite civil young fellow rang the bell and left with Kitty a large, official-looking document, obviously not a quack medicine almanac. She noticed too that he knocked or rang the bell at every door on the block. Curious, she peeked at the paper. It was headed "Internal Revenue — Income Tax," and contained a schedule of questions of an intensely personal nature, such as "What was your income last year?" "Have you any Real Estate?" What about carriages, silverware, and yachts? And so on.

Well, Kitty and Arthur — we do not learn their last name or the place where they lived — did have, speaking of real estate, an eight-by-ten-foot plot in the Sylvan Cemetery and they owned some quite genteel though plated silverware, a piano, and the little silver cup her father had given the baby, who was his namesake. Diffidently, that evening, Kitty laid the unwelcome form before Arthur, but not before he had had his supper. Anxiously she searched his face as his eyes ran down the schedule. She felt enormously relieved when he laughed out loud at the idea of his owning carriages or pleasure yachts, or of his receiving dividends or interest money.

"Well, little wife," Arthur said cheerfully, "we need not distress ourselves, for our income is exempt; six hundred dollars are allowed us you will observe, besides our house-rent, and that is all we have, you know." Their liability worked out at two dollars on the piano.

"A single performance on it by you, especially when you add the song," said Arthur gallantly, "is worth that — at least to me."

A few days later the internal revenue man, good as his word, returned to pick up the completed return and looked around the premises somewhat too searchingly, Kitty thought. But there was no contretemps. The following year he was back again, this time like an old friend, and again took away only the two dollars for the piano, for, said Kitty sadly, "our income had not kept pace with that of others around us . . . We struggled on, and hoped for better times."

Then Arthur was drafted for the army. But he returned safely from the war and got his old job back at a splendid advance in salary. Meanwhile their friend at the Bureau of Internal Revenue had been turned out of office and a quite different character appeared at the door. Let Kitty tell it the way it was. The agent was "a man of very coarse appearance . . . Without even taking off his hat, or bidding me good morning, he sat down on the sofa, and . . . with great abruptness demanded:

'What's your income?'"

Taken aback, Kitty said she hardly knew.

" 'But I want to know how much it is . . . how much silver plate have you? — how many watches? — and what do you live on?' "

Greatly agitated, the young housewife said that she would have to get the information from her husband, and suggested that the man from the revenue office leave the paper and return for it later.

" 'Indeed, I won't,' he replied . . . 'You may bring it yourself to my office.' "

That night Arthur filled in the form, calculated the tax at his new wage level. They owed, it appeared, $47. A few weeks later Kitty and Arthur had the disconcerting experience of finding their names in a list of taxpayers printed in the local newspaper. Kitty read the entire list and found it "certainly quite interesting," and commented that "everybody wanted to see it." But her conclusion on tax publicity was negative: "The satisfaction of knowing how much our neighbor was worth was no compensation for the exposure of our own affairs." [12]

Despite the public's complaints regarding the publication of their intimate financial affairs, the practice of releasing lists of taxpayers and their incomes was not abolished until Congress responded by stopping it in 1870. Disseminating the information may, as proponents of the public notice argued, have increased the assessments and consequently the dollar return. It also aroused much resentment and undoubtedly contributed to the growing unpopularity of income taxation.[13]

When it seceded from the United States, the Confederacy used every expedient known to public finance. It confiscated federal specie, impressed military supplies, seized alien property, levied export and import duties (disappointing in yield because of the vigilance of the U.S. Navy), established numerous license fees covering trades and businesses, and issued bonds payable not only in money but in commodities that the army could use directly — foodstuffs and forage, blankets, transportation, coal, and iron. But the policy of the Confederate government, despite the fiscal skill and enormous energy of its Secretary of the Treasury, C. G. Memminger, was to muddle along with taxation as a last resort. In consequence, a solid foundation was never put under the principal and interest of the various loans or Treasury notes that were issued. Meanwhile the disintegrating military situation eroded the economy.[14]

The personal income tax scarcely figured in the fiscal calculations of the Confederate states. The Richmond government, hampered by its states-rights doctrine and an unrealistic belief in a short war, found it less painful to borrow or issue printing-press money than to tax incomes. George Cary Eggleston, who had fought under Colonel J. E. B. Stuart, General Fitzhugh Lee, and General James Longstreet, described, in his *History of the Confederate War*, the approach of his compatriots to finance as having "all the flavor of the Princess Scheherezade's romances, with the additional merit of being historically true." By the time the Confederate Congress passed its first adequate tax act, the Treasury was in a state of collapse, the Cause was lost and with it the social structure of the South.[15]

The direct cost of the Civil War to the North and the South was about $5 billion, not including the cost of Reconstruction, another $3 billion, and leaving out the value of property destroyed, of future pensions, or of human losses.[16] In fairness to the Confederate government's management of its fiscal affairs, it should be said that stability and credit required a support that no financial policy could provide. That was military success. The United States eventually met its obligations. The South's were held to be "illegal and void" by Section 4 of the Fourteenth Amendment to the U.S. Constitution.

"Winning," in the late Vince Lombardi's well-known aphorism, "isn't everything — it's the only thing."

4

Taxes, Tariffs, and Revolt

AFTER THE SURRENDER at Appomattox, when patriotic fervor
had subsided and government finances were improving, cor-
dial feelings toward the income tax evaporated. There was
a broadly held opinion that succeeding generations should
assume as much of the war debt as possible. The public
recalled with embarrassment that the tax on incomes had a
socialistic tendency, and the *New York Times*, wrote Randolph E. Paul, tax expert and Treasury official, in describing
the period, "made the less than startling discovery that the
tax had never been popular with persons with high incomes." [1]
Looking back at the finances of the war years and the role
of the income tax, Justin S. Morrill philosophized in 1866:
"The law was new and therefore not polished and perfected
by experience or revision, but first put into operation . . . it at
once vindicated the propriety of its principles and policy.
Often amended subsequently in consequence of the increasing wants of the Treasury . . . it soon brought forth most
bountiful supplies and disclosed a resource of unequaled magnitude that can be used in any sufficiently urgent crisis . . ."
Looking ahead, Morrill predicted a rapid scaling-down of the
tax. This in fact occurred. But he registered firm objections
to an income tax as a permanent policy. Such a tax "tends

to undermine public morals," he noted, and emphasized that the tax was to be phased out by 1870. Also scheduled for elimination were many miscellaneous nuisance taxes, which "imposed domiciliary visits, always obnoxious to a spirited people." [2]

Congress lost no time in walking around the problem. It promptly lowered the rates, raised the exemptions, and so liberalized the deductions that the legislators, fearing a deficiency at the Treasury, reversed course and extended the income tax for two years beyond the original 1870 cutoff date. Many taxpayers who had stood foursquare behind the tax during the national emergency were seized with tax fatigue under postwar conditions. The price rise was over. Profits were under pressure. Evasion of the tax was widespread, as were ugly rumors, later confirmed, of irregularities in the Bureau of Internal Revenue itself. As was noted in the previous chapter, the confidentiality of tax returns was restored in 1870. This protection may have made a considerable number of taxpayers more willing to compromise with conscience; certainly there was a new tolerance toward tax-dodging among the public generally.[3]

Mark Twain expressed his disgust with this shifting and waffling at tax time. Under the guise of humorous autobiography, he describes an encounter with a tax assessor. Mark Twain comes off very much the antihero in the story, but whether the "I" was really the author is extremely doubtful: satire cast in the first-person form was one of his most effective literary devices. Anyway, Mark Twain's persona receives a visit from a revenue agent whose line of work the author did not quite grasp during the stranger's visit. So he thought to himself that he would draw out his caller, who seemed rather uncommunicative, by being very candid and even exaggerating a bit about his own affairs. He said:

"Now you never would guess what I made lecturing this winter and last spring?"

"No — don't believe I could, to save me. Let me see — let me see. About two thousand dollars, maybe? But no; no sir, I know you couldn't have made that much. Say seventeen hundred, maybe?"

"Ha! ha! I knew you couldn't. My lecturing receipts for last spring and this winter were fourteen thousand seven hundred and fifty dollars. What do you think of that?"

"Why, it is amazing — perfectly amazing. I will make a note of it. And you say even this wasn't all?"

"All! Why bless you, there was my income from the *Daily Warhoop* for four months — about — about — well, what should you say to about eight thousand dollars, for instance?"

"Say! . . . Eight thousand! I'll make a note of it. Why man! — and on top of all this I am to understand that you had still more income?"

"Ha! ha! ha! Why, you're only in the suburbs of it, so to speak. There's my book *The Innocents Abroad* — price $3.50 to $5.00, according to the binding. Listen to me. Look me in the eye. During the last four months and a half, saying nothing of sales before that, but just simply during the four months and a half, we've sold ninety-five thousand copies of that book . . . Think of it. Average four dollars a copy, say. It's nearly four hundred thousand dollars, my son. I get half."

"The suffering Moses! I'll set *that* down . . . Upon my word, the grand total is about two hundred and thirteen or fourteen thousand dollars! *Is* that possible?"

"Possible! If there's any mistake it's the other way . . ."

Well, the gentleman got up to go and handed the writer an envelope. He said "that I would find out all about his business in it; and that he would be happy to have my custom . . . and that he used to think there were several wealthy men in the city, but when they came to trade with him, he

discovered that they barely had enough to live on . . ." In
fact it had been so long since he had seen a rich man face to
face that "this simple-hearted stranger" actually embraced
the wealthy author and shed tears down the back of his neck.

Alone, Mark Twain opened the supposed "advertisement."
It was "nothing in the world but a wicked tax-return — a
string of impertinent questions about my private affairs, oc-
cupying the best part of four foolscap pages of fine print —
questions, I may remark, gotten up with . . . marvelous ingenuity . . . By working on my vanity, the stranger had
seduced me into declaring an income of $214,000. By law,
$1000 of this was exempt from income-tax — the only relief
I could see, and it was only a drop in the ocean. At the legal
five per cent, I must pay to the Government the sum of ten
thousand six hundred and fifty dollars, income-tax!"

So the author called upon a certain rich man who lived
in opulent fashion yet had no income "as I have often noticed
by the revenue returns . . . He . . . put on his glasses, he took
his pen, and presto! — I was a pauper! . . . He did it simply
by deftly manipulating the bill of 'Deductions'. . ." And when
he was done, Mark Twain's income had been reduced to
"one thousand two hundred and fifty dollars and forty cents."

"Now," he said, "the thousand dollars is exempt by law.
What you want to do is to go over and swear this document in
and pay tax on the two hundred and fifty dollars."

The author inquired if his friend worked up the deductions in this fashion in his own case. The answer was, of
course, yes; otherwise "I should be beggared every year to
support this hateful and wicked, this extortionate and tyran-
nical government."

And so since the gentleman was "among the very best of
the solid men of the city . . . I bowed to his example. I went
down to the revenue office, and under the accusing eyes of
my old visitor I stood up and swore to lie after lie, fraud after

fraud, villainy after villainy, till my soul was coated inches and inches thick with perjury, and my self-respect gone for ever and ever.

"But what of it? It is nothing more than thousands of the richest and proudest, and most respected, and honored, and courted men in America do every year." [4]

The New York *Tribune*, spokesman for the Standing Order, expressed its displeasure with the extension of a tax that was "odious, vexatious, inquisitorial, and unequal . . . a tax on honesty . . ." The upper-class New York outlook appears also in a confidential remark of Clarkson N. Potter, himself a member of Congress at the time. Potter was sure, early in 1870, that the "demoralizing, unequal, unconstitutional income tax will *not* be repealed or essentially modified . . . Of course, all who evade the tax," Potter continued bitterly to a friend who cordially agreed with him, "like to see it continued." [5]

At the end the tax ran out the clock at the minuscule rate of 2.5 percent above a generous exemption of $2000. The last time the tax was assessed, in 1872, only 72,949 citizens filed returns that required the payment of a tax. The states west of the Alleghenies put up a fight to keep the tax since it fell largely upon the East. But the moneyed interests wanted the revenue from the personal income tax cut off so that the Treasury would be compelled to retain import duties at a high level. Plainly, the income tax had become a political liability to the Grant administration though it was, the historian Allan Nevins has written, "the fairest single element in the revenue system . . ." During the whole period of the act's existence, the constitutionality of the Civil War income tax was never tested in the courts, but it was sustained in a case that reached the Supreme Court in 1880. William M. Springer, of Springfield, Illinois, had refused to pay an income tax due under the act of 1865 and raised the issue of the law's constitutionality. The government took Springer's two town lots, dwelling, and barn by distraint — seizure of property to enforce a claim — and assessed a penalty of 10 percent in addition. The high court decided that this did not deprive the delinquent taxpayer of due process and that the tax could be levied against his income, because it was not a direct tax within the meaning of the Constitution, but an excise or duty.[6] Fifteen years later the Court said precisely the opposite.

After 1868 and extending all the way to 1913, nearly 90 percent of all collections came from excises on spirits, fermented liquors, and tobacco. The Bureau of Internal Revenue no longer had a complicated income tax to administer. But the country was now well acquainted with the tax as a fiscal device of enormous potential: it had a bright future. The internal revenue collection staff, meanwhile, was not dismantled. It was heavily engaged with taxation employed as a regulatory tool, as in the enforcement of the tax levied in 1886 on oleomargarine and in the later use, for a further example, of the taxing power to eliminate the manufacture of dangerous white phosphorus matches. Another duty of the staff was to enforce the federal excise taxes on beverage alcohol, a function that produced a major scandal in the early 1870s, when distillers and revenue officers conspired to run untaxed whiskey. A special problem for the revenue agents was moonshine whiskey. In the states of the Old Confederacy the distillation of untaxed "brush whiskey" was not merely an ancient folkway; among unreconstructed rebels it was a positive act of patriotism based upon the legalistic states-rights argument that there really hadn't been any general government since the South withdrew from the Union.[7]

The postwar years were a *belle époque* for the Republican Party, which claimed credit for winning the war — "Vote as you shot," it urged the veterans of the Grand Army of the Republic — and the Republicans blamed the Democrats for the war debt and the millions spent for bounties, pensions, and other war claims. If they dared not say that all Democrats were rebels, they could at least make a plausible case for saying that all rebels were Democrats. Meanwhile, with the economy growing spectacularly, the manufacturing interests wanted high prices, low interest rates, a highly protected domestic market, taxes that would fall on the consumer and on agricultural products. What prevailed was orthodox economics, whose pious study "was an attempt to ascertain the will of God" and led directly to "the idea that the Almighty had ordained the use of gold and silver as money." [8] Business boomed on easy credit until speculation got out of hand in the Panic of 1873, which strengthened the hand of those money theorists who wanted soft currency and led to the formation of the Greenback Party. In the subsequent clash of philosophies, however, the advocates of hard money, called derisively "Gold Bugs" by the Greenbackers, won out, and the gold standard was revived in 1879.

The crisis of '73 was followed by six years of distress, with industrial warfare in the cities, drought and crop failures on the western plains. When wheat fell below fifty cents a bushel and corn was worth more as fuel than as feed, thousands of pioneers backtracked eastward, leaving behind bitter legends of defeat, like the one found chalked on the door of a deserted cabin. It ended: "6 inches to hell. God bless our home! Gone to live with wife's folks." Or the contemporary ballad:

> How happy I am on my government claim,
> Where I've nothing to lose and nothing to gain.
> Nothing to eat and nothing to wear,
> Nothing from nothing is honest and square . . .
> There's nothing will make a man hard and profane
> Like starving to death on a government claim.[9]

Various events and policies served to keep the income tax issue alive as a mechanism for equalizing economic opportunity. Among them were:

- Depressions in 1873–1879, 1882–1885, and 1893–1897.
- The increasing drift toward plutocracy in a race for wealth that appeared to middle-class Americans to be fixed.
- In the West, the memory of "The Crime of '73" (dropping silver from the monetary standard).
- The price system under which the agricultural population sold at wholesale in a competitive world market but paid for the products of industry at the retail level in a controlled economy.
- A stubborn hostility to taxes on consumption, which the intellectual heirs of Alexander Hamilton thought quite reasonable since payment was entirely voluntary. As Hamilton had explained long ago: "The rich may be extravagant, the poor can be frugal." [10]

But congressmen with agrarian constituencies regularly introduced bills favoring railroad regulation, cheap money, free silver, trust-busting, income and inheritance taxes. All these tax proposals, of course, were referred to the Committee on Ways and Means, where they had a persistent tendency to disappear.[11]

The recurring debate on the income tax question after the tax was supposedly dead was accompanied on both sides by mordant denunciation and bloodletting adjectives. For instance, George Templeton Strong, New York lawyer, Columbia University trustee, and Trinity Church vestryman, a member of the Upper Ten, exploded in a diary entry dated April 28, 1874: "Here is a bill introduced to restore that iniquitous, unconstitutional, demoralizing, infernal income tax. It's supported by the spite of Western and Southern inflationists against the East. If it passes, I'll expatriate myself." And when Congress took up the issue seriously, Senator John Sherman of Ohio, a former chairman of the Senate Finance Committee and a Republican with the highest conservative credentials, called the proposal "socialism, communism, devilism." [12]

All the elements — farmers, trade unionists, small businessmen, and Greenbackers — that were soon to coalesce into the Populist Party lined up against the leadership in the House of Representatives. But Republican administrations continued to prefer financing the operations of government through taxes on consumption. The business of America was business, as President Calvin Coolidge said so memorably a generation later. More than that, it was big business, and it was sheltered by the due process clause of the Fourteenth Amendment. The last part of Section 1 of the amendment became a Magna Charta for the protection of flamboyant industrialism. The language reads: ". . . nor shall any State deprive any person of life, liberty, or property, without due process of law; nor deny to any person within its jurisdiction the equal protection of the laws." [13] Due process was no idle phrase. As interpreted by the Supreme Court it became the rationale for the economic theory that the government must keep its hands off business. The Fourteenth Amendment merely incorporated into constitutional law the law of "survival of the fittest" as expounded by Herbert Spencer, and for some fifty years the justices of the Supreme Court handed down decisions that in essence expressed a profound lack of faith in the democratic process.[14]

It was in 1868 that the Fourteenth Amendment was ratified, its purpose being at the time to secure for the freedmen all the rights of citizens of the United States. But from the middle eighties on, the chief beneficiaries of the amendment were those who pooled large amounts of capital and operated under the corporate form of organization. Much ink has been spilled over how this diversion came about. Corporations had been legislated against severely by the individual states. Yet they were wanted and needed for the development of the natural resources of the country because they solved problems of liability, adequate capital for undertaking large affairs, and diffusion of ownership among a wide public; and they operated on the broad scale necessary to serve national markets. Furthermore, they provided the element of permanence absent from small proprietorships or partnerships. Those who lived in the agricultural economy, despite their discontents, wanted the sewing machines, the gang plows, disc harrows, and improved reapers; they wanted top buggies, fancy whips, and pretty laprobes — and these the new industrialism could provide. Yet the corporations were at the same time hated and feared for their size, their behavior, and their ingratitude for favors received. As Justice Samuel F. Miller once observed, "Corporations lack the human affections." [15] Nevertheless, the Supreme Court decided unanimously in 1886 that corporations are persons, artificial to be sure, lacking the human affections, yet entitled to the same protection as human persons.

According to the "conspiracy theory," which historians have elaborated over the years, the language of the Fourteenth Amendment, guardian and shield of corporate capitalism, was not the consequence of inadvertence or faulty legal draftsmanship. Rather, the due process and equal protection clauses were supposedly slipped in by clever Republican lawyers who, according to Howard Jay Graham, a leading modern student of the Fourteenth Amendment and its history, "had intentionally used language which gave corporations and business interests generally increased judicial protection as against state legislatures." [16] Graham rejects the conspiracy theory and the point of his influential book is to lay it at rest, but he concludes regretfully that constitutional history makes duller reading without it.[17]

The significance of the judicial tilt favoring property rights and large enterprises may not have been apparent to the average citizen. But the agricultural South and West felt fervently about the price level created by high protectionism, which in their view consolidated financial power in the hands of the few to the disadvantage of the many. For a complex of reasons, but notably because of the tariff wall, the prevailing feeling of the average American was one of resentment and distrust of institutions and trends. There was a sense of being fenced in by malign influences personified as the Money Interests, the Trusts, the Railroad Barons. As the sympathetic economist Willfred Isbell King versified in a scribbling mood:

> . . . the fact still remains
> That monopoly gains
> Are paid for by those outside.[18]

The social unrest of those who felt themselves on the outside culminated in the formation of the Populist Party. Western and southern farmers and their sometime allies in city factories were populist in sentiment before there was a political movement to which they could rally. Grievances, in addition to those already mentioned, included practices of the grain-elevator companies, the weather, congressional generosity with subsidies, and a sense that public morality was everywhere in decline. Examples were numerous and sordid: the gold conspiracy of 1869; the "Whiskey Ring" prosecutions, which revealed corruption in the Bureau of Internal Revenue itself; the plundering of the municipal treasury of New York City by the Tweed Ring. During President Grant's administration an Assistant Treasurer of the United States "was allowed to resign after revealing that he had used the special knowledge of his office to gamble with profit on the gold exchange; a secretary of war . . . resigned after being impeached for bribery; and two Vice Presidents, as well as many senators and congressmen, were involved in the Union Pacific Crédit Mobilier scandals." There was a call for broad reform that would reinvigorate the spirit of direct democracy and enable the scattered majority to place some check upon the disciplined minority. Mingled with such proposals as the initiative and referendum, the direct primary, the popular election of senators, was a demand for the restoration of the personal income tax. This issue was kept alive by farm organizations, union labor, the Populists, and the splinter parties that also made it a part of their protest.[19]

The Democratic national platform staked out a position on the individual income tax, demanding as well economy in government expenditures, equalization of the burden of taxation, and simplification of the internal revenue system, including the "discontinuance of inquisitorial modes of assessing and collecting." With regard to the tariff, the Democrats conducted a cautious crusade, sometimes sitting on both sides of the fence by advocating a moderate or "incidental" degree of protection for domestic manufactures adjusted to promote the prosperity of the country as a whole, denouncing quadrennially the Republican "masterpiece of injustice," which impoverished the many to subsidize the few. To which the Republicans replied magisterially, "We reaffirm the American doctrine of protection," and congratulated the people on being able to vote for a party that had saved the Union and developed the industrial plant and the jobs it provided.[20]

In 1892, after the Republicans had nominated Benjamin

Harrison for a second term and the Democratic Party hoped
to capture the executive department with Grover Cleveland,
the Populists, under the formal name of People's Party of
America, held their first national convention at Omaha,
Nebraska. There they nominated James B. Weaver on July
2 and produced their platform on the carefully chosen date
of July 4 as a kind of new Declaration of Independence,
summarizing the ills of the nation. The protest expressed
total disenchantment with Grantism, upper-class liberalism,
and the jejune "struggles of the two great political parties
for power and plunder." The Populist Party platform included a plank advocating a graduated income tax and an
attack on the McKinley Tariff of 1890.

According to Finley Peter Dunne's Mr. Dooley, fictional
saloon keeper–philosopher in one of Chicago's Irish wards,
the principles of the "Pops," as he called them, were "anny
ol' thing that th' other pa-arties has rijected . . . Others want
th' gover'mint to divide up the rivinues equally among all
la-ads that's too sthrong to wurruk. Th' Pops is again th'
banks an' again the supreme court . . ." And he went on to
describe a Populist convention as reported by an eyewitness,
"a ma-an be th' name iv Cassidy, that thravels f'r a liquor-
house . . . an' he come fr'm Saint Looey." Cassidy said that
at the convention a man was discovered wearing a coat.
Cries of "Hang him!" arose until the man explained that he
wore the coat because he had no shirt. The chairman announced that despite the suspicious appearance of being a
plutocrat the delegate "is all right underneath."

Cleveland won both the popular and the electoral vote in
November. But the Populists gathered a surprising amount
of support in the November election — over a million votes
— and elected five U.S. senators, ten congressmen, and three
governors. This achievement was, however, the high point

of rural America's bid to retain power in a rapidly indus-
trializing nation.[21] The party faded, but its doctrines showed
an amazing vitality.

The revolt took place under colorful leaders. Among them
were Jerry Simpson, the "Sockless Socrates" of the prairies;
the white-maned orator from Iowa, General James B. Weaver;
Mary Ellen Lease, the "Kansas Pythoness"; and the political
and literary theorist Ignatius Donnelly of Minnesota, who
insisted that Plato's lost isle of Atlantis had actually existed
and that Bacon wrote Shakespeare's plays. No less idiosyn-
cratic was the southern agrarian Benjamin R. "Pitchfork
Ben" Tillman, governor of South Carolina, who yelled at
enthusiatic supporters, "Send me to Washington and I'll
stick my pitchfork into his [Cleveland's] old ribs." [22]

Hard times returned in the nineties to embarrass the Democratic Party, then in control of both houses of Congress and
with Cleveland again in the White House after the Benjamin
Harrison interregnum of 1889–1893. The tariff was to be
lowered; that was understood. But politics and the state of
the economy intruded. For there were Democrats, too, especially in the Senate, who were not eager to incur the wrath
and possible retaliation of important trade associations, such
as the National Association of Wool Manufacturers or the
American Iron and Steel Association, or the owners of coal
mines and railroads. In 1894, nevertheless, the Congress,
sounding an uncertain trumpet, passed the Wilson-Gorman
tariff bill. The House slashed the McKinley tariff in accordance with party pledges. But protectionist Democratic
senators introduced no less than 634 changes, most of them
upward. Even so, the Treasury faced a deficit in revenue.
To make up for the loss in customs duties, Congress hitched
an income tax on to the tariff bill. The debates over the income tax proposal were conducted with mingled acrimony
and partisanship, the arguments buttressed by quotations,

apt or not, from Adam Smith, David A. Wells, John Stuart Mill, Major William McKinley, Montesquieu, the elder Mirabeau, Jean-Baptiste Say, Sismondi, and the Chicago *Times*. There were many moving references to patriotism, protection, and the Stars and Stripes. George William Cooper (D.-Indiana) apologized for introducing a quotation from a book: "To my Republican colleagues . . . I suppose I must apologize for introducing a book . . . because if there is anything that will stir up a Republican . . . it is a work on political economy . . . If there is anything that the Republican politician can not stand it is a theory."

The intimation that Republicans were unlettered recalls an anecdote told with gusto by Thomas Beer. According to Beer, Marcus A. Hanna, the powerful Ohio senator who managed McKinley's triumphal campaign for the presidency, thought that Thorstein Veblen's famous treatise, *The Theory of the Leisure Class*, was a chronicle of high-society life and fancy-dress balls.[23]

There was dirty pool on the other side of the aisle on the part of George Washington Smith (R.-Illinois), who slyly introduced the idea that when the Democrats talked about constitutionality he feared they had lingering in their minds another constitution, that of the rebellious Confederate States of America, which specifically barred any tax assistance to industry but collapsed, thank God, at Appomattox. There were the customary extraneous interruptions in the progress of major legislation: a bill to validate the war claims of an old soldier, a bill for dredging Sheyboygan Harbor in Wisconsin, long deliberation on the nomination for postmaster at Pocatello, Idaho.

The rate of the income tax was fixed at a low figure — 2 percent — and not graduated. The personal exemption was high — $4000 — which proved to the East that this was a sectional tax, the sacrifice to fall on New England, New York,

New Jersey, and Pennsylvania. "The Democratic hen," said the New York *Tribune*, "has hatched a Populist chicken at last." And in the Brooklyn *Eagle* words were not minced. There the supporters of the income tax were categorized as "Western repudiators and Southern ex-rebels." [24] There was a replay of all the arguments that had ever been raised against the income tax concept. It was socialism, or worse. The tax penalized thrift. It was a tax of tyrants. It encouraged dishonesty and perjury, bringing on inevitably a cloud of spies and informers, setting class against class. Much of the dialogue was carried on by epithet. As the Washington tax expert Louis Eisenstein has tolerantly remarked, "Taxation is a political process and we should not expect the clichés to be more illuminating than they are in other areas of political contention." [25]

The Senate debated the bill from February to August, thus depriving the taxpayers of fundamental information to which they are entitled: certainty as to who is going to pay what. Business languished and trade stagnated while the country waited for the Democratic concept of what a tariff ought to be. It turned out to be only slightly different from what a Republican Congress might have produced. President Cleveland, who insisted that he was not doctrinaire about the tariff but thought the rates were too high, considered the act to be so inadequate a response to the Democratic pledge of honest tariff reduction that he was unwilling to associate himself with it. The Wilson-Gorman Tariff Act became law without his signature.[26] Almost as an afterthought on the part of those statesmen who had their minds fixed on pig iron, the sugar schedule, and similar regional interests, the country was visited for the second time with an income tax on personal gains and profits.

The visit was to be a short one.

5

The Second Income Tax

THE WILSON-GORMAN TARIFF ACT made an income tax a part of the law of the land on August 28, 1894, effective January 1, 1895, and continuing in force until January 1, 1900. The tax applied to all income of residents of the United States or its citizens residing abroad, with no allowance for dependents. Gifts and inheritances were classed as income, along with profits from the sale of real estate held less than two years and all interest on securities except such federal bonds as had been exempted from federal taxation at the time they were issued. Though the tax was not graduated, beyond the fact that any exempt amount introduces some degree of progression, it spread a wide net.[1] The measure stamped the Democratic party as the income tax party. The Democrats were also charged in Republican rhetoric with responsibility for the horrors of the late Civil War and — George Washington Ray speaking, a war veteran and Republican representative from upstate New York — for arraying "the idle, the lazy, the shiftless, the discontented, the ignorant, the socialist, the anarchist and the Mugwump" against the beneficent high protective tariff that had made America rich and prosperous. "The very roosters," Ray told the House, "were crowing more proudly, and every hen, as she came from her nest, having deposited the freshly laid egg, cackled forth the praises of protection . . . [Applause]." [2]

Republican chieftains heartily hoped that the income tax law would bring about the demise of the Democratic administration, and their wattles shook as they applied to the new law such harsh terms as "unmasked confiscation" and "flagrant spoliation." Actually, with its very high exemption and low rate of assessment, the revenue potential was not great. But the politicians well understood that the statute could always be amended, for the Democrats controlled both houses of Congress and the White House. As an old Arab proverb has it, he who owns the camel decides who will ride. There was a further disagreeable fact: unlike taxes that fall on the consumer, income taxes could not be shifted to somebody else. One consolation: Congress provided stiff penalties for divulging information taken from any income tax return.[3]

Eastern Democrats, aware of the substantial income levels of their constituencies, generally were quiet about the income tax or openly opposed it, though the influential Simeon Eben Baldwin of Connecticut, a founder (1878) and recent president (1890) of the American Bar Association, who usually expressed conservative views on economic issues, gave strong support to the tax. Baldwin said that he believed it "one of the fairest measures that can be devised, to fill up the treasury, without burdening the people at large. Its inquisitorial features are not much worse than those of our town tax list system, and it throws its burden on those who can bear it best." [4]

The new law was received in the West with great satisfaction. In a lyrical mood a prominent Democratic congressman from Missouri predicted that there would be surprising improvements under the Wilson-Gorman act: "The passage of the bill will mark the dawn of a brighter day, with more of sunshine, more of the songs of birds, more of that sweetest music, the laughter of children well fed, well clothed, well housed," and he saluted the law as "the first leaf in the glorious book of reform in taxation . . ." [5] A more down-to-earth explanation of western enthusiasm for the income tax was given to Supreme Court Justice David J. Brewer by a genial friend from Arkansas, who told him that the people of Arkansas were all for the law because no one had income above that exempted by the law and were perfectly content that citizens of New York should pay. By way of homely comparison, he added that "the people of Arkansas were as patriotic as Artemus Ward was during the Civil War, who was willing that all his wife's relations should be drafted into the service." [6]

Contributing to the popular support for the tax was a feeling among the people at large that too much money and property were being concentrated in too few hands for the safety of American institutions. William V. Allen, senator from Nebraska, had scored, for example, in the Senate debates on the income tax bill when he drew from census statistics the fact that 91 percent of the twelve million families in the United States owned only about 29 percent of the national wealth and 9 percent controlled the other 71 percent. Many were persuaded by arguments drawn from the benefit theory of taxation, under which it was a given that the rich man received more protection and service from the national government than others less endowed with material possessions and should therefore pay more for what he got, not proportionally, but according to another, though related principle, his ability to pay. With no pretense at disguise, the tax was "designed," as Louis Eisenstein has written, "for the pecuniary discomfort of the rich." Yet in the minds of a people feeling the winds of change, a great social goal seemed to be within reach.[7]

But certain receivers of large incomes thought otherwise, and commenced a number of injunction suits in the form of stockholder actions to restrain corporations from paying the tax. The issue was rushed with the greatest haste to the Supreme Court. The suit chosen for judicial immortality — several raised the same issues — was brought by a resident of Massachusetts, one Charles Pollock, who held ten shares of stock in the Farmers' Loan & Trust Company of New York. Pollock sued to prevent the trust company from voluntarily filing an income tax return and paying the tax. The constitutional issue turned on whether the income tax was a "direct" tax. The U.S. Constitution required that a direct tax be applied uniformly (Article 1, Section 8, Clause 1) and that it be laid in proportion to the population of the states as established by the census (Article 1, Section 9, Clause 4). The appellants advanced the rather attenuated argument that the income tax was a direct tax, which violated the principle of uniformity since the $4000 exemption let some go free but not all, and so was not consistent with the principle of equal treatment for all. Arguing from yet another premise, the appellants declared that the income tax, being a direct tax, was unconstitutional because the statute did not provide for apportioning the levy in each state according to its population. They well knew that a proportional levy could not be devised: the object to be taxed — money — was unequally distributed. The burden would fall heavily on states that had more people than money, lightly on states with relatively higher per capita wealth. It was calculated, for example, that a poor man in South Carolina would have to carry a load of taxation three-and-a-half times as heavy, according to his means, as a Massachusetts taxpayer, a Maine man twice as much as a New Yorker, and in North Carolina the burden would be four times as great, relative to income, as in New York State. Personal income simply did not bear any relationship to the statistics of state populations. In effect, the income tax became a political impossibility, which was, of course, the object of the litigation.[8]

In 1894–1895 the circumstances were very different from the exigencies of wartime, and a court of different complexion was sitting. It was deeply conservative, in temper a Marshall court, conceiving of society stratified along economic lines. It reacted with alarm to the peacetime innovation of a tax on incomes, which it saw as an assault by the many on the property of the few. Thus the legal issues were inextricably mingled with the social views of the justices, and these became, indeed, the controlling factor in the bench's interpretation of the Constitution. Attorneys for the appellants artfully played upon this political orientation of the Court as their strongest card.

The government's lawyers defending the income tax statute took the position that uniformity as inserted in the Constitution meant only geographical uniformity, a meaning that it applied generally throughout the United States. But it was not required, in their view, that the object of taxation, income, must exist uniformly in the several states. This position was upheld. The question remained as to what the words "direct tax" meant. In 1798, 1813, 1815, and 1816, Congress had levied direct taxes and the Supreme Court had shown "a strong disposition to limit the definition of direct taxes so as to include only capitation and land taxes." This construction was extended to cover the income taxes of 1861 and 1864. But by the last quarter of the nineteenth century the inequality involved in apportioning taxes according to the number of people living in a state had sharpened the issue because of a phenomenon that had not been anticipated: heavy concentration of wealth in the manufacturing states.[9]

The 1894 law was substantially the same as the Civil War statute that had been reviewed and sustained, but the climate had changed. It was not passed under the duress of national peril, representing rather a confrontation of opposing social philosophies.[10] The first decision of the Supreme Court, delivered on April 8, 1895, struck down certain provisions of the income tax law but not all. It left the law in so uncertain a position that both parties joined in requesting that the tax be clearly vindicated or completely annulled.

The justices of the Supreme Court faced a particularly difficult task because they had to try to fill a *casus omissi;* that is, they had to guess what the shapers of the Constitution would have thought about the personal income tax if they had thought about it. There is no evidence that they had or that they appreciated all the implications of the term "direct taxes." Direct taxation by apportionment was adopted as a part of one of the famous compromises of the Constitutional Convention in 1787. But the journals of the proceedings throw little light upon the question.[11] Rufus King asked for the precise meaning of "direct taxation," a phrase Gouverneur Morris had introduced during the convention. There sat Madison and Hamilton and Martin and Pinckney and all the rest of the great lawyers of the day. But no one answered. In 1796, incidentally, Alexander Hamilton argued that direct taxation referred only to poll taxes and taxes on land and houses, and he was paid a handsome $500 for convincing the Supreme Court that a tax on carriages was not direct, but was an excise. "That this tax cannot be *apportioned* is evident" (emphasis added), the Court said. Its decision included a hypothetical example showing that the result of taxing on one basis and measuring the result on another is "manifestly absurd." [12]

At the rehearing in May 1895 the justices must have felt themselves under the tutelary spirit of Chief Justice Marshall, who had led the way in the early eighteen hundreds in asserting that the Court had the power to nullify an act of Congress, as they heard the argument against the income tax law advanced by tall, handsome Joseph H. Choate. In an era of fighting lawyers, Choate was perhaps the period's greatest courtroom advocate. The precedents were all against him. Therefore, skilled jury lawyer that he was, Choate shifted his emphasis to class and sectional feeling, to the political and social arguments that the income tax was aimed at property. Such suggestions, he knew, were congenial to the Court's thinking and might give him the victory through judge-made law. Rising to the challenge of the most important case he had ever tried, Choate told the justices that if this "communistic march" was not summarily halted, there was nothing to prevent action by Congress to increase the exemption from $4000 to $20,000 and increasing the tax from two percent to twenty percent. Eloquently he invoked frightening images of the poor coercing the rich through control of Congress. And then in a happier vein the great orator led the judges up to the top of a high mountain and showed them a Beulah land for the well-to-do, in which everyone, including John Jacob Astor, paid or swore off his taxes. And he shook them with his solemn demand: "Protection now or never. If it goes out as the edict of this judicial tribunal that a combination of States, however numerous, however unanimous, can unite against the safeguards provided by the Constitution in imposing a tax which is to be paid by the people in four States or in three States or in two States, but of which the combination is to pay almost no part, while in the spending of it they are to have the whole control, it will be impossible to take any backward step." [13] Actually, the bill was far from a model of legal draftsmanship and would have been difficult to administer.[14] But the problems of enforcement were not related to the substantive questions before the Court.

Justice Stephen J. Field shuddered and was put in mind of a historical parallel, an English statute of 1691, in the third year of the reign of William and Mary, that taxed Protestants at a certain rate, Catholics at double rate, and Jews "at another and separate rate"; and Chief Justice Melville W. Fuller, who wrote the opinion, was thoroughly aroused and got off some rather cutting remarks on "the speculative views of . . . revenue reformers." And so, under the leadership of Justice Fuller, on May 6–8, 1895, the Court declared the whole law unconstitutional, by the barest of margins, 5 to 4, one justice having changed his opinion. The decision left the matter in this position: the income tax was a direct tax and could not be levied except on a basis proportional to the population of each state. Justice Henry Billings Brown, dissenting, called this "an impossible theory of apportionment," and the decision "the first step toward the submergence of the liberties of the people in a sordid despotism of wealth."

Men of large means felt that the republic had been saved. Choate received a well-earned fee, reputed to have been $200,000, and the 4047 known millionaires in the United States rejoiced as the bridegroom rejoiceth over the bride.[15] Among the public at large the closeness of the decision and the class consciousness evident in the courtroom created consternation and a feeling of alienation. Some good people thumbed their Bible and wondered, "What portion have we in David?" The middle class, the small businessman, the trade unionists, and the agricultural West were convinced that the federal government was run as a plutocracy; indeed, that the Supreme Court, adopting the view that the poor might mulct the rich through manipulation of the taxing power, was out of touch with American political institutions.

E. L. Godkin, influential editor of the journal of opinion the *Nation,* called the decision frank class legislation, and the New York *World* reacted vigorously:

> The overthrow of the income tax . . . is another victory of greed over need. Great and rich corporations, by hiring the ablest lawyers in the land . . . have secured the exemption of wealth from paying its just share towards the support of the Government that protects it . . . No dictum or decision of any court can make wrong right. And it is not right that the entire cost of the Federal Government shall rest upon consumption . . . A way will be found . . . to revoke what Justice Brown well calls this "surrender of the taxing power to the moneyed class."

Professor Allan Nevins summed up the views of most modern students of the period: "It was one of the unhappiest decisions in the history of the Court."[16]

Choate anticipated the wrath of the public. With the magic words of a conjuror he prepared the justices for it while at the same time subtly flattering them:

> I have more than trespassed upon the kind indulgence of the court . . . No member of this court will live long enough to hear a case which will involve a question of more importance than this, the preservation of the fundamental rights of private property and equality before the law . . . If it be true, as my friend said in closing, that the passions of the people are aroused on this subject, if it be true that a mighty army of sixty million citizens is likely to be incensed by the decision, it is the more vital to the future welfare of this country that this court . . . declare, as Marshall did, that it *has* the power to set aside an act of Congress . . . and that it will not hesitate in executing that power, no matter what the threatened consequences of popular or populistic wrath may be.[17]

Not only the redoubtable Choate and his happy clients, but persons of all shades of opinion thought the income tax was dead, and indeed it looked so for a time as other issues — free silver, antitrust legislation, government regulation of public utilities, tariff reduction — occupied the center of the stage. Yet for the rest of the nineteenth century the federal income tax remained, in the consciousness of the West and South, a symbol of fiscal reform.

Early in 1895 an income tax division had been organized in the Bureau of Internal Revenue. Circulars of instruction were prepared, regulations and thousands of forms printed and distributed to the collectors. Some 48,672 individuals had already paid their income taxes, amounting to more than $6 million, when the Court decided the whole law was null and void. All income tax work stopped, and the division disbanded on June 30, 1895. Agents and chiefs were thrown out of their jobs and all returns and tax papers were ordered returned to headquarters under seal. Since they contained much private information, the Commissioner of Internal Revenue recommended to Congress their complete destruction. Congress complied with an appropriate resolution and a committee appointed by the Secretary of the Treasury assumed control of all returns and tax documents and presumably destroyed them by burning on May 5, 1896.[18]

The word "presumably" appears as a qualification in the previous sentence because of a curious episode that occurred in England in connection with the income tax levied to pay for the wars against Napoleon. After peace was concluded at Amiens in 1802 it was generally felt that too much personal information had been given to the government by private citizens. So Parliament ordered all records and returns to be cut up into small pieces and committed to the mash tubs of a paper mill under the eye of a Commissioner for the Affairs of the Taxes; and so it was done. After the breakdown of this peace, however, a new income tax was imposed, and in 1815, when Napoleon had finally been defeated, the pulping operation was, according to tradition, repeated. But in 1939 a modern scholar with an intuitive grasp of the bureaucratic mentality had a bright idea. Possibly *copies* had been made and sent to the King's Remembrancer. Pursuing this surmise, the historian rummaged diligently in the Public Record Office. And there he found what he was looking for in sacks and bundles: the tax records, almost complete, never opened since Waterloo. Who then can say positively that our American functionaries are less faithful in making and saving a copy of everything? Perhaps we shall yet find, in some musty basement or attic, duplicate records of the income tax that the Supreme Court struck down so long ago.[19]

The option of amending the Constitution remained open. It was a possibility that many regarded with reluctance. And it was a slow and uncertain procedure whose outcome could not be predicted. Nevertheless, this was undertaken, though it took twenty years to get the amendment ratified, pass the necessary enabling legislation, and make the first assessment. When the income tax came it was indeed discriminatory. Yet communism did not follow, as the prophets of gloom had warned. "Nor," as one modern historian has remarked, "were all comforts and riches quite lost."[20] As the 1896 presidential campaign, one of the great canvasses in American political history, began to heat up, the question of the personal income tax appeared to be settled. But the country was not satisfied to let the matter rest. Subsequent events demonstrated that the issue was merely in a state of remission.

6

Protecting
the Protective Tariff

WILLIAM JENNINGS BRYAN's brilliant campaign for the presidency in 1896 drew most of the scattered Angries into the Democratic Party. The canvass reflected the metrophobia of the fast-fading small town, the malaise of the Nebraskans who had chanted at the formation of the People's Party: "What is home without a mortgage?" The Bryan campaign train would pull into a dusty town on the Great Plains, the band playing "El Capitan." The handsome, earnest man with inexhaustible energy, longish black hair, and that thrilling voice began to speak of the despoilers and the wicked. Sharply felt, also, was frustration at the defeat of the income tax, the hope that free silver would bring moral as well as fiscal redemption, the fear of remote abstractions, such as "Wall Street," a strong sense of being victimized by a vaguely defined conspiracy. These are only a few of the complex factors that produced disenchantment in the 1890s; and Bryan enjoyed the reputation "of being the most marvelous campaigner America has ever known," wrote a contemporary observer, Arthur Wallace Dunn, veteran Washington newspaper correspondent. The voters turned out to see and hear him. Yet when the ballots were counted, it was clear that Bryan with his devil theory had not been able to convince the country as a whole that his moral millennium would be as prosperous as the here-and-now of his opponent, Major-Congressman-Governor William McKinley, who ignored the income tax but offered the protective tariff, sound money, and generous pensions for Civil War veterans. Even Nature smiled upon the Republican Party and provided an abundant harvest. McKinley won handily in both the electoral and popular vote. Many men who had served in the government departments under Cleveland turned Republican and enjoyed the offices for sixteen more years and didn't recall that they were really Democrats until after the election of 1912.[1]

The Democratic Party platform of 1896 had excoriated the McKinley tariff and the Supreme Court decision in the income tax cases. The Populist wing that had not joined up with the Democrats called on Congress to amend the Constitution so that a graduated tax on incomes and inheritances could be laid, and the other splinter party, the Socialist Labor, similarly demanded progressive income and inheritance taxation, with the lower incomes to be exempt. The haves and have-nots were never more sharply aligned against each other. No matter. The Republicans had the astute campaign management of Marcus A. Hanna and plenty of money, advertising, bunting, posters, placards, supplemented by ready-plated editorials for the small western newspapers, brass bands, marching clubs, hired orators, farmers paid to haul voters to the polls, and golden elephants. They also had a train of Pullman cars, well stocked with bourbon whiskey, liver pills, and mineral water. It was called the Old Soldiers' Touring Special and carried a complement of Civil War officers and a few privates, exhibited to the war veterans, who needed to be braced up for comrade McKinley. The Irish voters received an incendiary pamphlet entitled *How McKinley Is Hated in England*. The Republicans had the lawyers. The legal brotherhood had never liked Bryan and were deeply offended by the Democrats' attack on the Supreme Court and their lack of reverence for the "aristocracy of the robe." So on election day frightened Republicans who had talked of moving their lares and penates and railroad bonds to Paris rethought their position and decided it would not be necessary to exchange the amenities of Fifth Avenue for those of rue Saint-Honoré. In fact, the Republicans seem to have expounded more convincingly than their opponents the answers to the dilemmas of a nation yearning for unity, identity, and prosperity. The Republican campaign itself, Thomas Beer wrote in his biography of Hanna, "was mass production, politically applied . . ." and Beer added that Theodore Roosevelt had once told his father, the elder Beer, that Hanna "advertised McKinley as if he were a patent medicine." Even little Republican children came with the expense-paid political pilgrims who visited McKinley at his home in Canton, Ohio. They trampled the grass around the front porch and chanted with childish voices the jingle provided for them:

> Governor McKinley, he's our man.
> If we can't vote for him our papas can.

As for Bryan, "People liked him," Senator Peter Norbeck (R.-S.D.) said in analyzing his defeat, "but did not have confidence in his judgment." [2]

With the decisive victory in 1896 the Republican Party entered into a period of dominance that lasted until 1910. The order of the day for fourteen years was, quite simply, that business and party leaders together ran the country on the principle that a high tariff wall around the United States would provide ample revenue and ensure prosperity for industry and jobs for the working people. As the benefits trickled down, wage-earners would enjoy what was called symbolically "the full dinner pail." A bill to revise the tariff, drafted by Nelson Dingley, Jr. (R.-Maine), chairman of the Ways and Means Committee, was rushed through an extra session of Congress in the spring and summer of 1897. While it was being marked up there was a mad scramble for pecuniary benefits. Tariff-fixers haunted hotel lobbies and committee rooms to look after the interests of wool, granite, hides, and other commodities. There was the usual trouble over sugar. "Aldrich (R.-R.I.) had formed the schedule and it was a wonderful production," Arthur Dunn wrote. "He devoted several hours to an explanation in the Senate, and when he concluded everybody knew less than before." [3] Maine and Wisconsin joined to save the lumber schedule and rolled logs to achieve their common goal. Even Senator Aldrich, who sincerely believed in government by and for the industrial plutocracy, was filled with disgust for "the trooping of the beggars" through his committee room and the less refined Mark Hanna exploded that the manufacturers were "squatting behind the tariff like a lot of God damn rabbits."

But the mind-set of the Senate was to raise the tariff even beyond the level contemplated by the House, and the Conference Committee accepted most of the increases. President McKinley signed the bill into law on July 24, 1897. The Dingley tariff stood undisturbed for twelve years, the ultimate expression of economic nationalism. Prices rose. "The High Cost of Living" became the phrase of the day. But the public was apathetic and cynical after three revisions in seven years (1890, 1894, and 1897). There was relief that the policy was settled and hope that business would revive now that it knew where it stood. And there was hope, too, that the Treasury, which was in a deficit position, would be replenished. Whether the Dingley tariff would have achieved that object cannot be determined. Before it had time to demonstrate its merits the war with Spain upset the normal course of commerce and business and made crisis-financing necessary to meet the military emergency.[4]

The Republican Party needed a diversion that would nullify the political axiom that the party that passed a tariff bill is doomed to defeat in the next election, and found it in the war with Spain. A tenacious native insurrection against the heavy-handed colonial rule of Spain had maintained a precarious existence in Cuba for a decade, and American popular sentiment strongly favored "Cuba Libre!" There were a number of reasons: genuine humanitarian idealism, the indignation of Protestant small-town America, easily aroused against Catholic Spain. There were commercial relations and investments in sugar plantations to be considered, and indefatigable efforts on the part of the newspaper publishers William Randolph Hearst and Joseph Pulitzer to produce a "Yanko-Spanko" war. Their journalistic enterprise was inadvertently assisted by some indiscreet comments on President McKinley by Enrique Dupuy de Lôme, the Spanish minister to the United States. In a private letter stolen from the mails by Cuban revolutionaries, de Lôme described McKinley as "weak." His remark seems rather innocuous, compared with the fulminations of Theodore Roosevelt, who was, after all, as Assistant Secretary of the Navy, a member of the President's official family. A leading jingo, fearful that war might not come, Roosevelt, who could mix his metaphors in moments of excitement, said of his chief that he had the backbone of a "chocolate éclair." But it was the unfortunate de Lôme's gaffe that was spread across the front page of Hearst's New York *Journal,* under the streamer: WORST INSULT TO THE UNITED STATES IN ITS HISTORY.[5]

When the U.S. battleship *Maine* was blown up on February 15, 1898, by a submarine mine of unknown provenance, the course of the United States was set. The fever for war was beyond control despite last-minute concessions by the Spanish government, which would have fully justified further negotiations. But the "gunpowder men" were determined. As Roosevelt jauntily said to Mark Hanna, "We are going to have this war." The war was mercifully short, a thrilling triumph from the American point of view. Roosevelt promptly resigned from the administration, organized the First Volunteer Cavalry Regiment, a motley gathering-in of cowboys, gamblers, football players, Pawnee Indians, and young gentlemen from Harvard and Yale universities. The cavalrymen were dubbed by the press "the Rough Riders," though they fought dismounted since there was no transport available for horses. Lieutenant Colonel Roosevelt managed to have a mount.

In a smart charge, their only significant military action, the Rough Riders took casualties and captured a hill. Roosevelt, whose elbow had been nicked by a bullet, returned home from what he called his "crowded hour" a full chicken colonel, eager for the Congressional Medal, which, however, he didn't get. But in New York he seized a prize greater than Kettle Hill: the governorship. On campaign swings through the state, Roosevelt was flanked by Rough Riders in uniform. A bugler sounded the cavalry charge "just as had been done at Santiago," and Buck Taylor, a former member of the regiment, testified for his old commander and hero, "He was thar in the midst of us . . ."

A jubilant John Hay, President McKinley's Secretary of State, summarized the expansive mood of the country when he called the four months of hostilities a "splendid little war." An offset to this self-congratulatory frame of mind should not be overlooked: many thoughtful Americans denounced the visions of American imperial grandeur as a falling away from our professed ideals and a threat to our own liberties.[6]

But all wars, even splendid little ones, bring in their train — taxes. The War Revenue Act of June 13, 1898, in effect until June 30, 1902, raised money through the sale of bonds, pushing part of the burden into the future, and through the imposition of nuisance taxes on businesses and recreational facilities patronized by the working classes, such as circuses and other shows, bowling alleys, billiard and pool rooms. Stamp taxes were levied on many commercial transactions, patent medicines, and chewing gum. Pawnbrokers, who were a feature of economic life below a certain level, felt the weight of the tax. The existing rates were nearly doubled on tobacco and beer, both prime examples of commodities with inelastic demand, meaning that manufacturers and vendors could pass the tax along to the consumer as part of the retail price without the risk of diminished sales. Thus business interests escaped any real increase in their tax burden while there opened new prospects of extending the markets for American goods abroad. In the case of tobacco, the packages were allowed to be reduced in size as a war measure. But when Congress removed the war tax in 1902 it allowed the manufacturers to continue with the short weight.[7]

An income tax was considered. But it was not considered very seriously. The constitutional obstacle remained, of course. And the congressional majority had no desire to put the Supreme Court in an awkward position, even as their spokesmen talked of sacrifice for "one cause, one country, one flag." And certainly the men at the levers of power did not wish to run the risk that an income tax might be continued in peacetime. One fiscal novelty did appear — a temporary tax on legacies, enacted as a concession to popular sentiment. It was attacked on constitutional grounds but sustained by the Supreme Court. Fortunately, the brevity of the war relieved Congress of the necessity for further painful decisions.[8]

The successful conclusion of the Spanish-American War, the lift to national pride, the prospect of a reduction in war taxes, buoyed Republican hopes of winning the presidential election of 1900, again with McKinley at the head of the ticket. The Democrats put forward Bryan once more, emphasizing in their platform "the burning issue of imperialism," the evils of monopolies and trusts, and the iniquities of the Dingley tariff. Again those populists who refused to merge with the Democratic Party demanded a graduated income tax, by constitutional amendment if necessary, and oddly enough so did the platform of a splinter group of Republicans, mostly from the silver-producing states, who clung to free silver and income taxation as the salvation of the debtor class.[9]

Since the country had endorsed the Republican theory of protectionism in 1896 and the administration's conduct of the war in 1898, and prosperity was returning, the chief problem facing the party was to settle on McKinley's running mate. New York's Governor Roosevelt toured the country in 1899 for the party, escorted again by a corps of his faithful Rough Riders. There were tumultuous receptions, western jamborees, and an enormous volume of favorable publicity, which put Governor Roosevelt in a leading position for the vice presidency. Hanna disliked and distrusted him, as did Senator Thomas C. Platt of New York. Platt may have been "a little old mangy rat in his nest," as William Allen White thought during an interview, but his well-oiled political machine dominated New York politics and patronage. Platt wanted no part of a Civil Service reformer and

colorful popular leader, a potential troublemaker highly un-
attractive to the New York bankers and possibly able to run
New York's affairs without the advice and consent of the
senator. As early as February, Platt, with the enthusiastic
cooperation of Matthew Quay of Pennsylvania, a Hanna
enemy, decided to transfer Teddy to the office of Vice President to get him out of New York. To no avail was Hanna's
agonized cry: "Don't you understand that there is just one
life between this crazy man and the presidency if you force
me to take Roosevelt?" [10]

Roosevelt insisted that all he wanted was a second term
as governor of New York and assured McKinley and Hanna
that he was not a candidate for Vice President, an announce-
ment they found supererogatory since they entertained no
such thought either. This was before they had heard from
Platt, or fully understood the governor's strength with the
delegates to the Republican convention. But when the faithful gathered in the muggy June heat of Philadelphia, with
torchlight parades and all the trappings of the quadrennial
frenzy, there was Theodore Roosevelt as a delegate-at-large
from New York, teeth gleaming, eyeglasses flashing, grinning
and reveling in his role as a booming national personality,
frankly delighted by the cheers that rose from onlookers,
making sure he would be identified by wearing his trade-
mark, his old Rough Rider slouch hat, a reminder of his late
military glory.

"Gentlemen," one political veteran chuckled, "that's an
acceptance hat."

Sure enough, it was. The convention chose Roosevelt by
acclamation. The band struck up a tune of the Spanish War
era, "There'll Be a Hot Time in the Old Town Tonight," and
Teddy said he felt "strong as a bull moose." The party duti-
fully closed ranks. But Hanna, as H. Wayne Morgan has

written, "had some terrible premonition of Roosevelt's suc-
cession, a faint but undefinable feeling that Teddy had not
been shelved." [11]

With Roosevelt doing most of the campaigning, stressing
the "full dinner pail" and the newly won overseas empire,
McKinley won a sweeping victory for orthodox Republicanism over Bryan, the Democrats, and the Fusion Populists.
Nine months later, at an afternoon reception in the Temple
of Music at the Pan-American Exposition at Buffalo, New
York, while a Bach sonata was being played in the background, two shots cracked from a .32 revolver, draped with
a handkerchief, as President McKinley reached out to take
the hand of anarchist Leon F. Czolgosz.[12] Eight days later
McKinley died, Theodore Roosevelt was President, and the
history of the United States was set on a new course, moving
from an individualistic republic toward the centralized power
of a social democracy. The new President took up his task
with a caution that has often been overlooked because of his
later reputation as tribune of the people. His position on
such issues as the tariff, the inheritance tax, and the income
tax failed to justify either the worst apprehensions of the
bosses or the eager hopes of the reform elements within the
Republican Party. This is perhaps not surprising, considering that Roosevelt had the election of 1904 very much in
mind and that his counselors at the time included the arch-
conservative Senator Aldrich from Rhode Island, Mark
Hanna, two partners in the House of Morgan, and the president of the Pennsylvania Railroad.[13]

After Roosevelt was elected President in his own right in
1904 over the colorless Alton Brooks Parker, he began to
show a new independence. But his program could scarcely
be termed a serious departure from what went before except
from the point of view of the extreme conservatives or the

troglodytic Speaker of the House, Joseph G. "Uncle Joe" Cannon, who, like the ancient Romans, regarded as unfavorable any portent that appeared on the left. As a matter of fact, Roosevelt was trying to reinvigorate the economic system, not radicalize it, to prune away excesses and remedy abuses, but not to upset the values of individualistic capitalism. Under his policies, known collectively as the New Nationalism, even the misbehavior of the giant corporations, as Roosevelt saw it, did not invalidate the old maxim *abusus non tollit usam* — abuse is no argument against popular use.[14]

In his message to Congress of December 3, 1906, President Roosevelt expressed the judgment that the United States ought to have an income tax and an inheritance tax. "The man of great wealth," he said, "owes a peculiar obligation to the state, because he derives special advantages from the mere existence of government." The burden should be distributed so as to attain "absolute equality between the rich and the poor man. True democracy requires this." But then the President climbed down the pole by expressing uncertainty as to whether an income tax could be devised that was constitutional. He ended rather lamely by saying, "If possible, it is most certainly desirable."[15] But he did not press vigorously for action, and indeed his power for action diminished with the approach of the end of his elective term. There were indications that the President intended to make adjustments in the tariff, ark of the Republican covenant and the sharpest issue that had separated the two major parties for more than two decades. But wiser heads prevailed. Especially sharp was Speaker Cannon's reminder that the party that put through a new tariff law always lost the next election. Roosevelt kept returning to the topic but never sent Congress a message advocating revision. So tariff changes and possible new objects of taxation were left as dubious legacies for T.R.'s successor and political heir, William Howard Taft. Joseph Keppler, the trenchant political cartoonist of the period, caught the moment well when he cast Roosevelt in the role of Hamlet, seated in deep meditation and leaning heavily on the arm of his chair. "Thus," said the caption, "the tariff does make cowards of us all." [16]

Roosevelt was handicapped in dealing forthrightly with the tariff question. Despite evidence that representative government was being manipulated by powerful economic groups, T.R. had learned laissez-faire economics as then taught at Harvard, and an understanding of how the economic system worked had never become his forte. Perhaps he sensed the gathering of explosive new forces more progressive than he was. But for whatever reason, he left the problem to Taft, who easily defeated Bryan, the only presidential candidate of a major party to be rejected three times. Taft took the oath of office on a snowy March 4, 1909, and two weeks later sent a special message to Congress, urging "prompt revision" of the Dingley tariff, which had stood like a stone wall since 1897.[17] On the following day a bill was introduced in the House of Representatives by Sereno E. Payne, the plodding but hard-working chairman of the Ways and Means Committee, whose major interest was the tariff and whose name was attached, for better or worse, to the fateful measure that became law before the year 1909 had passed.[18]

7

Clearing the Way
for the Sixteenth Amendment

In 1908 the Republican platform pledged the party to a revision of the tariff. Although the language used was somewhat Delphic as to whether revision meant upward or downward, it was generally assumed by the public, then struggling with the "H.C.L." (high cost of living), that the impact of high protectionism on the pocketbook of the ordinary citizen was going to be eased.

It was Taft's understanding that this pledge was in the nature of a contract to lower import duties and he honored it promptly by sending his special message to Congress. The bill that emerged from the House provided for moderate reductions. But the Senate was protectionist in sentiment and firmly under the control of Senator Nelson W. Aldrich, who saw nothing grotesque in the idea of "The Senator from Steel," "The Senator from Wool," or "The Senator from Sugar." This last special interest was represented by deaf old Samuel D. McEnery (D.-La.), who came up to Aldrich one day during the debate, cupped his hand behind his ear, and shouted to the amusement of all within hearing distance, "If I don't vote right, Senator, you'll understand it's because I don't hear what it is you want."

Aldrich completely captivated men. When he wanted to

pass or defeat a bill he sat down beside a senator, sometimes even a Democrat, and used what a Republican colleague, Senator Henry Clay Hansbrough (R.-N.D.), called "his chloroform bottle," which Hansbrough was convinced Aldrich carried in his pocket: "The first thing that the Senator knows he has been chloroformed."

Some 600 out of 847 revisions in the Senate version of the bill went *up*. All were laid on necessities of life, consumed by the population generally. The reductions or eliminations of customs charges were on articles that needed no protection anyway.[1] Finley Peter Dunne's Mr. Dooley explained the free list to his friend Mr. Hennessy: "Th' Republican party . . . has been thrue to its promises. Look at th' free list if ye don't believe it. Practically ivrything nicissry to existence comes in free . . . Here it is. Curling stones . . . teeth . . . sea moss . . . newspapers . . . nux vomica . . . Pula . . . canary bird seed . . . divvy-divvy . . . spunk . . . hog bristles . . . kelp . . . marshmallows . . . silk worm eggs, stilts, skeletons, turtles, an' leeches. Th' new tariff bill puts these familyar commodyties within th' reach iv all." [2]

Congressman Charles A. Lindbergh, progressive Republican from Minnesota and father of a son who was to become famous, said he would vote reluctantly for the Payne-Aldrich tariff measure because it had been amended and improved somewhat. Still, he thought many of the provisions that remained, such as the tariff on hosiery, gloves, shoes — "most of the things that we eat and wear" — were "outrageous." They reminded him, he said, of a poem, which he proceeded to read to the House. One verse was:

> Build a tall old tariff wall,
> Thus produce a dearth.
> Make the honest workman pay
> Twice what things are worth.[3]

A friendlier estimate of the Payne-Aldrich Tariff Act came from Representative Asher C. Hinds of Maine: "Massachusetts," he said, "never went away from Congress carrying more in her craw than she's got in that tariff bill." But the new law was widely denounced throughout the country as being, in the words of the *New York Times,* a "fine old farce . . . revised by its friends"; and the *Financier,* contemplating the schedules, recalled, though not quite accurately, the Cheshire cat of *Alice's Adventures in Wonderland* — the longer one watches the bigger the grin becomes.[4]

Reluctantly, President Taft signed the bill into law in August 1909. He wrung a few concessions from the Republican leadership, but they were minuscule, rather like getting a $50 discount on a Pierce Arrow automobile. A coalition of Republican dissidents — called "Insurgents" at the time, a word on everyone's tongue because of the recent uprising in the Philippines against U.S. rule — joining the Democrats, had attempted to include a provision for a statutory income tax. The Senate balked when Aldrich opposed the idea. But it appeared that the tax had many friends among the voters. It became respectable, at least among southern and western congressmen and senators. As a consequence a serious split between the Insurgents and the eastern Establishment threatened Republican Party unity. The President stepped in to work out some arrangement.

There were cool evening rides in Rock Creek Park with congressional leaders. White House dinners. Golf at the Chevy Chase Country Club. The President got a deal that enabled the advocates of the income tax to claim an immediate modest success and a kind of political promissory note — a call on the future that appeared from the point of view of Republican elder statesmen to be harmless because uncollectible. Under the compromise the Senate accepted a tax on corporate profits at once and agreed to sponsor a joint resolution of the Congress, as recommended by President Taft in his special message of June 16, 1909, to submit an amendment to the Constitution to the states. If approved, the amendment, which would be number sixteen, would make possible a tax on incomes at some time in the future.[5]

President Taft would have preferred an income tax at once. But since the Supreme Court, only fourteen years earlier, had held such a tax to be unconstitutional, his instinct and training inclined him to avoid another Court review, accept the 1895 decision, and change the Constitution. Many good constitutional lawyers both in and out of Congress thought that the Supreme Court had erred in its income tax decision in the *Pollock* case. They bowed, however, to the sensibilities of the Court and conceded that the matter had been settled. Thus courtesy among the brotherhood and respect for *stare decesis*, the doctrine that preceding court decisions be allowed to stand, led to the dubious conclusion that old error was better than new truth. As a consequence, the country had to go through the elaborate ritual, whose outcome was of course uncertain, of changing the Constitution rather than embarrass the Supreme Court. The corporation tax was passed and levied at 1 percent on net above $5000. This was one half of what the President had asked for. It was an income tax under another name, called an excise on the privilege of doing business. The Supreme Court reviewed the corporation tax and sustained it.[6]

As for the distasteful resolution submitting the proposed Sixteenth Amendment to the states, the Republican Congress passed it for several reasons. First of all, Aldrich, like President Taft, did not want the constitutionality of the income tax to be resubmitted to the Court because the respect in which the Court was held might be severely damaged whichever way it decided. Both the President and Senator Aldrich were in chancery. They knew that the Insurgent Republicans, in association with the Democrats, had the votes to put through the resolution. Also, they faced a Treasury deficit of a hundred million dollars, a large sum for the first decade of this century. So the corporation tax was designed to meet the shortfall. Together with the income tax amendment, it was the price that had to be paid to save the high-protection tariff. It was widely hoped and believed that the eastern states would never ratify the amendment. Actually, as John D. Buenker has shown, ratification received unexpected support in the urban, industrialized states.

Also operative was a sense that the government needed greater freedom to tax in times of national emergency. This consideration was strengthened by the still-vivid recollection of John Hay's Open Door note in 1899, the imperialistic adventures of the Spanish-American War, Theodore Roosevelt's interference in Colombia in 1903 to secure both the independence of Panama and the lease to the U.S. of the Canal Zone, the new American presence on the world stage in mediating the Russo-Japanese War in 1905, and the xenophobia manifested in the phrase "Yellow Peril." Finally, as already indicated, the amendment scheme had political appeal because it pushed the day of reckoning into the future.[7]

As a spokesman for the conservative position, Sereno Payne, coauthor of the tariff bill, supported the idea of submitting the income tax question to the states because he wanted the United States to have "the longest pocket-book" in time of war. But he made abundantly clear his aversion to such an exaction in time of peace. "I believe with Gladstone," he said, "that it tends to make a nation of liars. [It is] . . . a tax upon the income of honest men and an exemption, to a greater or lesser extent, of the income of rascals."[8]

The amendment was simplicity itself, consisting of these thirty words: "The Congress shall have power to lay and collect taxes on incomes, from whatever source derived, without apportionment among the several states and without regard to any census or enumeration." By this draftmanship the government achieved a clarification of its taxing power that had escaped from the strained construction of the Constitution on which the *Pollock* case was decided. It put the graduated income tax beyond successful challenge.[9]

While the states deliberated, moving somewhat more rapidly than had been expected, it was politics as usual in Washington. If the Payne-Aldrich tariff cemented the alliance between the administration and big business, it also produced rebellion in the progressive wing of the Republican Party, and contributed substantially to the Democratic capture of the House of Representatives in the fall of 1910.[10] The Democrats also picked up ten seats in the Senate. This, with the help of Insurgent Republicans, gave them de facto control of Congress. This loss was followed by the debacle of 1912, when Theodore Roosevelt drew off enough Republican votes to his temporarily powerful Progressive (Bull Moose) Party to elect Woodrow Wilson, though Wilson became President without receiving a majority of the popular vote. The Democrats also achieved a sweeping victory in both houses of Congress under the Wilsonian slogan, the New Freedom, which called for a Congress more responsive to the people and the restraint of great concentrations of economic power. Both the Democratic and Progressive Party platforms of 1912 favored ratification of the pending amendment giving Congress unquestioned power to lay an income tax.[11]

On February 3, 1913, Wyoming became the thirty-sixth state to ratify the Sixteenth Amendment, providing the necessary approval by three fourths of the states. Connecticut, Florida, Rhode Island, and Utah, the only state west of the Mississippi River to vote no, rejected the proposal. Pennsylvania and Virginia failed to act. The Secretary of State, Philander C. Knox, affixed the Great Seal of the United States to the document on February 25. The event attracted little attention. Far more newsworthy at the moment was the resumption of the first Balkan War, between Bulgaria, Serbia, and Greece on the one hand, and Turkey on the other, the fighting in front of Adrianople (now Edirne), the tragic death of the English Antarctic explorer Robert Falcon Scott, and the fact that Woodrow Wilson had declined honorary membership in the Chevy Chase Country Club.[12] Incidentally, the Sixteenth Amendment was the first modification of the Constitution to be adopted in forty-three years. Brooks, the White House valet, was already packing up President Taft's personal baggage when the Secretary of State acted, and Woodrow Wilson took the oath of office on March 4, at one minute after one o'clock in the afternoon on the east portico of the Capitol.[13]

During the hot summer of 1913 the Sixty-third Congress, holding its first session, whipped the income tax legislation into shape, though not neglecting those other important matters in which Congress takes an intense interest, such as the purchase of a site for a U.S. post office in Carrollton, Illinois, home of an influential member of the House on the Democratic side (Henry T. Rainey, who later became Speaker of the House), and the allocation of cannon and cannonballs to villages, towns, cemeteries, and Grand Army of the Republic posts. In the case of national unity even the Daughters of the Confederacy were recognized with four field pieces, mounted, "and suitable outfit of cannon balls," for a park located on the Prairie Grove battlefield at Prairie Grove,

Arkansas. The income tax measure, as usual, was not set forth in a separate bill but tucked into a new tariff act, known as the Underwood-Simmons Tariff Act, officially entitled "An Act to Reduce Tariff Duties and Provide Revenue for the Government, and for Other Purposes." Section II, which assessed the new income tax, was buried among bauxite, gloves, false teeth, wool, beads and spangles, human hair, sheep dip, statuary for bona fide orphan asylums, and wild animals not for sale.[14]

With the passage of a permanent, peacetime income tax, the United States turned a sharp corner in its thinking about taxation. The accumulation of influences and circumstances that led to the tax has been the theme of the preceding chapters. To summarize, the tax was the result of a developing leveling movement, a sheet anchor in case of war, and a reaction to the rapid concentration of wealth.

As reformist thought gained ground, concerned as it was with individual liberty, with freeing the channels of economic opportunity, bringing to life again principles espoused by Jefferson and Jackson, the nation turned to the direct election of senators as it did to the income tax, and shortly after the income tax amendment became law it was followed by another amendment, the Seventeenth, on May 31, 1913, which provided for the direct election of U.S. senators. It was a question of the day much discussed and thought about, involving as it did the question of how every rich man got his money, and the people, as William Allen White put it, "were ready to believe — and too often were justified in the belief — that he was a scamp . . ."[15] The method by which senators were elected became an issue because it was through the senators that commercial interests controlled the judiciary. The system worked as follows: The corporations or "trusts" found it easy to dominate the state legislatures. The legislators elected the U.S. senators. The senators controlled the appointment of federal judges. The judges could be counted on to construe the Constitution strictly when property rights were affected. The members of the power group that dealt in the mutual favors that passed between the business community and the federal government were known as Standpatters, from a term used in an address in 1902 by Mark Hanna. He advised Ohio to "stand pat and continue Republican prosperity." The Standpatters in the Senate were, wrote the late Samuel Eliot Morison, "pungent personalities" who fancied they were renewing Hamiltonian policies, and Admiral Morison added, being a pungent personality himself, "Some were gentlemen, most were not . . . [but] all became very rich." Senators were known by the company they kept. In Massachusetts it was bankers and owners of textile mills. In Kansas it was railroad attorneys. In Montana, copper moguls. Aldrich, certainly, felt no need to apologize or make secret these relationships, for he was a man of candor and firm conviction, believing "that the mass of the people are not the final sovereign." [16] Demonstrating a paranoid resistance to any substantive change in society or their own operations, the entrepreneurial capitalists of the day called upon biology, psychology, and Herbert Spencer to show that human beings were fixed structures and to defend their philosophy of elitism. Some men were born to succeed, the argument ran; others, foredoomed to failure. It was all determined by the genes: "The Rockefellers were born to be Rockefellers," as Professor Eric F. Goldman has phrased it, "and the slum-dwellers to be slum-dwellers." [17]

But the people generally rejected the theory that gross inequalities of wealth came from some iron law of nature, and the reformist Sixteenth Amendment symbolized their conclusion on the matter. And it soon became evident that the proceeds from the income tax would be deployed for social purposes as well as for operating the machinery of government. In the near future even the Supreme Court would be responding to the needs of an expanding society, and shifting to a broader construction of how Congress could use the taxing power to promote the general welfare, as provided in Article I, Section 8 of the Constitution. Most of those who pushed the idea of the income tax sought a Square Deal, as Theodore Roosevelt had expressed it — the career open to the talents under a free market system. There was no thought of making fundamental changes in society. For in a fluid society formed of many disparate elements, the hope springs eternal of getting into the surtax brackets tomorrow or sometime, and sharing rather than destroying the material joys of the gross national product. To think otherwise, we believe generally, is to keep bad company, to linger over the destructive notion that the majority's power to tax will be wielded by the poor to strip the well-to-do. To think otherwise is to misread the whole tendency of American life and to accept, as Justice Edward D. White warned in the inheritance tax case that came on in 1898, the "assertion that free and representative government is a failure." [18]

8

The American Taxpayer
Faces His First Form 1040

IT IS ONE of those fascinating paradoxes in which history abounds that our all-embracing income tax, made possible by the action of one of the most reactionary Congresses ever to control the machinery of legislation, was shaped into law according to liberal Democratic ideas. After the election of 1912, which made Woodrow Wilson President and assured Democratic control of both houses of Congress, the Republicans who opposed the tax gave up and from that point on the desirability of a tax on personal incomes has never been seriously questioned by either major party, although large areas remain for disagreements and delicate negotiations as to the size of the pie and how it shall be sliced up.[1]

The new measure, the Underwood-Simmons Tariff Act, contained sections explaining and justifying the imposition of the tax. These were written by Representative Cordell Hull of Tennessee, an old-fashioned southern progressive Democrat and "a quiet fanatic" on the particular issue of the income tax as an equalizer of opportunity.[2] The tariff act, with its provisions for the income tax, was signed by President Wilson on October 31, 1913, and the money meter began to tick retroactively back to March 1, 1913.

The first $3000 of income, or $4000 for married couples,

was relieved of the tax, the equivalent in the dollars of April 1976 of $18,360 and $24,480 respectively. Mercy and expediency joined in indicating the desirability of such exemptions because subsistence, the fuel for the human furnace, was considered to be necessary to maintain the output of the work force. Certain business deductions were allowed: normal and necessary expenses, interest on indebtedness, other taxes, casualty losses not compensated for by insurance, bad debts, depreciation, dividends of corporations that had paid the corporation tax, and income on which the tax had already been collected at the source. State and federal bond interest was excluded and the President of the United States, U.S. judges, and state officers were exempt from paying.

Since for the year 1913 only ten months' income was subject to the tax, only five sixths of the allowed deductions could be taken for the year. Returns were made under oath and were public records. But inspection was restricted under regulations issued by the Secretary of the Treasury. Eight hundred thousand dollars were appropriated to administer the tax section of the tariff law. The needed forms had to be devised and printed and a hundred clerks had to be quickly recruited and trained. It took thirty just to handle the flood of letters and telegrams that poured into the Bureau of Internal Revenue. Thirty-four field agents examined the returns, for which task they were paid up to five dollars a day plus three dollars for subsistence. Their work was no bureaucratic sinecure, not only because of the lack of regulations and legal precedents and sloppy compliance through taxpayer ignorance, but also because the tax was assessed on net income. The Bureau of Internal Revenue had no information on gross incomes. This important omission greatly hampered the tax-collection process, as it left the taxpayer in the agreeable position of deciding what was net. However, the taxpayer who filed a fraudulent report risked a fine of up to $1000 and a prison sentence of up to a year.[3]

And so the personal income tax, with escalation built into its table of rates, arrived gently and quietly, by no means ignored, yet not the object of any great public excitement either. In 1914 the corporation tax was merged into the new income tax law. There were a number of reasons why the American people reacted with such composure to this major turning point in their fiscal history. First of all, they didn't have to get up the money until March 1, 1914. This lag in time diffused the impact. Furthermore, the exaction fell on a very small proportion of the population, estimated to be about 1 percent. Actually, the figure turned out to be even smaller. The number of returns filed was 357,598, or less than one half of 1 percent. The taxable few were required to pay 1 percent on the first $20,000 of income above the exemption, with a surtax rising through several brackets to an additional 6 percent for those with taxable income above $500,000. In view of the value of the dollar in 1913, the ability-to-pay theory does not seem in retrospect to have been stretched unduly by the first tax code. Yet the conservative economist Charles J. Bullock, at the time professor of public finance at Harvard University, blew his circuits when he saw the tax schedules and warned that the percentages imposed by the law approached a dangerous limit for direct taxation on large incomes. A factory worker, incidentally, earned at this time about $500 a year, and a rib roast of beef cost twenty cents a pound. The exemptions, originally generously conceived, have moved sharply downward during the two generations that have since lived under the income tax. The present meager allowance is not concerned with allowing the taxpayer a comfortable living standard but with collecting as much money as is politically possible — plucking the most feathers with the least honking.[4]

Form 1040.

INCOME TAX.

THE PENALTY
FOR FAILURE TO HAVE THIS RETURN IN
THE HANDS OF THE COLLECTOR OF
INTERNAL REVENUE ON OR BEFORE
MARCH 1 IS $20 TO $4,000.
(SEE INSTRUCTIONS ON PAGE 4.)

List No. ....

District of ....

Date received ....

File No. ....

Assessment List ....

Page .... Line ....

UNITED STATES INTERNAL REVENUE.

RETURN OF ANNUAL NET INCOME OF INDIVIDUALS.
(As provided by Act of Congress, approved October 3, 1913.)

RETURN OF NET INCOME RECEIVED OR ACCRUED DURING THE YEAR ENDED DECEMBER 31, 191....
(FOR THE YEAR 1913, FROM MARCH 1, TO DECEMBER 31.)

Filed by (or for) .... of ....
(Full name of individual.) (Street and No.)

in the City, Town, or Post Office of .... State of ....
(Fill in pages 2 and 3 before making entries below.)

1. GROSS INCOME (see page 2, line 12)	$		
2. GENERAL DEDUCTIONS (see page 3, line 7)	$		
3. NET INCOME	$		

Deductions and exemptions allowed in computing income subject to the normal tax of 1 per cent.

4. Dividends and net earnings received or accrued, of corporations, etc., subject to like tax. (See page 2, line 11).......... $

5. Amount of income on which the normal tax has been deducted and withheld at the source. (See page 2, line 9, column A)..

6. Specific exemption of $3,000 or $4,000, as the case may be. (See Instructions 3 and 19)

Total deductions and exemptions. (Items 4, 5, and 6) .... $

7. TAXABLE INCOME on which the normal tax of 1 per cent is to be calculated. (See Instruction 3). $

8. When the net income shown above on line 3 exceeds $20,000, the additional tax thereon must be calculated as per schedule below:

			INCOME.		TAX.	
1 per cent on amount over $20,000 and not exceeding $50,000....		$			$	
2 " " 50,000 " " 75,000....						
3 " " 75,000 " " 100,000....						
4 " " 100,000 " " 250,000....						
5 " " 250,000 " " 500,000....						
6 " " 500,000						
Total additional or super tax					$	
Total normal tax (1 per cent of amount entered on line 7)....					$	
Total tax liability					$	

2

GROSS INCOME.

This statement must show in the proper spaces the entire amount of gains, profits, and income received by or accrued to the individual from all sources during the year specified on page 1.

DESCRIPTION OF INCOME.	A. Amount of income on which tax has been deducted and withheld at the source.			B. Amount of income on which tax has NOT been deducted and withheld at the source.		
1. Total amount derived from salaries, wages, or compensation for personal service of whatever kind and in whatever form paid.	$			$		
2. Total amount derived from professions, vocations, businesses, trade, commerce, or sales or dealings in property, whether real or personal, growing out of the ownership or use of or interest in real or personal property, including bonds, stocks, etc.						
3. Total amount derived from rents and from interest on notes, mortgages, and securities (other than reported on lines 5 and 6).						
4. Total amount of gains and profits derived from partnership business, whether the same be divided and distributed or not.						
5. Total amount of fixed and determinable annual gains, profits, and income derived from interest upon bonds and mortgages or deeds of trust, or other similar obligations of corporations, joint-stock companies or associations, and insurance companies, whether payable annually or at shorter or longer periods.						
6. Total amount of income derived from coupons, checks, or bills of exchange for or in payment of interest upon bonds issued in *foreign countries* and upon *foreign mortgages* or like obligations (not payable in the United States), and also from coupons, checks, or bills of exchange for or in payment of any dividends upon the stock or interest upon the obligations of foreign corporations, associations, and insurance companies engaged in business in foreign countries.						
7. Total amount of income received from fiduciaries.						
8. Total amount of income derived from any source whatever, not specified or entered elsewhere on this page.						
9. TOTALS.	$			$		
NOTE.—Enter total of Column A on line 5 of first page.						
10. AGGREGATE TOTALS OF COLUMNS A AND B				$		
11. Total amount of income derived from dividends on the stock or from the net earnings of corporations, joint-stock companies, associations, or insurance companies subject to like tax (To be entered on line 4 of first page.)				$		
12. TOTAL "Gross Income" (to be entered on line 1 of first page)				$		

It had taken twenty-five years of argument, debate, and psychodrama, the bitter defeat in the Supreme Court during the second Cleveland administration, and the ratification of the Sixteenth Amendment to clear the way for an income tax. When it finally came, the feeling about it was generally positive. It was contended, and widely believed, that the new law would put some restraint on the concentration of

3

GENERAL DEDUCTIONS.

1. The amount of necessary expenses actually paid in carrying on business, but not including business expenses of partnerships, and not including personal, living, or family expenses...... $............

2. All interest paid within the year on personal indebtedness of taxpayer.........................

3. All national, State, county, school, and municipal taxes paid within the year (not including those assessed against local benefits) ....

4. Losses actually sustained the year incurred in trade or arising from fires, storms, or shipwreck, and not compensated for by insurance or otherwise ....

5. Debts due which have been actually ascertained to be worthless and which have been charged off within the year...

6. Amount representing a reasonable allowance for the exhaustion, wear, and tear of property arising out of its use or employment in the business, not to exceed, in the case of mines, 5 per cent of the gross value at the mine of the output for the year for which the computation is made, but no deduction shall be made for any amount of expense of restoring property or making good the exhaustion thereof, for which an allowance is or has been made.........

7. Total "GENERAL DEDUCTIONS" (to be entered on line 2 of first page) ....

AFFIDAVIT TO BE EXECUTED BY INDIVIDUAL MAKING HIS OWN RETURN.

I solemnly swear (or affirm) that the foregoing return, to the best of my knowledge and belief, contains a true and complete statement of all gains, profits, and income received by or accrued to me during the year for which the return is made, and that I am entitled to all the deductions and exemptions entered or claimed therein, under the Federal Income-tax Law of October 3, 1913.

Sworn to and subscribed before me this.........................

day of ...., 191   ---
                                                                 (Signature of individual.)

SEAL OF
OFFICER   --
TAKING
AFFIDAVIT.   --
                        (Official capacity.)

AFFIDAVIT TO BE EXECUTED BY DULY AUTHORIZED AGENT MAKING RETURN FOR INDIVIDUAL.

I solemnly swear (or affirm) that I have sufficient knowledge of the affairs and property of ....
to enable me to make a full and complete return thereof, and that the foregoing return, to the best of my knowledge and belief, contains a true and complete statement of all gains, profits, and income received by or accrued to said individual during the year for which the return is made, and that the said individual is entitled, under the Federal Income-tax Law of October 3, 1913, to all the deductions and exemptions entered or claimed therein.

Sworn to and subscribed before me this.........................

day of ...., 191   ---
                                                                 (Signature of agent.)

                                    ADDRESS { --
                                    IN FULL.   --

SEAL OF
OFFICER   --
TAKING
AFFIDAVIT.   --
                        (Official capacity.)

c 2—7357   [SEE INSTRUCTIONS ON BACK OF THIS PAGE.]

wealth and income in the hands of the richest 1.6 percent of families in the United States who between 1890 and 1910 had nearly doubled their share of the national income (from 10.8 percent to 19 percent), chiefly at the expense of the middle class.[5] And it was further believed, as a matter of equity or fairness, that the personal income tax would place the burden of supporting the federal government in some reasonable relationship to benefits received and the ability to pay. The House Committee on Ways and Means did not think the task of filling out the income tax blanks would prove to be onerous. In recommending the bill to the House for passage, the committee declared that "those citizens required to do so can well afford to devote a brief time during some one day in each year to the making out of a personal return of income . . ." The bill had been drafted to meet a long-felt need for an elastic and productive system of revenue and the committee remarked hopefully that "all good citizens . . . will willingly and cheerfully support and sustain this, the fairest and cheapest of all taxes . . ."[6]

Gently ascending though the 1913 tax rates seem to us now, a new era had opened. "It is probable," wrote Edwin R. A. Seligman, the Columbia University economist, in 1914, "that the income tax has come to stay [and] will play its important part in bringing about greater justice in American taxation." The liberal historian Charles A. Beard, also of Columbia, who interpreted American history in terms of economic interests, also welcomed the social consequences of an attempt to redistribute the burdens of taxation, which recalls an anecdote concerning Nicholas Murray Butler, Columbia's durable president and a tough old Hamiltonian strayed into the twentieth century.

"Have you read Beard's last book?" an associate asked.

"I hope so," Butler replied.[7]

Dissidents were not lacking, or silent. Those who took a catastrophic view of the graduated feature of the tax rates reacted with cold hostility, and would have agreed unreservedly with the opinion voiced by Friedrich von Gentz, conservative German statesman and economist, whose opinion of progressive taxation was that it was not much better than common thievery; or with Anne Robert Turgot, finance minister to Louis XVI, who, when presented with a memorandum recommending progressive taxation, wrote on the margin of the proposal, "We must execute the author, not the project." [8] One American who shared such opinions was Ward McAllister, New York social leader and coiner of the term "the Four Hundred," who had threatened to abandon the United States if an income tax became law. By dying early in 1895, he was spared the ordeal of packing up. In 1913, with such a law actually in force, the idea of British citizenship became suddenly attractive. But so spins the whirligig of time that in 1975, when the British Labour government proposed an annual tax on wealth, on top of a stiff income tax, Michael Caine, the British movie star, announced that if the plan went through he would move to California. "The proposal," as he put it, "is to hammer nest eggs." But in the first year of the American income tax, persons of large means were appalled at the prospect of paying at the rate of 7 percent and learned to quote sententiously, and not strictly in context, Chief Justice Marshall's famous dictum already alluded to (see Chapter 2): "The power to tax involves the power to destroy." [9]

Alarmed, the Woman Suffrage Party of New York raised the historic issue of taxation without representation, and Dr. Charles W. Eliot, president of Harvard University, expressed the fear that the fiber of the American people would be weakened by the income tax and that they would "surely lose those sturdy, independent, honest and just qualities which alone befit free men." He was right to a degree, since the first of many arrests and convictions for tax evasion came soon after he spoke.[10]

Vigorous objections were also registered by proponents of an economic theory highly regarded in Wall Street and in the executive suites of the largest corporate enterprises: the general welfare was best promoted when the possessors of large fortunes were lightly taxed. On the happiness of the few, ran the argument, hinged the happiness of all. The rich must be encouraged to save and invest or initiative would dry up and the economy wither. This ideology has often been eloquently articulated in the reports of the House Ways and Means Committee, where revenue bills originate, and has been printed at government expense, especially when the Republican Party has been in control of the House.[11]

Though the income tax portion of the 1913 tariff act covered only fourteen pages in the *United States Statutes at Large* (as against today's code, with amendments, running to more than 2000 pages),[12] the necessity to comply with the first income tax generated a good deal of taxpayer irritation. The law was not explicit on many points. There were no administrative rulings to fall back on, and the leveling social philosophy implicit in the act made the calculating and the paying especially detestable to those who held the belief that the good things of life trickled down when the affluent were secure and happy. Many individuals, it turned out when tax time came to America, had not kept their accounts so as to show net income. Formidable financial problems often arose, with philosophic overtones. What was gross income? What constituted property? Even income was found to be a troublesome and ambiguous concept. An Undersecretary of the Treasury once theorized that Mr.

Hull, the architect of the act, "must have had some idea in his own mind of what he regarded as income." It became evident, but only gradually and over a long period of time, that income is whatever the Supreme Court thinks it is at a particular time. But the question was hard to resolve in those first, disordered days. One congressman, not overly sympathetic with the law, noted with amusement that some of the income tax's staunchest friends in Congress gave up in despair on filling out their own returns and had to ask the sergeant at arms and his assistants to do the job for them.[13] That functionary thus became a pioneer among a host of income-tax-return preparers "other than taxpayer," as the modern Form 1040 describes them.

Now that the Sixteenth Amendment had sanctified what a bare majority of the Supreme Court of 1895 had said the Constitution had condemned, those hostile to the tax could no longer call on our great organic document as a friend in time of need. It was freely predicted that men of talent, energy, and capital would cease to exert themselves, that the national wealth would be dissipated, that even such odd-ball types as artists and writers would desert their studios and battered typewriters to go to work for the government or even enter the ministry.[14] These melancholy forecasts, representing the pecuniary desires of those making them, were not fulfilled. There has never been a successful challenge to any provision of the income tax law. The last serious constitutional challenge to the progressive feature of the 1913 law occurred in 1916. Again, opponents took the issue to the courts, relying on an asserted violation of the due process clause of the Fifth Amendment because of the arbitrary sliding scale of rates and the exemption of some income. They also cited a violation of the uniformity clause and some other miscellaneous contentions, which Chief Justice White

described as "numerous and minute, not to say in many re-
spects hypercritical." Altogether twenty-one elaborate propositions were advanced in the case, *Brushaber* v. *Union Pacific Railway Company.* A stockholder sued the railroad to
restrain it from voluntarily paying the income tax imposed
by the 1913 tariff act, and the Attorney General of the United
States appeared as amicus curiae in support of the constitutionality of the act. The case was argued in October 1915
and decided in January 1916. The court found that that the
appellant's arguments were based on mistaken theories about
history, the U.S. Constitution, and the Sixteenth Amendment.
This decision gave the government "every conceivable power
of taxation," and made the principle of graduation forever
immune from attack on constitutional grounds, although the
constitutional issue continues to be raised, sometimes frivo-
lously, down to the present time. (See Chapter 11). But by
1916 the *Pollock* case had yielded to changing times, "becoming a footnote in history — an error of law and of political
judgment by the Court."

"Don't get excited," the *New York Times* said helpfully
when the time for filing approached. "Look blank 1040
squarely in the face . . . Read carefully the instructions on
Page 4." The numbered lines provided a guide to line 7 on
page 1, "which will contain the fateful entry of your taxable
income." [15]

The 1913 act defined income as including proceeds from
"any lawful business carried on for gain or profit." But three
years later, with Europe at war, "Preparedness" in the American air, and a sense of impending fiscal crisis, Congress passed
a new revenue law that dropped the limiting word "lawful."
Thus for the first time the Treasury skimmed the crock for
the cream rising from commercial extortion, bribery, the
rackets, referrals to abortionists, gambling, moonshining, and
housebreaking.

Several burglars inquired anxiously about the confidentiality of their tax reports. So successful were the Treasury's appeals to patriotic sentiment after America was actually a combatant in the First World War, that one professional at breaking and entering, who described himself as a hardworking burglar with a large family to support, was moved to write to the Collector of Internal Revenue for the Upper Manhattan Revenue District. He expressed his strong desire to file an honest report on his 1917 income "so that," he wrote, "the Government can use the money to fight the biggest burglar in the world — the Kaiser." There was just one difficulty: "Will the records be turned over to the police? I wish to be patriotic," the correspondent continued, "but naturally must keep in business on account of my dependents." Neither this larcenous patriot nor his colleagues need have worried. The income tax statute explicitly barred revealing such information, however attractive it might have been to other agencies of government. Even long-suffering wives, inquiring about the income they suspected was received by their spouses but never reached home, could not be accommodated by a regretful Bureau of Internal Revenue. Shunning the domain of morals, the tax law required of the U.S. citizen only that he pay in full the correct amount of tax on his taxable income.

"The object of this bill," declared Senator John Sharp Williams (D.-Miss.), a ranking member of the Senate Finance Committee, "is to tax a man's net income . . . what he has left at the end of the year after deducting from his receipts his expenditures or losses. It is not to reform men's characters . . . The law does not care where he got it from, so far as the tax is concerned . . . although the law may very properly care in another way." That made it official: money does not smell of its origin. The social basis for the rule that Congress may tax what it also forbids is that not to tax illegal income would simply shift the taxes due from lawbreakers to honest citizens. This well-established concept was tested and sustained again in 1961, when the Supreme Court noted that "the federal income tax . . . is not a sanction against wrongdoing . . ." and that "the statute does not concern itself with the lawfulness of the income that it taxes." [16] After the passage of the National Prohibition Act bootleggers and "alky" cookers learned, in an opinion delivered by Supreme Court Justice Oliver Wendell Holmes, that the Fifth Amendment was not a refuge that could save the recipient of unlawful income from the necessity of making a return. But with exquisite tact the Bureau of Internal Revenue permitted profits made through breaking the law to be reported as "other income," without disclosure of the source.[17]

Rascals posing as revenue agents added a new leaf to the world's roster of confidence games. A native of Scotland, happily on his way home to Glasgow, approached Pier 64 in New York City, carrying his grip and humming. " 'Twas Your Voice, My Gentle Mary." Suddenly he was stopped by a well-dressed youth, who said crisply, "Your ticket and income tax receipt, please," and relieved the Scot of $90. It was the traveler's misfortune not to know that fake tax collectors were plying their ingenious trade, though the Washington headquarters of the bureau had warned of the racket at least two years before. "In the payment of the income tax," the bureau pointed out, "the public is required to seek the Government and not the Government the public."

Within the Bureau of Internal Revenue itself problems arising from the frailties of human nature appeared at an early date as the bureau addressed itself to its mandate for getting the last legal bit of catsup out of the bottle. One case that got into the newspapers called attention to the precocious tax trainee who managed to pad his expense account even before completing the course he was taking to learn to be a revenue agent. Another malefactor was the enterprising first deputy collector at Newark, New Jersey, who went into business for himself, selling the names of Jersey taxpayers for three cents each to a New York firm dealing in mailing lists.[18] These were minor and inevitable incidents involving human depravity. They do not obscure the fact that the income tax administration and receipts improved with each succeeding year as the Bureau of Internal Revenue struggled to master complexity and achieve equity. By 1916 the contribution of the income tax to the national safety was apparent to all who could read the unrolling history of their own times. Sereno E. Payne's "longest pocket-book" in time of war was about to meet its first test.

9

War, Boom, Bust

THE WAR IN EUROPE, known at the time as the Great War in the belief that no other could be greater, dragged on from August 1914 for more than two years without effect on the American income tax, which remained unchanged from 1913 to September 8, 1916. The top effective rate was 7 percent, only a slight inconvenience to the well-to-do. For the middle class, the effective rate was only 2.2 percent. But beverage alcohol was declining in importance as a source of revenue, and the income from customs duties was falling at the same time because the German submarines were strangling foreign commerce. Yet government expenses were rising rapidly.

Perhaps the income tax would have had hard sledding even had the world remained at peace. That can be only a surmise. The reality was that reports of German ruthlessness in Belgium and the violation of the rights of neutral shipping on the high seas pushed the United States into the Preparedness campaign of 1915. Thus, paying taxes became equated with patriotism, ultimately with national survival. If the machinery for picking up the revenue load existed more through historical accident than intent, it was, nevertheless, in place, a fact that a professor of public finance, writing soon after the end of the war, observed "should strengthen our belief in Divine Providence."[1]

By 1916 the German submarine warfare and the fantastic Zimmermann telegram of January 1917, in which the German Foreign Secretary, Arthur Zimmermann, generously offered Texas, New Mexico, and Arizona to Mexico in exchange for an alliance against the *gringos* in case war came, increased the possibility of American involvement. The Preparedness campaign reflected the trend, with President Wilson's stubborn hope for peace tied to the idea of "adequate national defense." [2] The President had actively opposed the idea of arming in 1914 and 1915. But events outran the policy. By the end of 1915 Wilson began to lean toward what he called a reasonable increase in the armed forces, despite the efforts of a very articulate opposition, suspicious of European diplomatic rivalries and with no appetite for overseas military adventures. In January and February of 1916 Wilson went before the country to call for serious military preparations. Theodore Roosevelt added to the President's burdens by announcing that he and his four sons were ready to fight, and the songsmiths of Tin Pan Alley exploited Roosevelt's popularity in a song, "If We Had a Million More Like Teddy."

The National Defense Act of 1916 provided for the gradual expansion of the regular army and navy and a naval building program. Though destroyers were urgently needed, the emphasis was on battleships, which the military historian Harvey A. Deweerd explains as "something a congressman and a blue-water admiral could get excited about." Congress added emergency taxes on alcoholic beverages and gasoline and some other special excise taxes. The administration talked of possible changes in the income tax, such as reduction in personal exemptions and a lower starting point for the surtax, which was in principle a graduated tax added to the normal income tax when net income exceeded a certain amount. There was a noticeable shudder on the Democratic side in Congress, which found arming merchant ships, the purchase of massive amounts of military hardware, and universal military service highly repugnant in an election year.[3]

Reluctantly, Congress locked up a new revenue act, signed by President Wilson on September 8, 1916. It was the first income tax law considered on its own merits and not tacked on to a tariff bill, and was hailed by progressive economists as a historic step toward the substitution of direct taxation for the protective tariff as a source of revenue. Exemptions were not changed, but the rates were doubled for both individuals and corporations, the surtax on incomes of over $2 million rose to 13 percent, and a progressive and permanent inheritance tax was laid on estates larger than $50,000. Manufacturers of munitions were charged a special added tax of 12.5 percent on their net profits. This introduced the principle of the excess profits tax.

Government receipts fell behind appropriations as the latter expanded not only to prepare for possible intervention in Europe, but also to pay the military costs of current troubles with Mexico, the charges for bringing home stranded Americans from Europe, war-risk insurance to cover American business losses, and other extraordinary expenses. At the same time the success of the Prohibition movement threatened to cut off some $237 million in liquor taxes. Congress could lower the exemptions on income taxes, but that was not an appealing option: it would remind new taxpayers of the cost of getting ready for war and increase the probability that taxpayers of frail moral fiber would fudge on their tax returns. So the politicians backed away from bringing the small taxpayer, who had already seen the price of gasoline double in a year to twenty-two to thirty cents a gallon, into the revenue system. Indeed, Representative Henry T. Rainey, who felt the income tax rates had already reached "the very highest notch," wondered where the money would come from to accomplish the national purpose.[4]

Woodrow Wilson was re-elected in 1916 on the promise, or the implied promise, that he could keep America out of the war. Avowed interventionists were few before 1917. But by April the President's neutrality policy was eroded by Germany's unrestricted submarine warfare against U.S. shipping as well as by the Americans' sympathy with the Allies. The American declaration of war came at 3:00 A.M. on April 6, 1917, and in Greak Neck, Long Island, George M. Cohan scanned the day's headlines, stepped to the piano, and wrote "Over There," his great war song with the stirring climax ". . . and we won't come back till it's over Over There." That night Nora Bayes, the Empress of the Two-a-Day, introduced the song in her own show. It was the song of songs of World War I, and Congress awarded Cohan a gold medal.

The Revenue Act of 1916 was quickly found to be inadequate and was followed by the War Revenue Act of 1917, passed on October 3. It was a sweeping measure. Exemptions were lowered and rates raised in an almost vertical ascent to a top of 67 percent. "This is the high water mark thus far reached in the history of taxation," wrote Seligman in 1925. "Never before, in the annals of civilization, has an attempt been made to take as much as two-thirds of a man's income by taxation." Even so, deficits in millions became deficits in billions. Appropriations for the calendar year 1917 approached the total cost of operating the federal government from 1791 to 1917.[5]

The War Revenue Act of 1917, passed on October 3, was not a new entity but an amendment to the act passed on September 8, 1916, and represented many compromises among divergent interests. Various provisions of the law were inconsistent with each other and extremely complicated to administer, provoking sarcastic comment from "Uncle Joe" Cannon, who said that reading the conference report on the bill, marked up by the Democratic majority, of course, gave him an anxious Sunday: "I did not say my prayers or read a chapter in the Bible or go to church [and] . . . I went to bed at 1 o'clock this morning . . ." He said that he did not think he could understand the bill without three months of study. Regardless of such partisan sparring, the United States, once in the war, lived up to its best fiscal theory, borrowing by means of long-term bonds and raising taxation to a level that left no question as to the nation's ability or will to meet the debt charges.[6]

It was devoutly hoped by many people of good will that the toughening military experiences on the Mexican border and the modest increase in the regular army and National Guard, authorized by the National Defense Act of June 3, 1916, had put the United States in readiness to fight a major foreign war. But conscription was inevitable and twenty-four million potential soldiers were registered as the provost marshal gave the "work-or-fight" order. Five million men were inducted under the draft. This, like the concurrent income tax experience, required a flood of printed forms and introduced bureaucratic red tape into American life on a scale never known before.[7]

The Revenue Act of 1918, which codified all existing income tax laws, took effect on February 24, 1919, after the end of the war, but was applied retroactively to 1918. Under this act the total tax on incomes over $1 million reached 77 percent, although there were relief provisions that lowered the effective rate and stretched its length to 106 pages. A constitutional question arose at this time. The issue was whether Congress had the power under the Sixteenth Amendment to tax stock dividends as income. It was a nice, lawyerlike question. The majority of the Supreme Court decided that Congress could not tax such dividends. The decision saved the wealthy a great deal of money.[8] The law also contained a provision making a public record of the names and addresses of everyone who had filled out an income tax return. This publicity feature was enacted again in 1921, and a revision of 1924 added more fascinating information — the *amount* paid, which could be published in the newspapers. The release of names and payments was an accomplishment especially dear to the hearts of Robert M. La Follette, the Progressive Senator from Wisconsin, and "country Democrats," who believed that passing the information around would help to make men honest and were perfectly willing to run the risk of a kidnaper or a bond salesman combing the returns for his prospect list.

To break with chronology for a moment and finish with this topic: The publicity feature of the tax law was abolished in 1926, then tried again in 1934, when all taxpayers were required to file a special pink slip disclosing much private information. But the resistance was so great that this section of the act was repealed before any public snooping occurred. Since that time personal tax returns continue to be defined as public records, but the right to inspect is restricted to those who have a legal right rather than a dilettante's interest in having a look. The question of the improper use of income tax information and the manipulation of the Internal Revenue Service became a cause célèbre during the second Nixon administration and continues to be a sensitive subject as these lines are written. (See Chapter 14.) Almost all countries that have a personal income tax provide for complete secrecy, and the experience of the United States with any modification of confidentiality has not been a happy one. The trend now is away from exposing private affairs to the public gaze. It has presumably helped to maintain the kind of taxpayer morale that is clearly an essential of a self-assessment system.[9]

Any thoughtful reader searching for a rationale to explain the extraordinary vitality of the income tax can easily find it in one word: war. The fundamental reason for an income tax is just what some members of Congress thought it was in 1913, the necessity for paying for wars past, present, or future, though tax-supported humanitarian programs may now obscure that fact. World War I built an acceptance for the income tax that might never have existed otherwise. Under the auspices of the Committee on Public Information, volunteer speakers known as Four-Minute Men, seventy-five thousand of them, their rubric invoking the memory of a glorious past, Lexington and Concord and Bunker Hill, and implying a pledge to talk for four minutes only, fanned out in churches, chambers of commerce, and lodges to explain "in a popular way" how all persons who were liable should pay promptly and cheerfully. Movie houses showed on their screens "suggestive sentences," such as "Give till it hurts" or "No white feather in our family"; and at the end of the "first show," as the hero and heroine walked into the sunset, the pianist shifted from "Hearts and Flowers" to "Over There," and a slide was thrown on the screen announcing the name of the Four-Minute Man who would speak.

Cheerful compliance was well publicized when John McCormack, the famous Irish lyric tenor, appeared at the office of the Collector of Internal Revenue for the Third District in New York City with a check for $75,000 and a broad smile. Paraphrasing Scripture, he said, "America gave and America taketh away. Blessed be the name of America." [10] The Bureau of Internal Revenue itself engaged in a massive propaganda campaign to explain the law and persuade the taxpaying public that the bureau was "actually serving the public." There were daily handouts to Washington correspondents and the wire services, plate-matter prepared for the small country weeklies, stories tailored to business, religious, medical, and farm papers, prefab editorials, streetcar cards. The clergy were urged to preach at least one sermon on taxation and the collectors of internal revenue were always affable and accessible to reporters, though their message may have been a stern reminder to "tax slackers" that they would be ferreted out and punished just as surely as draft slackers were under the Selective Service Act.

In addition to direct government efforts, artists and cartoonists contributed their special talents, banks paid for advertisements explaining and supporting the income tax, public utilities mailed out leaflets, and telegraph offices mounted posters. All these activities added up to the most massive propaganda effort ever seen in America. And they signaled something more: a turning point in our fiscal history, the end of one period of taxation and the beginning of another, "not merely the transference of the tax burden from one to another set of objects, but rather a transformation from a system of heterogeneous taxation based on expediency to a system of taxation comprehensive in scope and conforming consistently to a new and essentially different economic theory." [11]

The war imposed on the tax agency a tax-gathering task of such magnitude that some concerned people wondered whether the law, with all its quiddities, could be administered, and whether the financial system of the country could stand the strain of the withdrawal from circulation of the gigantic sums owed to the goverment. Under the 1917 act, for example, the actual amount collected was $3,694,619,638.72. The bureau had to interpret the intent of Congress while realigning, increasing, and training its forces to carry out audits, handle the new estate taxes, the excess profits tax, admission and stamp taxes, special levies on public utilities and insurance companies. And it had to keep up to date on frequent technical changes. Thirty-one blank forms had to be drafted quickly in language as clear and precise as possible, paper stock found in a time of paper shortage, and immense editions printed and shipped out of Washington during a transportation crisis.

After the adoption, on January 29, 1919, of the Eighteenth Amendment, which prohibited the manufacture, sale, or transportation of intoxicating liquors, or their importation into the United States, the Bureau of Internal Revenue was also charged with the enforcement of Prohibition until this task was shifted to the Department of Justice in 1928. War profits and the high tax rate overstrained the integrity of certain taxpayers and revenue agents. Need for an internal policing agency became evident in 1919, when bureau personnel reached fourteen thousand. A special intelligence unit of the Treasury Department was formed on July 1, "intelligence" then being a word in high repute because of an aura it had acquired during the war. The unit was organized around six postal inspectors brought in by the late Elmer L. Irey, himself a former post office inspector. Irey, who headed the unit from 1919 to 1936, became legendary as a "giant killer" because of his success in obtaining convictions of those who employed all kinds of tricks to defraud the revenue — extortion, bribery, embezzlement.[12]

Despite the collection of billions of dollars through the income tax, which financed about one third of the cost of World War I, the balance being paid for by borrowing, only slightly more than 5 percent of the population paid an income tax. Thus it was still a tax on the relatively rich, a group that is always articulate and quick to raise the cry of class legislation. A comment on this argument should be made. All taxes are levied according to some theory of classification,

either explicit or cloudy, in the minds of legislators. A tax
on real restate is class legislation. So is a tax on horses or on
horsepower of motor vehicles. A tax on any kind of property
specified by law is a tax on those who hold that kind of property. A tax on incomes, therefore, is no more an example of
class legislation than is any other tax. But the mood of the
country after the peace was for demobilization in all its
forms, including the financial. The national platforms of both
major parties reflected this in the 1920 presidential campaign.
The Democrats called war taxes in peacetime indefensible.
The Republicans called them a staggering burden. And the
New York Times complained that a law simple in its principle had become a source of nationwide exasperation because it attempted to be too nice in its "threadlike distinctions
for the laymen to decide." The law fails to take account of
the human element, the *Times* continued, making tax time,
in fact, a repellent aspect of spring.[13]

In 1920–1921 a short, sharp depression occurred in business; it lasted longer and cut deeper in agriculture. Economic
conditions, war weariness, and the repudiation of the League
of Nations swept Warren G. Harding to victory in November
1920.[14] The new Republican administration moved promptly
to meet the demand for tax relief. Congress wrestled all
through the summer of 1921 and into the autumn over a new
revenue bill. The war was over. But the expenses of government were still rising because of increased population, enlarged government functions, interest on the public debt,
veterans' benefits, even the operation of the Bureau of Internal Revenue itself as it dealt with Prohibition, narcotics,
and child-labor laws. And the bureau was bringing in less
money because war profits were vanishing and the agency
was clogged with a backlog of audits involving intricate disputes over taxes assessed for the war years. Still, the Com-

missioner of Internal Revenue saw a pot of gold at the foot of the rainbow. The average number of cases closed per revenue agent in 1920 was 174, up from 123 the preceding year. One of the reasons the commissioner gave for the improvement was the "maintenance of individual production records." This is the first official reference I know of to the existence of a quota system, a subject of perennial interest and curiosity to the taxpaying public.[15] (See Chapter 14 for the subsequent history of this administrative procedure.)

The result of the tug of war between opposing forces in 1921 was a modest scaling-downward of the revenue system. President Harding signed the new act on November 23. Each war brings vastly enlarged expenditures, which drop back afterward but never to the same level as before. Perhaps the most notable new feature of the Revenue Act of 1921 was the addition of a 12.5 percent tax on capital gains. Many of today's taxpayers may be surprised to learn that capital gains — the profit from the sale of capital assets — were taxed as ordinary income through 1921, which included the period of high wartime rates. The basis for this conception of income was the theory that any form of realized wealth increases one's power to satisfy his wants. The Sixteenth Amendment permits this levy. It confers on Congress, one must remember, the power to "lay and collect taxes on incomes *from whatever source derived.*" (Emphasis added.) Since 1921, however, capital gains have been subject to lower rates than ordinary income, and since 1923 capital losses have been offset against ordinary income, with varying limitations. The struggle between those who place primary emphasis on treating all dollars alike and those who argue that venture capital needs special encouragement has been long, fierce, sometimes tendentious, with no end in sight.[16]

Meanwhile it became one of the rites of spring for the

Commissioner of Internal Revenue to issue dire warnings citing the penalties that could be imposed by the agency, including warrants of distraint permitting seizure and sale of property of delinquents. Lawyers and accountants who helped their clients to falsify their tax returns would learn to their cost that the conspiracy laws applied handily to the situation. The bureau's annual foray into psychological warfare made solemn reading, often heightened by the spectacular indictment and/or the conviction of some prominent citizen. There was a widespread tax phobia in the country. Those opposed to Prohibition, for example, mourned not only the loss of their legal chalice but also the disappearance of alcoholic beverage taxes, which the income tax had to make up for. And they were infuriated by the use of income tax revenues to penalize behavior that the Anti-Saloon League and those who traveled with it regarded as undesirable.

Yet among the people as a whole, opinion had moved slowly to accept and endure, if not embrace, the graduated income tax. This more lenient sentiment was encouraged by the return of prosperity, the trimming back of the tax rates, and other meliorist gestures through successive reductions, between 1918 and 1929, of the effective rates for the middle- and upper-income classes.[17]

So far so good. But there was also a sense among those who still felt oppressed by the rates that the poor were not paying their proper share in support of the government that protected them and their property; and it was felt, further, that the interest in the conduct of public affairs of those lightly endowed with worldly goods would be strengthened if they paid something toward the public expense. Just what was their share, or anyone's share, is necessarily a recurring theme, entwined always with politics and subjective judgments. One patriot, a resident of Tacoma, Washington, sent in to an astonished district collector of internal revenue a check for $6.66. He explained, "I do not owe an income tax, but I do believe every man in the land should help support the government . . ." In suggesting that all should pay, the gentleman from Tacoma associated himself with a long and distinguished line of economic thinkers in the field of public finance. Manu, the Indian sage, made the same point three thousand years ago, long before Adam Smith formulated his proposition of tax equality. Jonathan Swift wrote, in a letter to the Lord Chancellor: "Every man who enjoys property hath some share in the public and therefore the care of the public is, in some degree, every man's concern."

In the last century, William Bourke Cockran (D.-N.Y.), famous in his day as an orator and spokesman for Tammany Hall, declared during the debate in the House on the short-lived 1894 income tax that paying taxes was basic to the right to control the government. It was a telling argument, echoed in the Senate by David B. Hill, also a New York Democrat responsive to the wishes of the New York City business class. Hill argued that the proposed $4000 exemption under discussion at the time deprived the poor of their proper share of responsibility for the way public affairs were handled. Similar views were expressed in the Senate by the Massachusetts aristocrat, Henry Cabot Lodge, when the relatively high exemption in the 1913 income tax bill was being debated. Lodge called it "vicious in principle," and insisted that the man with an income of $1000 a year would be a better citizen if he paid an income tax. Finally we come to a figure who looms large between March 4, 1921, and February 12, 1932 — Andrew W. Mellon, Secretary of the Treasury between those dates and tireless advocate, in the cabinets of three Presidents, Harding, Coolidge, and Hoover, of broadening the tax base in the tradition just described.

"Every citizen," Secretary Mellon said, "should have a stake in his country." And again, "An income tax is the price which the government charges for the privilege of having taxable income." It should be noticed that Cockran, Hill, Lodge, and Mellon all took the high ground. The poor should be taxed for their own good, to strengthen their characters and make them better citizens. These gentlemen were undoubtedly inspired by the highest motives and perhaps we should not try to go behind their words. Yet it is a curious fact that their recommended policy of spread-the-burden would in every instance have redounded to the fiscal benefit of the middle and upper classes. John Kenneth Galbraith, who stands tall among liberal economists and is a man of somewhat skeptical outlook, calls it a basic rule of economic discourse that "men of high position are allowed, by a special act of grace, to accommodate their reasoning to the answer they need," which is no more than "the simple unwillingness to give up the enjoyment of what they have." [18]

Andrew Mellon was a slight, frail-looking gentleman with a mournful countenance, a querulous voice, and a banker's chilly smile — not the kind of fellow one would easily approach for a ten-spot until Saturday night, although he was very, very rich. Robert K. Murray has written that Mellon was "seedy" in appearance; Arthur Schlesinger, Jr., that he was conservatively but exquisitely tailored. Perhaps a conflation of the two texts would show that the suits were elegant but the man inside looked as though he needed Geritol. However that may be, Mellon, who continued the tradition of McKinley Republicanism, knew what he wanted — economy in government; a reduction in the war debts; the repeal of the estate, gift, and excess profits tax; and a top personal income tax bracket of 25 percent, although as to this, his hope was for something better, "that some day we may get back on a tax basis of 10%, the old Hebrew tithe, which was always considered a fairly heavy tax." [19]

The policies referred to above became famous as the Mellon Plan. They were advanced on the ground that they would cut down on tax avoidance, increase the credibility of the income tax, and bring the maximum amount of money into the Treasury without stifling energy and initiative in the entrepreneurial world. Mellon cited, as confirmation of his views, the support he had received from Henry Ford; Richard Olney, former congressman and Boston wool merchant; Daniel Guggenheim, spokesman for the copper-mining family; and a woman dress manufacturer, who complained that high taxes were depressing her business. "It is the old story," she said, "of killing the goose that laid golden eggs."

After Harding, Coolidge. President Coolidge shared Mellon's outlook on fiscal policy, agreed that the correct rate of income taxation should not be over 25 percent. Harding had had no economic principles of his own to guide him and was overwhelmed when opposing tax proposals were presented to him, each supported with facts and figures. "I don't know what to do or where to turn in this taxation matter," he told his secretary. "Somewhere there must be a book that tells all about it, where I could go to straighten out my mind. But I don't know where the book is, and maybe I couldn't read it if I found it!" [20]

In all fairness, it cannot be said that the tax load was shifted sharply downward during the Mellon years, for actually only 8 percent of the population was being reached then by the income tax, and the Democrats, Progressive Republicans, and the farm bloc were vigilant and watchful when tax proposals were made. The principal reason why the Harding and Coolidge administrations, guided by Mellon,

with his towering reputation as the greatest Secretary of the
Treasury since Alexander Hamilton, could be generous toward wealthy taxpayers without bleeding those of modest
income was the unparalleled prosperity the country enjoyed
during the period. Five times taxes were lowered. These
years constituted, in Randolph Paul's phrase, "a fairy
tale with an unhappy ending," referring of course to the
onset of the Great Depression. As the rosy glow of material
prosperity and "manic optimism in economic matters" faded
away, so did the prestige of the rich and respectable, and the
economic beliefs of the financial Merlins. Critics charged:

> Mellon pulled the whistle,
> Hoover rang the bell,
> Wall Street gave the signal
> And the country went to hell.

According to one anecdote, which catches the flavor of
the times, a banker begged a friend not to reveal his occupation to his old mother. "She thinks I'm playing the piano
in a sporting house," he explained. As for income taxation
discouraging initiative, a favorite folk myth of the Coolidge-
Mellon era, Fiorello La Guardia, the Progressive Republican
congressman from New York, commented, "Well, we gave
them all the rope they wanted, gentlemen, and look at the
plight we are in . . ." [21]

Enter, the Dismal Decade. These were the years of the
greatest depression since 1873 — or ever. Certainly the Depression of the 1930s was the longest and deepest ever experienced in this country. Ways of living disintegrated, old values
were destroyed, and a fear of unemployment became deeply
rooted in the American psyche. Government spending rose
to stimulate recovery and to pay for new human resources
programs, such as the Social Security Act of 1935. Deficit

spending between 1932 and 1939 became, as one economics writer expressed it, "as commonplace . . . as the Saturday night bath was in 1900." Tax collections dropped sharply as jobs vanished. One taxpayer, who seemed to have reached the nadir of misfortune, wrote to the Bureau of Internal Revenue office in Louisville, Kentucky, to explain why he could not pay his assessment of $7.40; "My salary was $400 a month. Somebody got my job, the finance company took my car, the bank took my home, my wife took the furniture and somebody took my wife. All I have left is my health and education and I would be glad to have the opportunity to work out the bill in your department." [22] Unfortunately for the gallant proposal, the government had no arrangements for the payment of taxes through equivalents.

With the appearance of huge Treasury deficits during the Depression years the rates were again stepped up, for the first time since 1918. The Revenue Act of 1932 also broadened the base and lowered the exemptions. This reverse trend continued throughout the decade, pushed upward also by radical political pressures, such as Father Coughlin's League for Social Justice, the Townsend old-age programs, and Huey Long's seductive Share-the-Wealth movement. When President Franklin D. Roosevelt sent a surprise tax message to Congress on June 19, 1935, recommending a drastic overhaul of the tax system "to prevent an unjust concentration of wealth and economic power," Senator Long leered, postured, and almost waltzed as he crossed in front of the rostrum while the clerk droned through the President's message. Next day Will Rogers wrote: "I would sure liked to have seen Huey's face when he was woke up in the middle of the night by the President who said, 'Lay over, Huey, I want to get in with you.'" [23]

The euphoria of the booming 1920s had affected the Bu-

reau of Internal Revenue itself, where operations were often
casual and loose. The commissioner consistently exceeded
his authority to compromise cases. The fraud penalty was
not enforced. Division heads exercised practically unlimited
discretionary power, without adequate rules or instructions.
Formal rulings remained unpublished and lack of known
precedents meant that cases were settled in bargaining conferences rather than on principles; the most skillful and
dogged negotiator got the most favorable settlement. Deductions were lumped together under a general heading with
little hard information available as to their exact nature. For
example, Will Rogers's income tax return for the year 1924
showed earnings of $157,428, including $26,000 received
from weekly newspaper articles. "It says something for the
relatively easy-going attitude of that day's Internal Revenue
Service," wrote Rogers's recent biographer, Richard M.
Ketchum, "that all of the last amount was claimed as a deduction for salary paid to Betty Rogers." There was, moreover, a certain naïveté at the bureau about contemporary
developments in American life. In 1931 it released a remarkable booklet containing brief snippets of information about
income tax forms, filling-out requirements, and warnings of
penalties. The brochure was offered to radio broadcasting
stations, the bureau explained, "to fill the gap between scheduled programs." Evidently, the tax men did not know that
in the fall of 1931 forty million listeners were tuning in
"Amos 'n' Andy" as a nightly ritual and that the "gap" the
bureaucracy proposed to fill was prime commercial time,
booming the sales of Pepsodent toothpaste and underwriting
the solvency of the National Broadcasting Company.[24]

In 1933 and 1934 the general public got a look at the
income tax practices of the big guns of the financial world
through open hearings held by the U.S. Senate Committee

on Banking and Currency; a parade of Wall Street stars, "flanked by their hundred-thousand-dollar-a-year lawyers," took the witness stand and responded to sharp questioning by Ferdinand Pecora, committee counsel. Prestigious names that will never be forgotten by the generation that knew the Depression years passed in review — Charles E. Mitchell, chairman of the board of the National City Bank, who was indicted and convicted of tax evasion; Albert H. Wiggin, chairman of the board of the Chase National Bank; James V. Forrestal and Clarence Dillon, partners in Dillon, Read & Co. Inc.; Otto H. Kahn of Kuhn, Loeb & Co.; Thomas S. Lamont; George and Richard Whitney, who revealed under oath the methods used by the rich in escaping from paying the statutory taxes on income. But the big show was J. P. Morgan, the younger, from whom Pecora drew the acknowledgment that Morgan had, quite legally, paid no income tax in the United States in 1930, 1931, or 1932. Nor had the partners in his firm, through a delicate balancing of gains and losses, "real or technical," paid any tax in 1931 and 1932. It was during these proceedings that a circus press agent obtained a famous photograph when he slid a female midget onto the ample lap of the majestic leader of the House of Morgan. The picture shows her sitting up pertly against the background of the great head, the luxuriant white mustache, and an expanse of heavy gold watch chain. "The smallest lady in the world," the flack told the astonished banker, "wants to meet the richest man in the world." All in all it was a trying day for the international banker. Some of the findings of this famous investigation will be discussed further in Chapter 12.[25]

Tax avoidance and tax evasion reached a high in 1937. But the terms, often used interchangeably, differ widely in meaning and should be used with precision. Avoidance, often called "tax planning," was and still is legal, though it may represent the letter rather than the spirit of the law. It can be regarded as reputable or disreputable depending on who is involved and the circumstances attendant on its use. Evasion was and still is fraud. Lady Godiva's chilly ride was an act of tax avoidance, undertaken on behalf of the hard-pressed people of Coventry, and the ride made her a heroine of tax folklore. Tax-free "expense allowances" of ever-increasing generosity conferred by members of Congress on themselves are a modern example.

It was in 1937, or perhaps around the end of 1936, as tax rates were climbing to a top bracket of 75 percent under the Revenue Act of 1936, that President Roosevelt heard how a prominent New York financier had remarked to a group of friends in a bar in Paris: "My fortune is in the Bahama Islands, and is going to stay there as long as that bastard is in the White House." FDR was amused and surprised but less amused when he learned from Secretary of the Treasury Henry Morgenthau, Jr., how vulnerable the tax structure was to ingenious schemes. About that time, too, J. P. Morgan uttered the indiscretion of a lifetime when he told reporters, "Congress should know how to levy taxes, and if it doesn't know how to collect them, then a man is a fool to pay them." Later the mandarin of Broad and Wall streets tried to undo the damage by explaining that his "offhand remarks" were not to be taken as a defense of tax-dodging. But his observations undoubtedly gave comfort to those wealthy taxpayers who pressed on to the frontiers of the law and sometimes beyond, in the spirit of the French proverb: "Stealing from the State is not stealing." Sometimes, of course, the line shifted, or the question was one on which reasonable men might differ. Sometimes the venturesome taxpayer won; sometimes lost. But for players with not too nice a moral sense the game was frequently worth the candle.[26]

During the 1930s a veritable army of clever attorneys and

accountants emerged to circumvent the Internal Revenue Code. Often their expertise was gained in the bureau itself, as the Joint Committee on Tax Evasion and Avoidance must have reflected in 1937 as it viewed photographs of shacks maintained in the Bahamas as the headquarters of dummy corporations. This decade was also high noon for notorious violators of other laws, who were successfully prosecuted on tax charges, among them Irving "Waxey Gordon" Wexler, a high roller in beer-running circles during Prohibition days. Wexler was convicted of income tax fraud for the years 1930 and 1931, and changed his address from opulent digs on West End Avenue, New York City, to a cubicle in the federal penitentiary at Lewisburg, Pennsylvania. Surely the most spectacular instance of what the T-men could do with subpoena, gun, and camera was the termination of the career in crime of Alphonse Capone, the Chicago racketeer whose *nom de gang* was "Scarface Al." Capone committed murder with impunity but came to grief when he failed to file his Form 1040, and the sharp dresser who once rode to the opera in an armored limousine, escorted by eighteen bodyguards in tuxedos, found himself in a federal prison, cutting out overalls.[27]

"The underlying human reluctance to pay . . . the price of civilized society," Randolph Paul wrote, "remained in 1937 substantially what it was in 1894." There is always the question in the minds of taxpayers as to whether a particular taxpayer is transferring too much from the private purse to the public treasury or whether he feels that he is getting back enough civilization for his money. More painful still is the thought that others are shouldering less than their proper share of the general sacrifice. Thus a numerous corps of volunteer tax-collectors has been active ever since 1913, often including in its ranks disillusioned ex-wives, jealous mistresses, and business competitors. "We get floods of anonymous letters tipping us off to tax frauds," the chief of the intelligence unit of the Bureau of Internal Revenue said in a newspaper interview. "The authors point out that they are paying their taxes and don't see why their neighbors and competitors shouldn't pay, too." The motivation may be spite, a highly developed sense of justice, or a candid interest in the cash awards available to successful claimants who have filled out and filed Form 211, the form for informers. Some enterprising bounty hunters have even copied names at random from telephone books, hoping to make a lucky strike. The informer's best chance, by the way, is to cite unreasonable affluence. By an odd quirk of human nature, tax-cheaters sometimes tell on themselves. "If a tax evader's cup runneth over," Gerald Krefetz wrote in a newspaper feature article, "so usually does his mouth." The same writer mentioned one successful tipster who had IRS trouble himself when he omitted to include his honorarium on his tax return.

The citizen who turned revenue informer when the frontier was still open was treated like one of those who spread smallpox or cut a levee. He risked becoming the central figure at a lynching. Now if the informer claims a reward and the IRS collects on the helpful hint, he is given a commendation and a percentage. However, the revenue service is fully aware of the distasteful history of "spying," and no general appeals are made to the public to turn in potential cheaters. Most tipsters do not claim the reward. Their recompense lies elsewhere, as does that of those who turn in scofflaws for illegal parking. It just makes them mad.[28]

Against the background that has been sketched here, President Roosevelt sent a message to Congress on June 1, 1937, about the need for further revisions in the law to deal with such schemes as personal holding companies, family partnerships, multiple trusts for relatives, the yacht-and-country-home gambit. Congress responded promptly with the Revenue Act of 1937. A goodly number of loopholes were closed. But incomes and rates both rose during the defense boom of 1940–1941, offering new temptations to adventurous risk-takers. From the very beginning of the modern income tax to 1939, each major revenue act had contained a new set of ever more intricate provisions. To simplify compliance, in 1939 Congress undertook to codify systematically the accumulation of old and new laws. Legislation passed after that date, therefore, consisted of amendments to the basic code. It stood for sixteen years. Then it was overhauled again, to produce the Internal Revenue Code of 1954, which is still in effect. Its precise words are today the starting point in any tax dispute.[29]

The "high" for Depression expenditures was reached in 1935. By 1939–1940 the emphasis had shifted to defense, the nation responding to the Munich agreement, the fall of France in June 1940, and the air battle over Britain that autumn. After the Japanese attack on Pearl Harbor it was no longer necessary to give euphemistic "defense" titles to war-oriented agencies. A revenue act was passed on June 25, 1940, providing for increased individual surtax rates in most brackets and reaching down to tap more incomes by reducing exemptions. This was only a temporary expedient. In October came the second Revenue Act of 1940, increasing corporation tax rates and adding new excess profits taxation. The Revenue Act of 1941 in September of the next year lowered exemptions once more, boosting surtax rates to curb war profiteering and inflation and to help pay for national mobilization. Never before in the history of the United States was economic control, both macroeconomic and microeconomic, so tight.[30] New millions of Americans felt for the first time the weight of income taxation, war and taxes, as always, being bonded together and receipts always falling behind expenditures. The effect was to change profoundly the social structure of American society because everybody, or almost everybody, who had income was called upon to shoulder the burden of war.

10

The Class Tax Becomes
a Mass Tax

DURING THE SUMMER of 1942 the House Ways and Means Committee struggled with the first of several World War II revenue bills, hearing 250 witnesses, whose testimony came to 2376 pages. All who testified wanted to win the war — but not, when it came to finances, in the same way. With employment and incomes rising, organized labor discovered, as wartime basic rates soared from 4 percent in 1939 to 23 percent in 1944 and a new 5 percent Victory Tax appeared on gross incomes over $624, that it had a very direct interest in how the war was fought on the monetary front. Labor, therefore, wished to preserve the tax structure that had successfully underwritten the First World War; that is, a policy of keeping the exemptions high and the rates low, with steep graduation upward for the middle and wealthy classes. As late as 1939 only four million American citizens reported taxable incomes. But the figure jumped to about seven and a half million individual taxpayers the next year and by 1945 it rose to 42,764,000. The number of persons who were required to file returns though they did not have to pay taxes was even greater, by several million.

White collar or blue collar, there was no escape this time from the iron law of total war. But it was strongly urged that although Rosie the Riveter was performing her patriotic and essential function, yet was unable to buy a refrigerator, there should be no unjust enrichment of the wealthy.

Another group with different concerns feared that rigorous application of the egalitarian ethic to taxation might reach the point of forcing taxpayers to default on their fixed obligations, and this might dispossess or seriously discommode the middle class. Still other witnesses, representing the higher levels of capitalistic enterprise, demanded assurance that war taxation was not going to crush free enterprise, inhibit industrial expansion, interfere with war production, and so brake the drive for victory.

One point became clear: income taxes were going to affect the lives and personal plans of millions of Americans as they never had before. The issue of whether the low-income groups were to be brought into the income tax system or reached indirectly through excise and sales taxes was never perfectly resolved, but the decision was adopted to rely principally upon the income tax. The effective rate for the upper brackets increased moderately, and the receivers of middle incomes felt a sharp increase in their liability.

During the summer and autumn of 1942 Congress was not satisfied with knowing the general terms of the tax proposal. It wanted the details, but complained that they seemed awfully complicated, as indeed they were. James John Davis, who had been a steel puddler and had risen in the world to become Secretary of Labor under Harding, Coolidge, and Hoover, and a Republican United States senator from Pennsylvania, sat in on deliberations of the Senate Finance Committee while it marked up the bill. Finally he threw up his hands as the proposed legislation took shape. "It is too complicated," he declared, "for an ordinary man like me to understand." The committee was agreed, however, as Randolph

Paul expressed it, that "the geese that laid the golden eggs should be carefully nurtured," which means that standards of fiscal responsibility had guided the committee in its decisions. But it must have been a fatiguing operation, for the hearing record showed that the witnesses invariably proposed to preserve the health of the goose through achieving some preferential tax position for their own interests.[1]

The result of Congress's labors was described by President Roosevelt as "the greatest tax bill in American history" and was signed by the President on October 21, 1942. The Revenue Act of 1942 produced 36,528,000 personal tax returns, of which 27,719,000 reported on the bottom line money owing to the government. This was very nearly double the number from the year before.

"Almost overnight," as Surrey and Warren have noted, the income tax "spread from the country club district down to the railroad tracks and then over to the other side of the tracks." Yet the Treasury was so pressed for money that the act was inadequate before it was passed. The rules were tightened up in various ways. The Victory Tax was withheld by employers, representing a first step toward a permanent system of tapping income at its source. Taxes were made a current obligation; that is, the quarterly payments fell due as the income was earned. From 1913 to 1942 income taxes had been paid during the year following the receipt of the income. Now this one-year lag was eliminated. The wage earner was saved from hardship in case of a subsequent lean year or a lost job and the Treasury was relieved of the task of trying to collect that which might turn out to be uncollectible.[2]

Nineteen forty-three was a crucial year — the year of the U.S. offensive in the South Pacific, the year of the end of the African campaign, and the return of Anglo-American

forces to Europe through Italy. At home, the public appeared to favor financing the war with bonds rather than
taxes. Bonds represented future purchasing power, which
would be available when automobiles, tires, refrigerators,
and other big-ticket items would once more appear in the
marketplace. Taxes, on the other hand, were gone forever.
Thus the response was enthusiastic when stars from "The
Lucky Strike Hit Parade" or "The Aldrich Family" made
personal appearances at industrial plants during the lunch
hour in behalf of the war-loan drives. But tax propaganda
was not absent from the scene, *vide* the song Irving Berlin
wrote especially for the Treasury Department. Under the
title "I Paid My Income Tax Today," the lyrics represented
the taxpayer as singing:

> You see those bombers in the sky,
> Rockefeller helped to build them,
> So did I
> I PAID MY INCOME TAX TODAY.

The 1943 act made no changes in the personal tax rates
or exemption credits, but Congress introduced an important
change by putting income-tax payers on a current basis. The
new system of withholding made collections more efficient,
the yield greater, and it strengthened the effort to hold down
inflation. However, the act included so many tax favors
dear to Congress, though not to the administration or the
Treasury, that President Roosevelt vetoed it as neglectful of
the welfare of the low- and medium-income groups. A particular irritant was the complex nature of the 1943 act.
Aware that there were more than forty million returns to be
filed for that year and that the tax system ran serious risks
if it expected citizens to be bookkeepers, accountants, lawyers, tax experts, and war workers too, President Roosevelt

said in the veto message of February 22: "The American taxpayer had been promised of late that tax laws and returns
will be drastically simplified. This bill does not make good
that promise . . . These taxpayers, now engaged in an effort
to win the greatest war this nation has ever faced, are not
in a mood to study higher mathematics." It adds a human
touch to note that Robert L. Doughton (D.-N.C.), chairman
of the Ways and Means Committee which was responsible
for the legislation, admitted that he was caught in a web of
his own weaving; he found he had to hire a tax expert to
help him prepare his own return under the law for which
he bore major responsibility. Both houses of Congress, smart-
ing under the President's criticism, voted to override the
veto. The bill became law, therefore, without Roosevelt's
signature.[3]

In 1944 people dreamed of peace and complained about
cigarette, gasoline, and meat shortages and about filling out
tax returns as surtaxes rose from 20 percent on the first
$2000 to more than 90 percent on net incomes of over
$200,000. The taxpayer with less than $5000 in annual income got relief from unaccustomed mathematical labor because he could now compute the tax by using simplified
tables according to a schedule of standard deductions. This,
with other adjustments, unburdened some thirty million taxpayers with small incomes of the tedious task of declaring
estimates of their incomes and filing itemized returns.

The war was over when the Revenue Act of 1945 was
passed on November 8, 1945. It was a reconversion bill,
which provided for a moderate scaling-down of rates. The
expected traumatic experience of changing back to a peacetime economy, including a projected massive unemployment,
was avoided by a remarkable program and good cooperation
between government and business. The result was that the

gross national product by 1950 was greater than the peak wartime figure in 1944 — an enormous achievement.[4]

During World War II the individual income tax, in one of the most significant developments in American fiscal history, surpassed all other sources of revenue of the federal government. For the first thirty years of the income tax, the yield was controlled through changes in the rates applied to the middle- and upper-income receivers. The war changed all that. The revenue yield then and thereafter was determined principally by the resultant of two forces: the rate fixed for the first bracket and the level allowed for personal exemptions. An adjustment up or down of only $100 in exempt income was sufficient to move billions of dollars into or out of the Treasury. The income tax was most productive, it was found, when it reached the largest areas of income — not the largest incomes — for the lower-income taxpayers, taken collectively, had the most money. And it may be added as a fact of life that the wealthy can underreport and argue and work their way up the appeals system toward a satisfactory closing of their file, but those dependent on salary or wages are exposed to the rigors of the tax through payroll deductions.

The point where taxing personal earnings begins had been governed in the past by two carefully balanced theories. The first was to lift the bottom level of taxation high enough to permit the taxpayer a reasonable and even a generous allowance for the necessary expenses of living. The second, looking in a different direction, aimed to set the bottom rate low enough so that the working population would have an incentive to share responsibly in shaping government policies. This argument for taxing citizens with modest incomes was advanced by Joseph H. Choate in the *Pollock* case, by Bourke Cockran, the elder Senator Lodge, Andrew W. Mellon, and other spokesmen for the Standing Order, whom we have already met. As late as 1954, Raymond Moley, the repentant New Dealer, was fulminating against the Democratic leaders in Congress who wanted to ease the exemptions for low-income earners; he accused Jere Cooper (D.-Tenn.) and Sam Rayburn (D.-Texas), Speaker of the House of Representatives in nine Congresses, of raising "the grimy flag of class hatred." His fellow fiscal conservative, Henry Hazlitt, found that any reduction of the tax load on the common man would simply "relieve that many voters of any concern about government extravagance." Today exemptions are low, as Choate, Mellon, Moley, and others desired, but for quite different reasons from those they advanced: the government needs the money and cannot get it without reaching into the pockets of the millions of wage-earners.

The figures for those who were required to file returns during the defense build-up and the war period tell the story of the transformation of the income tax into a levy on Everyman:

$$1940 — 14,665,000$$
$$1941 — 25,855,000$$
$$1942 — 36,538,000$$
$$1943 — 43,602,000$$
$$1944 — 47,012,000$$
$$1945 — 49,865,000$$

The number of returns rose more than 350 percent while the population grew only 6 percent. These figures dispose of the polemic that the modern income tax is class legislation in the sense that Senator Lodge meant when he decried the "pillage of a class." For Congress had rediscovered, under the pressure of war financing, the principle Adam Smith set forth long ago when he wrote: "The whole consumption of the inferior ranks of people, or of those below the middling rank, it must be observed, is in every country much greater, not only in quantity, but in value, than that of the middling and of those above the middling rank. The whole expense of the inferior is much greater than that of the superior ranks." [5]

After the end of World War II, though personal and corporate taxes were moderately reduced, the federal budgets never returned to prewar levels. They had to meet the costs of the cold war, the quantitative growth of the modern mixed economy, and the assumption by the federal government of greatly enlarged responsibilities for dealing with social and economic problems that the private sector could not or would not handle. It had been held in 1937 that "the power of the purse could be utilized for whatever social purpose the legislature chose" so long as it was exercised to promote the general welfare. "The discretion," said the Supreme Court, "belongs to Congress."

This decision laid the constitutional foundation for the welfare state. Thus the United States, a late-comer to the idea in comparison with many other industrialized countries, adopted the principle that society had an obligation to protect the individual worker against the hazards that accompany advanced age, injury, infirmity, or loss of employment. And we have been able to have our cake and eat it too. As Paul A. Samuelson wrote, "The modern welfare state has been both humane and solvent." [6]

At 4:00 A.M. on Sunday, June 25, 1950, the Communist regime of North Korea invaded South Korea. President Truman, facing a crisis he saw as part of a historical process reaching back to the Japanese invasion of Manchuria and including the Hitlerian aggressions and World War II, decided within a week to commit United States military power, under the aegis of the United Nations, to block the Communist offensive. Income tax rates rose again, as did excise taxes on a long list of articles: gasoline, automobiles, and other consumer durables, and the old reliable workhorses of taxation, liquor and tobacco. The President received powers comparable to but not quite so extensive as those granted the executive branch in World War II. By the use of priorities and price and credit controls, the value of the dollar was stabilized, expenditures held down, and the war paid for by taxation rather than long-term borrowing.

By the end of the Korean War in 1953 the general character of the personal income tax was well established and well understood, its hoped-for elasticity fully demonstrated, its fiscal adequacy confirmed by its contribution toward the cost of the wars of the twentieth century and of the social programs assumed by the government in the last forty years. Further changes in the revenue laws, therefore, will not be pursued here in chronological detail. One does get a sense of this-is-where-I-came-in in observing that each new Congress bravely advances on the tax code under the banner of reform. But reform proves to be an elusive goal, never fully attained yet pursued with a delicate awareness of current feelings, attitudes, and beliefs among the electorate. Subsequent chapters will take up general topics that are always with us — the ever-hopeful income-tax-resisters looking for a constitutional loophole, the avoiders and cheaters, the Alice-in-Wonderland world of tax favors, the interplay of good and evil in the Internal Revenue Service itself, the humor of taxation (a necessarily brief treatment), and finally a summary of where we stand after some sixty-three years' experience with our most productive impost.[7]

PART TWO

11

Protesting the Tax:
Rhetoric and Action

Tax time in America, which is not merely April 15 but actually every day in the calendar year, has generated a substantial cadre of dissidents who fight on many fronts. Some object to the rising burden of the tax itself and point out that if what we have is taxation with representation, "we now need," as a *New York Times* reader wrote from Fayetteville, Arkansas, "to be protected from our representatives." [1] Others object to where the money goes — for current military spending, the space-shuttle program, farm supports, tax-exempt foundations, refrigerators for the Eskimos, or the high cost of supporting the average congressman. Still others get the fantods over the red tape involved in complying with the tax code.

On another front, tax-law amateurs and clever lawyers still search hopefully for some constitutional handle that may yet be grasped and used to strike down the authority of Congress to lay an income tax. Activists take to the streets. They form picket lines, write chain letters, dream of getting up a taxpayers' revolt, stage symbolic events such as Boston *tax* parties. A very few choose the desperate course of open defiance of the IRS.

Direct taxes have never met with popular favor or stayed

long on the statute books after the end of the wars of the United States except for the present income tax statute. "The tax-gatherer from earliest history has been an unwelcome presence, and his business an ungracious one," one Commissioner of Internal Revenue commented in describing the mission of his agency. The work of the revenue agent, the commissioner continued,

> is inquisitorial in its very nature, leading to inquiries into people's affairs, the condition of their business, their losses and gains, matters which most people prefer keeping secret . . . The process of assessment is summary, involving, in case of delinquency, penalties and sacrifice of property. The tax is a palpable thing to be paid, or some cherished possession is to be sold to meet it. No circumstances of poverty, misfortune, sickness, or death stay the distraint. Injustice in the assessment itself is relievable only by a circuitous process . . ." [2]

Against the background of so comprehensive a critique from so high a personality in the hierarchy of the Treasury Department, it is not surprising that the personal income tax generates a continuous flow of protests, some responsible, some self-serving, some highly imaginative, some governed by the comic muse. Various elites from within the Establishment have added weighty counsel — the American Bar Association, the National Association of Manufacturers, the United States Chamber of Commerce — on such topics as how the money should be collected, spent or not spent, and the perennial hope for simplification of the tax code. Radical-conservative groups, individual citizens, and even state legislatures have protested against the spending propensities of Congress and its unlimited power to lay an income tax. Judging by the volume of criticism and its varied sources, it appears that the American public is well aware of the connection between taxes and expenditures, including the tax favors that do not appear in the budget but are as much a charge on the Treasury as any other outlay.[3]

Three women, blooded in battle, stand out like modern Molly Pitchers in the fight against the income tax. The late, fiery industrialist Miss Vivien Kellems for over two decades devoted her not inconsiderable talents to an assault on the whole concept of a graduated tax on incomes as being un-American, unconstitutional, and, in fact, thoroughly communistic. She also conducted separate campaigns against withholding by the employer and the rate structure that discriminated between taxpayers on the basis of marital status. Included in her credentials for leadership were her study of economics at Columbia University and her eligibility for membership in the Daughters of the American Revolution eleven times over. For years she persistently but unsuccessfully sought victory or martyrdom. But when she flatly refused to collect the withholding tax from the employees of her cable-grip plant, then located in Westport, Connecticut, the wily tax men refused to seize her person. Instead, they attached her bank account, under an obscure provision found in Section 2707(a) of the Internal Revenue Code of 1939, which dealt with the tax on pistols, and collected the amount due according to IRS calculations.

Mrs. Irene Whetstone, an industrial engineer and long-time income tax rebel, went to jail rather than discuss her income tax with internal revenue officials. She refused to pay because her money would be spent on what she considered to be "illegal" projects, including the Marshall Plan. On another occasion Mrs. Whetstone had so many suits going against the U.S. Government contesting its right to collect income taxes from her that a federal judge in Chicago put her on an allowance. She could pursue the five actions already on the docket. But no more.

A movie actress of similar mettle, Corinne Griffith, smart

and pretty, though she refers to herself unconvincingly as "plain little ole me," organized the Crusade for the Abolition of the Individual Income Tax in Beverly Hills, California. She opposed the funding of congressional junkets abroad and federal expenditures for studying the psychology of the octopus. In support of her adversary position regarding military expenditures, Corinne explained that she had never been in "an actual shooting war," although she had been married for most of her life.[4]

Pacifist principles have a long history in America. Since the middle of the seventeenth century the population of this country has included elements that rejected not only military service but all forms of preparation for war, including the payment of taxes to support a military establishment. These settlers included Anabaptists, Mennonites, Moravians, and the Society of Friends. Historically, the Quakers did not fear persecution or prosecution. A modern instance of a religious group that caused the IRS much embarrassment was the Old Order Amish. The issue in this case was not war but the Social Security tax, which, because it is a form of insurance, was unacceptable to the Amish. Insurance, in the Amish view, implies a lack of faith in God's concern for the sick and aged. Their care is properly the responsibility of family and church. The trouble heated up in 1954 when the Social Security statute was amended to include self-supporting farmers. The hook-and-eye Dutch refused to pay. The IRS began seizing bank accounts, dairy checks, and finally, on a beautiful April day in 1961, three agents drove up into the field of a western Pennsylvania Amish farmer, Valentine Y. Byler, who was busy with his spring plowing. The revenuers unhitched Byler's handsome Belgian mares, took the harness and all equipment, and auctioned everything off, returning $37.89 to Byler, the excess received over his liability. National publicity followed. The public wrote angry letters to the press. Congressmen made indignant speeches, and in 1965 President Lyndon B. Johnson signed a Medicare–Social Security bill providing for the exclusion of the Amish as conscientious objectors to Social Security on the ground of its being a form of insurance. Ironically, many economists now say it isn't.[5]

The protest against the use of taxes to support war crested during the American intervention in Vietnam. As part of a demonstration in New York an outsized replica of a 1040 tax form was burned. A crowd estimated at six thousand rallied outside the downtown Manhattan district office of the IRS as the folk singer Pete Seeger introduced an ominous new lyric, "Last Train to Nuremburg — All on Board!" Other groups who gathered to picket and chant slogans in front of the IRS office have included the New York Workshop in Nonviolence, Women Strike for Peace, and the Peacemakers. In 1968, at the height of the American disaffection over the Vietnam involvement, eight members of the War Resisters League turned in their tax forms on April 15 without payment, while colleagues picketed with signs reading, "Don't Pay War Taxes." Another approach was taken by fifteen professors at Cornell University, who pledged to pay only 50 percent of their federal income taxes, the portion of the U.S. budget being spent on war.

Among individuals who have reacted, and acted, was Lorraine Cleveland. As a postwar relief worker in Europe for the American Friends Service Committee, she saw the devastating effects of war, and sent a check payable to the United States Children's Bureau in settlement of her tax liability. But the IRS got its money by attaching her assets. A sixty-two-year-old pacifist whose home had been seized for noncompliance handed out leaflets in front of the federal building in Cincinnati, criticizing the use of federal taxes for military purposes. Arrested for disorderly conduct, he went on a hunger strike while in jail.

The Reverend Abraham J. Muste, secretary of the Peacemakers, showed unusual ingenuity in 1951 in not paying to support what he called "this . . . paranoia race." He filed the Gospels and Thoreau's essay *On the Duty of Civil Disobedience* as supporting evidence since, as he said, tax returns have to be documented. Thoreau spent a day and a night in jail, it will be remembered, for refusal to pay a poll tax to a government that prosecuted the Mexican War. The late Edmund Wilson, distinguished author, influential literary critic, and polished stylist, became so angry over federal spending for the Vietnam disaster, along with some personal troubles he had with the Internal Revenue Service, that he wrote a book into which he poured the vials of his wrath. "I have finally come to feel," he said, "that this country, whether or not I continue to live in it, is no longer any place for me." [6]

The objects of taxpayer ire approach infinity, but these areas of spending, in addition to those already touched upon, may be noted as being representative: foreign aid, discrimination against single taxpayers, and the limitation on deductions for child care. This disincentive to married working women is especially repugnant to the National Organization for Women (NOW). Looking in a different direction, one finds Stockholders of America, Inc., advocating more favorable treatment of capital gains, while Lowell Ponte, national chairman of Taxpayer Democracy, wants more democracy in the way the money is spent and has proposed that each taxpayer be permitted to decide the proportion of his taxes that should go to each government service that he approved of — so much for welfare, so much to the Pentagon, the Micronesian Claims Commission, and so forth.

Notice should be taken at this point of citizens who hold no particular philosophical views but who just don't like to pay taxes. Their antipathy to the tax-gatherer sometimes overflows into violence, as was the case with a garage owner of Putnam Valley, New York, who assaulted a revenue agent with a jeep when the IRS representative tried to enforce a delinquent tax levy; or the California taxpayer who arrived at the IRS office in Stockton to discuss his tax problems equipped with eight sticks of dynamite and a revolver. The Scriptures remind us that this is no new thing: "Then king Rehoboam sent Adoram who *was* over the tribute; and all Israel stoned him with stones, that he died." Fortunately, in neither instance mentioned above did anybody die.[7]

Honorable men can differ over disbursements of tax money for health, education, and welfare, our military establishment, mass transit, the plight of the cities, the search for new energy sources, the sale of our wheat to ideological adversaries. Less well known are clearly ridiculous projects hidden in the budgets of important agencies and departments.

Senator William Proxmire (D.-Wis.), who makes a monthly "Golden Fleece" Award for outstanding examples of how the taxpayers get fleeced, told the Senate in April 1975 that the Award for that month had been won jointly by the National Science Foundation (NSF), National Aeronautics and Space Administration (NASA), and the Office of Naval Research, for spending in the range of $500,000 to determine why and under what circumstances rats, monkeys, and humans bite and clench their jaws, and for a proposal to appropriate an additional $150,000 for further work on alcoholism and jaw-clenching in the monkey world. "It's time for the federal government to get out of this 'monkey business,'" Senator Proxmire has declared.

The National Science Foundation has also passed out

$465,000 for the study of passionate love and sexual arousal, fascinating subjects, without doubt, but scarcely likely to yield their secrets to the NSF, which is also responsible for a twelve-month study called "Hitchhiking — A Viable Addition to a Multimodal Transportation System."

A few more examples of how our money goes that-a-way:

The Pentagon spent $375,000 to study the flight of the Frisbee and a modest $12,600 on research into the chromosomes of chipmunks.

The Federal Aviation Administration used $57,800 to quantify the body measurements of airline stewardess trainees, ostensibly for the design of safety equipment. It must have been interesting work, all right, taking seventy-nine measurements from head to foot. And what did the data accumulated so painfully — or should one say pleasantly? — amount to? It showed that "stewardesses are young women with the body measurements of young women."

Seventy thousand dollars of NSF money went into a study of the smell of the perspiration given off by Australian aborigines.

One bureaucrat, Jubal Hale (salary, $19,693), became something of a popular hero when he recommended to the House of Representatives that the agency of which he was director, the Federal Metal and Nonmetallic Mine Safety Board of Review, be abolished. It had not heard a case since its establishment in 1970. Congress accepted the unusual recommendation reluctantly and only after Hale himself had stirred up the press and the networks. A member of the House visited the board's suite in downtown Washington. He found the door open, the office empty, coffee on the desk, and a Beethoven disc turning on the record player.[8]

Many of the brainstorms like those already cited are funded through lump-sum discretionary appropriations to agencies, disguised by innocuous descriptions or grouped under headings so general that congressmen don't know what they are approving. The National Taxpayers Union (NTU) has been especially diligent in exposing to public gaze various little horror stories about what tax money is spent for. The NTU has been criticized for concentrating on trivial and ludicrous examples of government largess. Jim Davidson, the NTU director, insists that the charge is without merit. He says it is the media that go for the light stuff, and cites NTU positions on issues of great magnitude, such as the funding of the space shuttle, whose cost will probably hit $150 billion, or the grave problem of the ever-increasing non-budgeted debt. According to NTU's research director, Sid Taylor, the total liabilities of the U.S. Government stood at about $5 trillion in 1974, which may even be a low estimate because of "hidden liabilities, undiscovered commitments, or back-door spending" not yet revealed.[9]

Many but not all tax rebels are one-idea people. What is often involved is an anarchic or antigovernment outlook. Corinne Griffith has also opposed the UN, NATO, the CIA, and finds it significant that the Senate Office Building is known in the city rooms of newspapers as the S.O.B. She has claimed that the navy has enough hamburger on hand to last for sixty years, and mentions one department of the government, unfortunately not specified, that has on hand a century's supply of paper clips.

Liberty Lobby, a right-wing organization, held a convention in Washington at which four people were honored for nonpayment of income taxes. The Lobby also opposes the UN, foreign aid, "the pro-Soviet Washington *Post*," Zionism, black mayors and congressmen, the Federal Reserve System, foundations, immigration (especially of Asians), and gun control. Operating well to the right of the John Birch Society, the Liberty Lobby points to the graduated income tax as an entering wedge for international communism. It passes the word to its membership to store weapons and dehydrated foodstuffs against *Götterdämmerung* and instructs them to join together quietly under such euphemisms as "Jogging Group" or "Bird-Watchers." Liberty Lobby also offers literature on survival and guerrilla training. Similar views on taxation are held by the National Justice Foundation, which convened in 1974 in the ambience of H.M.S. *Queen Mary*, now berthed at Long Beach, California. Those who attended heard talks on the IRS conspiracy and the coming tax revolt; they hailed victories over the American Civil Liberties Union; and saluted the sheriff's deputies of Los Angeles for their zeal during civil riots. Needless to say, the unrestricted right to possess arms is precious to this organization.[10]

Constitutional challenges to the graduated income tax were disposed of by the Supreme Court long ago, which means the tax is safe from attacks based on strained interpretations of the Constitution. (See Chapter 8.) But adventurous taxpayers keep trying to find a basis for noncompliance. Gloria Swanson, the actress, argued that, being unmarried and taxed at a higher rate than are married couples, she was the object of discrimination when the IRS cracked down on her for back taxes of more than $14,000. This was tantamount, she said, to taking property without due process of law and was based on an unreasonable classification of property. But, alas for Gloria, at that point she bumped into *Carmichael* v. *Southern Coal Co.*, in which it was held that "neither due process nor equal protection imposes upon a state any rigid rule of equality of taxation," for inequalities "infringe no constitutional limitation," and "a legislature may make distinctions of degree having a rational basis."

Another gambit that has been tried is the Fifth Amendment protection against self-incrimination. Jerome Daly conducted a seminar on tax evasion (admission, $15) and sold packets of instruction for $100, giving details of his method for noncompliance. Taking his own advice, Daly filed his Form 1040 with only his name, address, occupation, and Social Security number filled in and the perjury statement at the bottom blacked out. But the Eighth Court of Appeals sustained his conviction, saying that if a tax return does not contain the information on which the tax can be computed, it is not a return. William Douglass, convinced that the internal revenue system is unconstitutional and that voluntary payment of any taxes constitutes treason, scrawled "Under Protest" in bold letters across the face of his return and gave no financial information. The Tax Court ruled against him: "One may not pick and choose which laws he will obey and which he will disregard . . ." It is all right to criticize, to write, to speak, to distribute literature challenging the constitutionality of the income tax. The right of free speech covers that. But when dissent moves into action, such as advocating evasion, filing a blank return, well, it is just like kicking a policeman — *mala in se;* and in a criminal case it doesn't strengthen the claim that the rights of the taxpayer have been violated for the defendant to arrive at the courthouse by ambulance and be carried to the scene of battle on a stretcher, as was tried in 1973 by a Mrs. Eugene F. House of Blossburg, Pennsylvania.[11]

Marvin L. Cooley, an Arizona man who once ran for Congress, and a leading tax rebel, wrote a book on tax evasion with the intriguing title *The Big Bluff*. The author took the same general line of attack as Daly did, and suffered the same fate as did Daly — conviction by a federal court jury for following his own advice. Karl Jack Bray was more adroit than Daly and Cooley. A big wheel in both the Utah Liberation

Party and Tax Rebels of America, Bray sold his followers instructions in the methodology of how not to pay. It was a commercial enterprise. Bray carefully reported his profits and meticulously paid his own income tax. He must be a man with an odd but well-developed sense of humor because he had printed up counterfeit IRS seizure stickers, as used by the IRS Collections Division, very official-looking — "Warning, United States Government Seizure, All Persons are warned not to remove or tamper with this property" — and slapped the labels at random on automobiles and other property in the Salt Lake area. Compared with the risk of fines and jail sentences these bold spirits willingly accepted, the mild activism of the National Conference of State Taxpayers Associations (NCSTA) seems like a boarding school pillow fight. The NCSTA got up a special protest stamp for taxpayers to stick to the envelopes containing their tax returns. The stamp pictured a taxpayer, his wife, and child all wearing barrels and standing in front of the United States Treasury building.[12]

Like the psychosis in the Old Confederacy over the terrors of a slave insurrection, the dread of a massive taxpayers' revolt hangs over Washington tax authorities as at least a theoretical possibility, though it has never occurred. The idea of job action of this sort does get tossed around among unhappy citizens from time to time. But the number of hard-core tax guerrillas is small, their sympathizers numerous but cautious, fatally flawed as potential revolutionaries by being bourgeois at heart. Vocal and skilled publicists, the active resisters, often get public exposure out of proportion to their numbers. The IRS watches them, understands their need for martyrs, moves in only when there is an overt attempt to impede the execution of the law. A bigger sensation than any the tax protesters have ever been able to create came, ironically, from the highest level of the government itself, when President Johnson's last Secretary of the Treasury, Joseph W. Barr, testified in January 1969 before the Ways and Means Committee and forecast a tax revolt of the middle classes because of revelations that some high-income Americans were paying little or no federal income taxes.[13]

Today the cry is seldom raised that the income tax is communistic except as it issues from extreme radical-conservative sources who continue to insist that it is Marxian doctrine that progressive taxation is a helpful device for establishing the classless society. Congress, certainly, has shown no appetite for tampering with the Sixteenth Amendment, nor has the executive. Even Calvin Coolidge approved of the income tax as a part of our revenue system, and he has never been accused, so far as I know, of harboring anticapitalistic thoughts. In sum, progressive taxation is now one of the accepted components of modern capitalism, though various proposals have issued from conservative power centers to impose some upper limit on the authority of Congress to lay the tax. Proponents of such mandated limitation, knowing that Congress would never take the initiative in the matter, have at different times turned to an alternative method, the calling of a constitutional convention by the state legislatures. This procedure is provided for in Article 5 of the U.S. Constitution. With two-thirds of the legislatures concurring, the states could call on Congress to pass legislation fixing a ceiling for the tax. The figure most often mentioned has been a maximum, on income, estate, and gift taxes, of 25 percent. A variation on the idea would allow Congress to increase the levy to 40 percent for a limited period in times of emergency, if the rise was ratified by three fourths of the states. The proposal to call a constitutional convention became active in some state legislatures as a postwar reaction to the burdens of World War II and the Korean War. Formal action was taken as far back as 1939 by one state, Wyoming. Then later a number of other states followed.

Private organizations also working for a tax ceiling at various times between 1939 and 1957 included the National Association of Real Estate Boards, the Committee for Constitutional Government, the American Taxpayers Association, the National Small Businessmen's Association, the Western Tax Council, and the National Association of Manufacturers. The NAM favored a 35 percent figure. In 1952 the House of Delegates of the American Bar Association adopted a resolution calling for a constitutional amendment. A special committee was appointed to study the question. It found that the country faced grave times: "To attempt to build an estate has become futile," it reported. "One earning in excess of normal needs serves only as a federal tax collector." The American Bar Association kept the question open for a decade. However, over a period of ten years the climate of opinion changed and the committee reported that the tax-limitation amendment was no longer a realistic goal. It recommended that the 1952 resolution be rescinded and the committee be dissolved, which was done.[14]

There was, however, considerable action in the legislatures. By 1958 both branches of the legislatures in thirty-one states and one branch of the legislature in six additional states were reported to have adopted resolutions calling for limiting the congressional taxing powers, this to be accomplished by repealing the Sixteenth Amendment and substituting a new one, which at that time would have become number twenty-three. An effort was also made to get Congress to act directly. Resolutions were regularly introduced during the 1950s, supporting what was commonly referred to as the Reed-Dirksen Amendment. But interest was marginal, and waned during the 1960s. By the seventies there was little evidence of a desire for the change either in Congress or the states. Only conservatives of deepest dye kept up the fight as required by their concept of "Americanism," which found a dangerous statism in the social aims of liberal democracy, and they continued to feel that they could be happier in palaces than cottages. They connected, quite correctly, money with power. As J. Bracken Lee, the ultra-conservative former governor of Utah, stated the position: "A weak government is the corollary of a strong people." [15]

For such antitax shock troops as the Organization to Repeal Federal Income Taxes and the John Birch Society, their support of the 25 percent ceiling was merely a reconnaissance in force. Their major objective was outright repeal of "the mistake of 1913." In their rhetoric they invoked the Founding Fathers as abhorring a strong government, although to do so required them to overlook the fact that it was the men of the Revolution who replaced the weak Articles of Confederation in 1787 with centralized government and a strong Constitution. A corollary line of argument was that if the United States eliminated foreign aid and got out of some 700 different kinds of business activities that would be conducted better by private enterprise anyway, the income tax would not be necessary. The amendment that would replace the Sixteenth would also provide that the United States Government should not engage in any industrial activity "except as provided in the Constitution" and that within three years after ratification all business properties and facilities "shall be sold." As Senator Carl Hayden (D.-Ariz.), chairman of the Senate Committee on Appropriations pointed out, that would mean a forced sale. The Joint Economic Committee made a careful study of what repeal would mean — a new federal sales tax at a very high rate, the end of all assistance to the states and localities, and the inability of the United States to carry out its obligations and responsibilities to the free world. The cost of government would fall on the general population through the sales tax, rising interest rates, and inflation, and the benefits would accrue to a very small number of wealthy taxpayers, donees, and heirs of large estates. Underlying the proposal, the committee suggested, was a profound distrust of our political institutions. Nevertheless, identical resolutions were enacted by four states, Wyoming, Texas, Louisiana, and Nevada, calling for absolute repeal. Colorado later joined the four in asking that gift and inheritance taxes be repealed.

The account just given of the push to limit or repeal the power of Congress to lay an income tax perhaps conveys an impression of greater significance than the movement actually had. Though the states can resolve for a constitutional convention, Congress retains the power of deciding when a convention has been validly called for. Thus, in 1963 when Colorado became the thirty-fourth petitioner, this at first glance seemed to provide the required two thirds of the states. Yet Congress could and did safely ignore the call. Why? The form and substance of many of the resolutions could have been challenged. They were not uniform in language. Some had been passed almost a quarter of a century earlier by legislatures long ago adjourned, and some states had changed their minds and rescinded. There was ample room for argument as to the number of resolutions outstanding at any given time. Precedent weighed heavily in the balance, for it is worth noticing that no amendment dealing with any subject had ever been proposed, passed, and ratified using the machinery of a constitutional convention. But above and beyond the circumstances that have been enumerated, despite well-orchestrated publicity campaigns for performing an amputation on the income tax law, and all the steam that was let off in the state legislatures, there never was any broad support for the scheme. The public undoubtedly had not read the careful and exhaustive study made by the Joint Economic Committee, analyzing the consequences of repealing the Sixteenth Amendment. But in their own common sense way the people saw the subject in all its bearings, reached the same conclusion as the staff study did, and decided to leave the power of Congress to levy taxes undisturbed. Americans can not be rushed, it appears, into changing their institutional structure.[16]

12

Endless Quest: The Privilege
of Paying the Least

THE NUMBER of individual taxpayers who are found guilty
of tax fraud in a given year is small, and indicates that most
Americans show up well under our self-assessment system,
either because the average man is honorable and patriotic or
because evasion carries with it the risk of quite disagreeable
consequences. The line between crude evasion and artful tax
avoidance is thin and often indistinct. But it exists. (See
Chapter 9.) Because the law is vague when applied to a specific set of facts, some critics, infected with cynicism, simply
call tax avoidance "legal evasion" by which some shift the
sacrifice to others.

Many virtuosos of the tax bar maintain that evasion is not
only antisocial but unnecessary. "Avoid collisions with authority," counsels Australian-born Dr. Peter Clyne. "Find
out if there is another route," Clyne says, "and go by
the round-about way . . . The courts will always uphold a
tax avoidance scheme if it is properly drawn, properly exe-
cuted and keeps within the law." Norris Darrell, the New
York tax lawyer, takes a sterner stance. He has written with
disapproval of schemes that neatly fit the language of Congress but not the intent.

However, there is no social stigma attached to tax avoidance. "Anyone may so arrange his affairs that his taxes shall be as low as possible," Judge Learned Hand said in one of his opinions. "He is not bound to choose that pattern which will best pay the Treasury..." Or, as the late Senator Pat Harrison (D.-Miss.), chairman of the Senate Finance Committee, put it in a more homely idiom: "There's nothing that says a man has to take a toll bridge across a river when there's a free bridge nearby." David Rockefeller, chairman of the board of the Chase Manhattan Bank, whose annual income is estimated to be $1 million, is well aware "that it doesn't look well for a person with a large income not to pay any taxes ... I have personally arranged my finances in such a way that I do pay substantial taxes for this reason." But the inference is clear that he could easily avoid the income tax if he chose to.[1]

The fiscal good health of the state is, in theory, of prime concern to all who are a part of it. But as Aristotle observed long ago, "What is good for the individual is for him a greater good than what is good abstractly considered." There are forces at work nibbling at the desire of the taxpayer to remain honest: government waste; the high tax rates; the propelling power of inflation, which thrusts the taxpayer into a higher bracket without adding to his real income; the feeling of injury that arises at the thought, frequently articulated in the halls of Congress, that the rich don't pay their share. Many taxpayers are not conscious of receiving benefits in return for their money, and so look on the collection of taxes "as though it were only a common disaster." This may explain, then, the mental processes of the taxpayer who asserted that his mother had left him forty thousand nontaxable dollars in an earthenware crock in a basement in Iraq; or the taxpayer who contended that he had received a gift of $200,000 for marrying a wealthy widow nearly four times his age. Incidentally, the Tax Court believed him.[2]

Over a long period of time, tax litigants who carelessly mingled business and personal living expenses had good reason to think gratefully of George M. Cohan, not only because he wrote "Over There" and entertained theater-going Americans for a generation, but because he established a tax precedent, irksome to the IRS, known as the "Cohan Rule" of approximation. In those easy-going days of the twenties, it was sufficient for a taxpayer to make an estimate of his Travel and Entertainment (T&E) expenses. Cohan flourished in an era when theatrical producers were celebrities who maintained an expensive way of life, traveled in elegance to Palm Beach, French Lick Springs, London, Paris, the south of France. None understood *les douceurs de la vie* better than Cohan, who was lavish in his expenditures but parsimonious when it came to furnishing details to the tax authorities. Despite the latitude allowed taxpayers of the period, Cohan found himself in court. He explained that in connection with the production of his plays he had to travel with his attorney, be free-handed in entertaining actors, employees, and, he added rather naïvely, dramatic critics. The sums expended were substantial but Cohan kept no account of them. The Circuit Court of Appeals decided in the producer's favor, conceding that he had spent *something* and ruling that absolute certainty was not required. Cohan thus provided for years a precedent invoked by taxpayers who were good to themselves when they calculated their Travel and Entertainment expenses. This delightful state of affairs was ended by the Revenue Act of 1962, which required meticulous substantiation and no more guessing.

Before leaving Cohan for more serious business, a sidelight is worth preserving. The actor-playwright-composer-producer once mentioned in a court appearance that under a certain arrangement he was receiving the very small salary of $1000 a week.

"Is $1,000 a week a small salary?" asked counsel for the plaintiff. Cohan answered: "For me it's small." [3]

Tax avoidance is mainly a high-bracket game, based on diligent study and familiarity with the rules. The opportunities for minimizing income taxes come alive when the taxpayer's financial assets are substantial and his affairs complicated — the more complex the better. So as long as there is no finding of fraud or "cooking the books," the prevailing judicial view of an avoidance plan that fails is generally that it was legitimate though futile; call it a good try. Cheating, on the other hand, is not the exclusive preserve of the elite. It is practiced up and down the economic scale, signified by misrepresentation, trickery, concealment, and "a patently lame and untenable excuse." [4]

Who evades? Steeplejack, gravedigger, lawyer, undertaker, society matron, prostitute, corporation executives, prominent figures from the labor, political, entertainment fields, small businessmen, abortionists, loan sharks, drug traffickers — all have been objects of prosecution. Occupations in which cash changes hands regularly are subject to special temptations, as the IRS well knows. And so the revenue service pays particular attention to nightclubs, liquor stores and automobile dealerships, taxi drivers, hotel waiter captains, gamblers, and doctors. A Pasadena oral surgeon's nurse informed the IRS office in Los Angeles that her employer kept a double set of books and the investigating agents found that it was true. A side effect was that the nurse was blacklisted by the dental and medical professions of the region and had to leave the area to get employment.

In 1973 the revenue service in Cleveland courteously invited 700 indignant waitresses to come to the federal building to discuss their unreported tips, promising that the encounter would be as brief and pleasant as circumstances permitted. Tips recorded on credit cards were reported, it was found. It was the cash that caused the trouble. The first twenty-four reviews produced an additional $463 per person. Down East, in Maine, there was some talk about the lobstermen and scallopers, who are customarily paid in cash, not reporting all their income. "In Vinalhaven they get away with quite a bit," it was said on another island, and at Stonington on Deer Isle there were jocular hints of tax shading that went on — elsewhere. Both insinuations were right. A special unit of the IRS set up a command post in a school at Ellsworth and collected about $600,000 in additional taxes and penalties.[5]

But the taxmanship of the rich and famous makes more compelling reading than the fiscal sinning of simple lobstermen or waitresses, or the resort to such commonplace dodges as putting in a veterinarian's bills for care of the family pet as a medical expense, or deducting for thefts that never took place. The decade of the thirties provides many a cautionary tale of tax liens filed against the stars of the entertainment world, among others Zazu Pitts, John and Elaine Barrymore, Gloria Swanson, Leon Errol, and the estate of Florenz Ziegfeld. After Joe Louis, the heavyweight champion boxer, lost his title he still had income tax liabilities of over $1 million. The IRS gathered in what assets it could find but finally gave up. Even the best of tax collectors cannot get it when it isn't there. Better success attended the effort of the U.S. Government to touch the heavy monies Ingemar Johansson, the Swedish boxer, received as personal income from his bouts with Floyd Patterson, in addition to movie, radio, television rights, and earnings from shows, exhibitions, and commercial tie-ups. Johansson tried to siphon off his assets to Geneva through a sham Swiss corporation but the feds followed the fighter from ringside to his dressing room after the 1961 fight, secured liens on his property, and terminated his tax year at once. He was warned not to try to leave the country by ship, airplane, automobile, or by swimming across the Rio Grande

River. A federal judge scored a knockout of the former heavyweight champion in the U.S. District Court at Miami with a ruling that the boxer owed the United States $1,009,801 on his 1960–1961 income.

The Senate Committee on Banking and Currency was only tangentially interested in tax avoidance in its 1932–1934 hearings, but the grilling of leading Wall Street figures turned up some tasty items about the tax maneuvers of the country's financial leaders, who lived like fine gentlemen yet did not have one cent of taxable income. "We know that," Ferdinand Pecora said, "because they paid no income taxes . . . The Bible tells us," Pecora continued, "that a good name is rather to be chosen than great riches. But it was vouchsafed to the members of J. P. Morgan and Company to enjoy both."

This pleasant state of affairs changed after the committee heard a pride of Wall Street lions reveal the lengths they went to to avoid paying taxes, using methods that were sometimes legal but were morally repugnant to a country floundering in the Great Depression. The findings of the committee led to the passage, on June 6, 1935, of the Securities Exchange Act, to correct unfair market practices and to curb speculation. (See also Chapter 9.) Among the tricks laid bare were juggling of capital gains and losses to eliminate all income taxes; special favors to powerful people, including the Secretary of the Treasury, who could return courtesies; short sales; family trusts; pretended sales to near relatives at a loss; funneling funds through paper corporations often domiciled in the islands of the Caribbean or Canada — "tortuous manipulation . . . in contrast to the simplicity of the ignoble purpose," as Broadus Mitchell has characterized the disclosures. Nor should it be overlooked that enforcement was lax. A tax return prepared by the House of Morgan was assumed to be correct.[6]

Former Secretary of the Treasury, and later Chief Justice,

Frederick M. Vinson once said of tax evasion, "There is no future in it." Among those who could confirm the truth of Vinson's remarks are many who should have known it and lived better — a governor of Illinois, a congressman from New Jersey, the one-time Democratic Secretary of the United States Senate, even, of all persons, a Commissioner of the Bureau of Internal Revenue, who did time for his derelictions. The pleading of former Vice President Spiro Agnew to a criminal tax charge is still fresh in memory. The reactions of the tax-paying public to Richard Milhous Nixon's tax delinquency are interesting because they point in two different directions. Some taxpayers were impelled to practice creative tax-dodging to the limit; others to be extra careful. In fact, many taxpayers leaned over backward to be safe and so failed to take perfectly legitimate deductions, a mistake Mr. Nixon would never have made since he found nothing too insignificant to deduct, including a $1.24 finance charge at Garfinckel's, the elegant Washington department store. But Richard Nixon is not the first President to have problems connected with a tax return. Rutherford B. Hayes confessed to his diary during the centennial campaign that "it appears in 1868 & 1869 I made none at all . . . because my attention was not called to the matter." Hayes considered issuing a public statement on the subject but was restrained by the Republican general staff, which successfully kept the lid on the story.[7]

"To underestimate your opposition and assume that you can glibly outsmart the Treasury investigator," Harry Graham Balter has written, "is probably the most tragic error which can be made by the taxpayer or his adviser . . . Do not assume that you will overwhelm the investigator with some 'novel' explanation . . . The chances are that the agent has heard that story many times before." Since the willful intent to cheat is subjective and involves a state of mind, it must be inferred from things said or done, or from personal attributes, such as education and knowledge of taxation and business practices. All of these circumstances bear on the ultimate question of whether the person under charges has committed a felony. For example, a North Carolina accountant lost his case because the court held it was a decisive factor that he knew what he was doing when he failed to keep accurate records. Proving fraud beyond reasonable doubt is a tedious task, often requiring close analysis of books of account and bank records, but it can be easier if the defendant is a Phi Beta Kappa because one element that influences judges to believe, or to doubt, that the IRS attorney has produced the required "clear and convincing" evidence is the degree of sophistication of the underpayer. Applying the same rule, the Tax Court threw out fraud charges against a Springfield, Ohio, turkey farmer because he had only a sixth-grade education.

The *Handbook for Special Agents,* the vade mecum of the intelligence arm of the IRS, includes a specimen report on an imaginary Mr. I. M. Bell, who was in the scrap steel business in Chicago. Bell attempted to underreport on his income over a period of three years. In the course of an excellent investigation described in the *Handbook* we learn a good deal about Bell, his wife, Eta, and daughter, Betty. For one thing, Bell had studied accounting, a fact that, unfortunately for him, he withheld from the IRS, claiming ignorance of such matters and throwing the blame on his accountant.

In the course of the combing-over that Bell received we also meet some of his customers and a bevy of bank officials, A. Buck, cashier at the National, and John Teller at the Second State Bank at Gary, Indiana. What with Bell's attorney being named Law, the report begins to sound a bit like *Pilgrim's Progress.* The cast of characters is crowded, the plot thickens, for this is a criminal proceeding. And then the *Handbook* leaves us with a cliffhanger. For though agent Charles, a modern Valiant-for-Truth, recommended that Bell be prosecuted, we never learn what happened.

The IRS fought doggedly to prevent the disclosure of the text of this *Handbook* and released it only under compulsion of the Freedom of Information Act. But one wonders why it was not given the widest possible distribution among taxpayers. Its description of investigative procedures, enforcement of summonses, scientific resources, surveillance, searches and seizures, its recital of criminal sanctions, methods of proving income, all provide a powerful incentive toward virtuous tax conduct. The police in totalitarian countries have found it effective in the interrogation of prisoners to exhibit the instruments of torture. Similarly, some familiarity with the book could only have a deterrent influence on potential tax gamesters.[8]

Fraud investigations may arise from routine audits, reports by banks of large currency transactions, informants, information obtained during third-party audits, or "chain" examinations, where one leads to another. The revenue agents keep their eyes and ears open to the life around them. They read the newspapers and are great clippers. A lavish wedding starts them to thinking. As the commissioner explained at a congressional hearing, "Today it is pretty hard for anybody, no matter what their income, to spend money freely except out of capital or by finding some way to get it out of their taxes." The IRS figures it has a fifty-fifty chance in most cases of lavish spending "of finding some little episode." In one case a corporation paid the sundry wedding expenses of its treasurer's daughter but the court was quick to observe that though the corporation acted as father of the bride, its name did not appear on the wedding invitation. Deduction denied.

The real estate pages of the newspapers are good sources of leads. If a man making $10,000 a year has just built himself a $70,000 home, the tax men get a little bit suspicious. A story of a robbery led to a tax indictment. A Bronx gas station owner, who reported that he earned less than $10,000 a year, was robbed by gunmen of $20,000 in cash, $20,000 worth of jewelry, and $250,000 in negotiable bonds. The IRS read the story, investigated, and a tax deficiency of $143,369 was uncovered.

And then there was a fellow riding around in a pretty expensive automobile and one of the IRS men saw him several times and on a hunch looked him up. It turned out that he had substantial properties scattered all over, and various bank accounts, a single one of which contained more money than he had reported as his total income. So for making a show he got tripped up. The commissioner, in telling of the incident, said of the prospective felon, "And if he does not go to jail I am going to be very greatly surprised, because the highest amount of tax he ever paid in any year in the last six years has been $18." [9]

Before 1952 there was a fairly well-defined policy in the then-designated Bureau of Internal Revenue that if a penitent underpayer voluntarily confessed that he had filed a fraudulent tax return before the machinery of the investigation was revved up, the criminal phase of the case would be forgiven. But after January 10 of that year, the BIR announced that it would no longer grant immunity to taxpayers who made a clean breast of their schemes. In a criminal case, unlike civil fraud, the burden of proof is on the government and the proof must be "beyond a reasonable doubt." But when a "jacket" is opened on a taxpayer and a special agent assigned to work up the case, the suspected taxpayer is in deep trouble. The criminal charge is not used indiscriminately, and cases for prosecution are carefully chosen. The recommendation of the special agent can be set aside. But it is only realistic to conclude that in any bureaucracy the managers will tend to support the findings of their own operatives, which was doubtless a factor in Justice Vinson's description of tax-dodging as a dead-end career and explains why Justice Holmes cautioned, "Men must turn square corners when they deal with the government." The costs of an unsuccessful defense, incidentally, are not deductible.

A sufficient number of taxpayers convicted of fraud go to prison each year, the IRS believes, to exercise a deterrent effect on those who are tempted to conceal their true income. Purely fortuitous circumstances, though, can change the odds of doing time behind bars. Location is a major factor, as is the attitude of the federal judge in any of the different U.S. district courts. When Randolph W. Thrower was commissioner he compiled some figures, covering three years, that showed these striking disparities: in New Jersey only about 2 percent of those found guilty got prison terms. In the western district of New York the figure was 4 percent. In New England a convicted offender stood a 65 percent chance of incarceration and in western Tennessee 91 percent of the defendants who were convicted went to jail. "We can pick districts where the taxpayer almost certainly will receive imprisonment, and other districts where he most certainly will not," Mr. Thrower said.[10]

Evaders normally lie low. But not Dr. Peter Clyne, mentioned at the beginning of this chapter, a complex man who has pursued a brilliant career in Europe operating as a tax-adviser. Opposite appears one of his advertisements, published in the *International Herald Tribune* of Paris, a daily newspaper read by Americans living in Europe.

Clyne recently expanded his operations to include an

International Tax Planning Office at Tulsa, Oklahoma, where he faced his greatest professional challenge — the American graduated income tax, which he considered to be discriminatory against different classes of people, "such as the wealthy," he said. Author of a scholarly work entitled *How Not to Pay Your Debts* and a lively promotional brochure, *How Not to Pay Any Taxes,* this modern Dr. Faustus has chosen oil country for an American debut, a scene where money is plentiful and appreciated. "I have a total lack of scruple," Dr. Clyne admitted cheerfully, adding, "All's fair in love, war, and tax planning." So far he has been able to fend off the tax authorities of several countries, earn a six-figure (untaxed) annual income, and indulge in conspicuous consumption at the Palais Schwarzenberg when in Vienna and the Dolder Grand when in Zurich. "I stay at the best hotel, wherever I am, if there isn't anything better," he explained. But Clyne found in the Dallas office of the IRS an adversary worthy of his steel and in March 1976 a federal judge sentenced him to the maximum

---

BUSINESS OPPORTUNITIES

DECLARE WAR ON THE TAX COLLECTORS. Turn Your Black Money into White Money!

We are a merchant bank for tax fugitives.

Your money is collected in cash no questions asked . . . and we open a Swiss account for each depositor, pay 10% p.a. interest in Switzerland (tax free, naturally) and repay your capital in Swiss Francs on 24 months' notice Bank references available. Write: PETER CLYNE INTERNATIONAL AG (Inc. in Zug), Palais Schwarzenberg, Vienna.

punishment of three years in prison plus court costs for helping to prepare spurious loan documents for presentation to the IRS. *Sic transit gloria mundi.*[11]

When Emperor Constantine I established Christianity as the official religion of the Roman Empire, certain attractive exemptions were granted to priests of the Church. Within a short time so many Roman citizens had become priests that it was necessary to take steps to remedy the situation: too many chiefs, not enough Indians. Apparently the lessons of history are not lost on certain American citizens who have a raised consciousness about taxation. The owner of a wood products company put the Reverend James Wardrop on the payroll at $7020 a year to conduct prayer meetings for employees to reinforce their "spiritual awareness" and to counsel the officers of the company on business problems that might yield to the power of prayer. When the matter came before the Tax Court the court said that the unusual portfolio occupied by the Reverend Wardrop did not meet the criterion of "ordinary and necessary" business expense. But it did allow $1000 of the clergyman's salary as a deduction because he was useful in the mail room and for running errands.[12]

In the early 1950s Lafayette Ronald Hubbard, an American and a former best-selling writer of science fiction, launched with spectacular success a system of psychotherapy called Dianetics. Dianetics evolved into a quasi-religious cult, the Church of Scientology. The IRS ruled that healing the body through treating the spirit, and the operation of a gadget called an "E-meter" by ministers without professional training, are nonmedical. Therefore nondeductible. And the Tax Court agreed. Counterattacking, the Scientologists have charged the IRS with "harassment," and a number of the churches have now received tax-exempt status. Hubbard has made a good thing out of his offbeat church. When the *London Daily Mail* reported that Hubbard had nearly three million pounds in a secret Swiss bank account, the Number One Scientologist, relaxing on his 3300-ton yacht off the coast of Tunisia, discouraged such materialistic thoughts. "I've got only a very small amount in Switzerland," he insisted.

Another sect with a charismatic leader is the Universal Life Church, based at Modesto, California, the brain child of an unlettered preacher named Kirby J. Hensley, who has ordained more than three million ministers since 1962 for only a $20 "free-will offering." Hensley has also created several thousand doctors of divinity. A skeptical IRS attacked the Universal Life Church but a federal court disagreed with the revenue service's anticlerical position. The court did not pass on the theology of the Modesto ecclesiastic but did affirm that "the ordination of ministers and the chartering of churches are accepted activities of religious organizations," and preferred, because of the First Amendment, not to look too closely at Hensley's disciples and their weird doings. Just recently, with more than half the property in little Hardenburgh, New York, owned by tax-exempt Zen Buddhists and Tibetan monks, the taxpayers of the Catskill mountain town got religion. At least the majority became ordained ministers of the California-based Universal Life Church, and so were able to thumb their noses at the tax assessor and address each other as "reverend."

Churches have much to recommend them to those who are acutely conscious of taxes. Their religious activities cannot be examined by the IRS except to make sure that the church is a church. Churches are exempt from paying taxes. They may engage in a trade or business unrelated to their spiritual mission, and did so for many happy years, without being taxed on their business income. But as of now they are taxed on the net profit from their commercial activities and, like other enterprises, must keep good records. Still, if you have a sense of urgency about minimizing your income tax bill, you might consider starting a church. John P. Roche, the political scientist and nationally syndicated columnist, has been thinking along those lines. He expresses regret that he was never able to afford a farm to lose money on, and that he was unable to convince the IRS that he needed an "idea depletion allowance." So, he reasoned, why not organize his family as a church and claim immunity to taxation under the First Amendment? Perhaps the recent indications of ecumenical tendencies in the IRS will encourage Professor Roche to try it.[13]

13

Loopholes, Deductions,
and All That

DISCUSSIONS of the federal income tax seldom proceed very far without recourse to the word "loopholes." This useful term in its metaphorical sense is often applied to an ambiguity in the Internal Revenue Code and the Treasury regulations that affords an opportunity for slipping in between the interstices of the code to accomplish a saving in a taxpayer's account with the federal government. "Loophole" is not a new word. It would have been understood in this extended sense by such literary figures of the seventeenth century as Sir Thomas Browne, John Dryden, and Andrew Marvell; by Macaulay and Thomas Jefferson in the nineteenth. And in our own time the word is so much a part of common speech that one tax authority is reminded of W. C. Fields reading the Bible: "Looking for loopholes, of course," Fields said; "looking for loopholes."

Loopholes may be inadvertent, but most are the result of deliberate congressional policy, shaped to create incentives of one kind or another. To make the subject more complicated and tax morality more difficult to define, one year's loophole may become another year's honored principle of tax justice. In 1950, for example, the profits of inventors were regarded by the Ways and Means Committee as loopholes that should be closed, but four years later the committee thought just the opposite. Indeed, the word is now so heavily charged with political and emotional overtones that those who are both knowledgeable and polite prefer to use neutral synonyms, such as differentials and preferentials, tax aids, shelters and havens, exceptions and special dispensations, of which there are sixty-eight categories in FY 1976, representing something in the range of $90 billion the government could collect under the tax laws but chooses not to. This huge subsidy to particular beneficiaries is a reminder of the pragmatic rule that equal incomes should be taxed equally — unless Congress decides they should be taxed unequally. If this seems like an absurdity or a serious miscarriage of justice, there are two possible consolations. First, the exceptions are perfectly constitutional. Or we can take the broad view, which contains the whole philosophy of the subject as expressed in the saying of Francis Bacon that "some things must be done unjustly in order that more may be done justly." [1]

Actually, instances of legislative error due to inept legal draftsmanship are not very common and are likely to be corrected promptly once the slip is recognized. One example may be mentioned from the Internal Revenue Code of 1954, Sec. 152(a)(9). It permitted the taxpayer to take a dependency deduction for a member of his household whose principal place of abode was the taxpayer's home, even though the dependent was not related to the taxpayer by blood, marriage, or adoption. The intent was to permit foster children to qualify as dependents. But the language did not exclude the possibility that the taxpayer could deduct $600 a year for the maintenance of a mistress, in violation of the criminal statutes of the state where he lived. A case of "adulterous cohabitation" did in fact come before the Tax Court when Leon took a dependency deduction for Tina. The court, however, reached the sensible conclusion that Congress did not intend to promote unconventional ménages and shot down the argument.[2]

When Congress does let a special-interest tax favor stand without change it usually means that the provision has wide support or that contending forces have reached a state of equilibrium — the conservatives, mostly Republicans, fighting to defend the existing special dispensation and introduce new ones; the liberals, mostly Democrats, wanting to knock out the "back-door spending," to raise more revenue for the social projects they favor. The lobbyists, for their part, can concentrate on one proposal, present it simplistically, disregard unintended consequences, and push the congressman to vote before he fully comprehends the measure. If some accidental goody appears along the way, the special-interest group that benefits declares fervently that it was a major tax objective always intended by Congress and defends the preference "with a loftiness of argument far removed from the origins of the benefit," Professor Stanley S. Surrey has written, adding, "There is much of the Daughters of the American Revolution in tax privileges."

Opposition to loopholes can bring into existence strange alliances — New Populists who want to redistribute the national income; academics who are looking for horizontal equity, that is, equal treatment of equals; welfare reformers with a guaranteed-income program; unorganized voters disenchanted with a swollen bureaucracy; and taxpayers in the middle-income levels who favor cuts in federal expenditures. It is they who feel with particular intensity that the foxes have holes and the birds of the air have nests, the rich have their snug tax havens, but for them there is no place to hide. Historically, tax favors, once granted through the IR Code, are seldom withdrawn, and tend to grow as they age.[3]

Amid swirling pressures the average congressman gives a political response, for the vote he racks up may determine whether he remains a congressman and whether his party will control Congress. All of the conflicting pressures are concentrated, as with a burning glass, on the tax-writing committees. They are expected to get action. As a senator on the Finance Committee once put it: "What's the good of being on this Committee if you can't get through a little old amendment now and then?" Another factor: congressmen may honestly not realize that tax fairness is involved in a given course of action. The representative or senator, amiable and generous by nature, leans toward granting, sees the problem not in the abstract or technical framework but from the point of view of his constituent, who is human and has desires that he is able to present skillfully and in appealing form, using such effective words as "special hardships" or "penalizing."

There is always, of course, the matter of viewpoint. What looks like a scandalous give-away to the United Auto Workers or Americans for Democratic Action is merely "relief from intolerable rates" to the American Bankers Association or the National Association of Manufacturers. Whether the pecuniary consequences of tax devices are benign or malignant is, it must be remembered, difficult to determine absolutely. In any event, tax decisions are usually made beyond the public gaze or are too complex for the common understanding, so the question of congressional accountability simply does not arise often.

The struggle between the supporters of the two concepts, a tax system that is equitable, efficient, and simple, and one deliberately arranged to lower the taxes on activities deemed especially worthy by Congress and the IRS, heated up in 1968. In that year Professor Surrey, then Assistant Secretary of the Treasury for Tax Policy, came forward with a catchy new name for tax subsidies. He called them "tax expenditures," and they are now officially listed under that heading by the Office of Management and Budget. The term refers to the dollar amount of taxes that are not being collected because of special assistance extended to those who feel they need it. The figure is rising rapidly from an estimated $40 billion in FY 1970 to $81 billion in FY 1975 and to almost $92 billion in FY 1976. And there are certain revenue losses not adjusted for in this last figure. All of the figures given above assume that people would not change their inclination to work, save, or invest. The assumption can be neither proved nor disproved and so remains conjectural.[4]

The achievement of justice is one of the great goals of civilized society, greater than production, greater than the gross national product; yet the fundamental doctrine of tax fairness is only intermittently honored by Congress. More frequently than not, the taxing power is used to promote aims quite remote from collecting the revenue. During the two world wars the excess profits tax was levied in part to strengthen the war spirit of labor and the armed forces. Oleomargarine was long taxed (1886–1950) not for revenue but to favor the dairy industry, and tobacco and beverage alcohol are heavily taxed, in part at least, as an instrument of social discipline. The Revenue Act of 1918 included a tax provision, later declared unconstitutional, aimed at discouraging the employment of child labor. The income tax has been suggested as a means of controlling population, and recently the IRS singled out for preferential treatment the National Astrological Society's School of Astrology because this seat of learning has a racially nondiscriminatory policy on admissions. Congress has also selected for favorable tax treatment the rental value of parsonages and of dwellings occupied by members of the Coast and Geodetic Survey and the Public Health Service.

Ever hear of trona? Trona is a natural vitreous gray or white mineral (Na_2CO_3 . $NaHCO_3$. $2H_2O$) used as a source of chemical soda ash. Produced mainly in Wyoming, trona received in 1975 a handsome improvement in its percentage depletion allowance for decarbonation of the ore. The benefit applied to only four taxpayers, all industrial giants. "I understand that there were no hearings on this," Senator James Abourezk (D-S.D.) told his colleagues, and he urged, "Instead of burying it deep in the tax code where the public cannot find it . . . let us put that subsidy regularly on an annual appropriations basis . . ."[5]

As exception continues to be piled upon exception, each departure from strict neutrality creates the need for new adjustments. And so we have anomalies and mysteries. An apple farmer is taxed at ordinary rates. A Christmas tree farmer files under the much more favorable capital gains schedule. But a Tp (taxpayer) who raises sod for sale isn't a farmer at all; he's a miner of an exhaustible natural resource, so he deducts sod as a "natural deposit" under the same dispensation as trona, oil and gas wells, limestone, and quartz crystals (radio grade). An airline stewardess was denied a business-expense deduction for shoes, boots, gloves, cosmetics, and a handbag. Bennie Blatt, a wholesale bakery salesman, was luckier. He was required to wear a specified uniform, with company insignia sewed on the cap and jacket and a double seat on his pants. Faithful to his trust, Bennie never wore the costume socially or at any places that would bring reproach upon the Peterson Baking Company. Bennie's uniform was tax-deductible and the Tax Court agreed that the cost of cleaning was too.

A girl lost all her hair. Her father was advised by a physician that a wig was essential to her mental health and the IRS bowed to the deduction as a medical expense. But when a thyroidectomy was performed on a mother for cancer of the throat and she could not speak above a whisper, she lost control of her healthy energetic children, and the surgeon advised sending them away to school. Was their tuition a medical expense? The Tax Court and the Court of Appeals said no, it was a family expense, not medical. Judge Frank dissented and protested destroying "what little humanity remains in the Internal Revenue Code." And he compared the majority opinion to "such old scholastic questions as to where a horse's tail begins and where it ceases." [6]

Some deductions, or tax expenditures, that have been claimed by the more imaginative clients of the IRS have included a daughter's debut into society, a honeymoon, beach house, a swimming pool (under the explanation "water purification experimentation"), boxing and tumbling lessons, religious confirmation party, marriage annulment, funeral, call girls, gifts of gowns, lingerie, flowers, perfume, and Cadillac rentals for lady friends, cruises and massages, and stamp collections charged as postage.[7]

The tax subsidies that loom big are those provided by resourceful practitioners who have pored over the IR Code, the Treasury regulations, and the case law the way good souls used to apply themselves to reading the Bible. One such lawyer, who invented a collapsible corporation (a device for transforming ordinary income into a capital gain through early liquidation of the corporation), claimed that the idea for his gimmick came to him under the most agreeable circumstances imaginable — while he was dining with a famous actress at Antoine's restaurant in New Orleans.[8]

Louis Auchincloss, the lawyer–novelist–social-historian, in his story of life in a highly regarded law firm in downtown New York, records a conversation between Beekman "Beeky" Ehninger, a senior partner with a fatherly interest in a fledgling law clerk, Ronny Simmonds. Ronny is six years out of Columbia Law School, just back from Vietnam, and somewhat adrift in life. He has a job with the firm but needs a specialty, yet backs off when Beeky suggests the tax department.

"'I'm no good at figures.'"

"'You don't need to be. We have accountants for that side of it.'"

"'But tax questions are so picky.'"

"'Modern life is picky.'"

"'Not as much as the Revenue Service!'"

Beeky replies: "'Everything today is taxes. Common law, constitutional law, even criminal law. They're all soaked in tax questions. What better seat on the grandstand of life can I offer you than that of tax counsel?'" Beeky rose to pace the room as he enthusiastically expounded his conception. "'Public and private morality, where are they? Submerged in a sea of exemptions and depreciations, of write-offs and loopholes, of fabricated balance sheets and corporate hocus-pocus. What is hospitality but deductibility? What is travel but business expense? What is charity, charity that was greater than faith and hope, but the taxpayer's last stand? Who is the figure behind every great man, the individual who knows his ultimate secrets? A father confessor? Hell, no. The tax expert.'"

So Ronny was assigned to formidable Mrs. Thelma Stagg in the tax department. One of her estate plans shocked him. She explained: "'Mr. Pierson does not come to One Orange Plaza for spiritual advice . . . It is my simple duty to accomplish what the client wishes accomplished.'"

The result is that "the rich, as usual, are well served . . . by the mandarins of the bar," whose clients "usually get what they pay for," according to Joseph W. Bishop, Jr., Richard Ely Professor of Law at Yale University Law School. "Their legal affairs are in better shape than those of poor people for the same reason that their teeth are — i.e., preventive measures. The main job of a Wall Street lawyer is not to get his clients out of trouble, but to keep them from getting into it in the first place." [9]

In looking at some of the ways those whose marginal income tax rate is, say, between 50 and 70 percent and who escape the full rigors of the rates, we must keep in mind two principles that sustain the wealthy in their annual scuffle with the income tax people. One was formulated over eighty years ago by the "sound money" orator of Tammany Hall, Bourke Cockran, who told Congress, "In the whole history of the world property has always been able to take care of itself." The other comes from our erudite contemporary Dr. Joseph A. Pechman, chief economist at the Brookings Institution, who has fathered this perceptive aphorism: "People with money always feel poorer than they are." [10]

It is commonly assumed that the price system in free markets will result in the best direction of our resources but it can be shown that tax subsidies have far-reaching economic consequences, such as directing more money than is socially desirable into catfish farming and the growing of pistachio nuts. Special benefits and exclusions reduce the tax base and cut down the flexibility, making something of a joke of the progressive nature of the statutory rates for many high-income individuals who do not pay what the schedules say but a figure more likely to be in the range of 40 percent. Since most of the millions of tax returns are taxable at only the first-bracket level and the taxpayer takes the standard deduction in lieu of itemizing, the big loopholes are of no help to the citizen of modest means.

An example: the ordinary middle-American taxpayer cannot charge off the costs of transportation to and from his regular place of work, although commuting costs weigh heavily in the family budget. There is one very, very tiny loophole. In the past, a worker was able to deduct commuting expenses if he customarily drove to his job in the family automobile and his employer required him to carry bulky tools along with him. That did not mean, however, a forty-pound flight kit bag. It meant heavy supplies, or equipment. Recently the IRS has taken an even harder line. The wage-earner must be able to prove that carrying the tools caused him extra expense and only that extra part of his travel costs can be deducted.[11] Proving the existence and amount of such a cost, obviously, is going to be a scholastic exercise comparable to determining the anatomical structure necessary for angels to fly. Such fine-spun technicalities of accounting and proof do not trouble the more than 800 high-ranking government officials who ride between home and office in free, chauffeured limousines. They are not supposed to under federal law, but . . .

Senator William Proxmire, who jogs five miles to work every morning, has suggested to the IRS that the cost of limousine-commuting was taxable income, and a discussion draft of proposed prohibitory rules is under consideration. The only persons who will not be affected by those rules are the President and Vice President of the United States, cabinet members, and a few other dignitaries. From now on, unless the IRS falters, limousine treats will be Dutch.[12]

Not to be overlooked on the expense side of the budget are globe-trotting congressmen who turn up in such attractive places as Stratford-on-Avon or the Isle of Capri, looking for military installations to inspect. "Somehow," muses *Dollars and Sense*, monthly publication of the National Taxpayers Union, "government business always seems to take members of Congress to the nicest places." This is especially noticeable in November of even-numbered years, when statesmen who have been relieved of their duties by the electorate go winging off to London, Paris, or Africa to observe and learn and be treated like royalty by the U.S. diplomatic missions abroad. There is a problem, however. The lame duck congressman is not in a position to make any practical use of the valuable knowledge he has acquired at public expense because when he returns he is going back to Pocatello. The cost of these broadening experiences cannot be computed by the folks back home because former Representative Wayne L. Hays (D.-Ohio), whose duties took him overseas at least twenty-five times in ten years, got the law changed in 1973 so that disclosure of the expenses of foreign travel is no longer required. However, a report of congressional travel by military aircraft only, released by the Defense Department and summarized by *Dollars and Sense*, names Representative Claude D. Pepper (D.-Fla.) as the leading junketeer in Congress during the first nine months of 1975, when the Miamian represented the interests of Florida's Fourteenth District in Austria, Yugoslavia, Egypt, Algeria, Morocco, Malaysia, Singapore, Denmark, Norway, Sweden, Iran, Israel, Spain, and England.[13]

Noncommuting business travel costs incurred by private citizens, often combined with the entertainment of customers and associates and possibly pleasurable, can be written off as a deduction from gross income by a taxpayer willing to bet on his ability to persuade the revenue agent in an audit session that the trip to Acapulco, Las Vegas, or sunny Spain was undertaken primarily for business purposes. Not only do the big earners eagerly pursue the tax-expenditure grant system, but there are promoters of prepackaged tax shelters who bring their commodities to the marketplace. Thus at a recent convention of the American Medical Association at San Francisco the talk was not confined to ophthalmology,

immunology, orthopedics, and osteoarthritis. The announce-
ment board at the Fairmount Hotel listed among the meeting
topics for one day "Tax Sheltered Investment — Financial,"
in the Bali Room; "Mountain Shadows Ranch Tax Shelter
Investments," in the Garden Room; and "Gemini Financial
Tax Counsel," in the Crocker Room.[14]

It may hardly seem necessary for a doctor to travel to
Nairobi to hear an instructor from the Harvard Medical
School present a lecture entitled "The Law and Clinical Medicine." Yet specialized travel companies, such as Seminars
& Symposia, are kept busy planning tax-deductible educational programs to be held at exotic locations, and their bro-
chures frankly tell their clients to bring along their golf
clubs, tennis racquets, and plenty of suntan oil. London is
always a nice place for a conference. The Rabat Hilton offers
glitter, Moroccan cuisine, 600 acres of resort facilities, and
the excitement of the native markets and the Old Quarter.
Monte Carlo, with its new luxury hotels and relaxed atmosphere, beckons the *congressistes* with their plastic badges
to come to the Côte d'Azur for their colloquia and to have
fun beside the blue Mediterranean just a step from the
Casino. If the conferee travels first class on a tax-deductible
ticket, those who ride in the no-frills coach seats pay through
the U.S. Treasury an estimated 48 percent, or half the price
of his comfortable seat with plenty of leg room and all jet
plane amenities.

Conferences are now held in such locations of high tour-
ism as Amsterdam, Paris, and the Caribbean Islands, where
accountants and members of the tax bar are wined and dined
as they learn how to be better guides to clients who are am-
bitious to become multinational individuals in a hospitable
country where the tax laws distinguish between profits
earned inside and outside its jurisdiction. Referring to one

such lecture, Representative Charles A. Vanik (D.-Ohio) called the attention of House colleagues and the IRS to the event, declaring, "This conference is a journey to the edge of the law." [15]

The IRS is of course quite aware of the Travel and Entertainment loophole, but closing it is often a strenuous exercise. There is no hard-and-fast rule governing T&E deductions. It all depends on the facts of a particular case. It has been possible for years, and still is, for a business executive to go to the Rose Bowl game, attend the running of the Preakness, take in a heavyweight fight, provided the diversion is followed or preceded by "a substantial and bona fide business discussion." This is not to suggest that the taxpayer isn't taking chances. To a doctor who attended six two-hour seminars in the course of a two-week trip to two countries, the IRS said sorry, he couldn't call a vacation a business trip. Entertainment expenses that teeter on the business-personal borderline have to be allocated, an exercise calling for a finely tuned conscience and a keen sense of the public weal. Is an evening spent in good seats at a hit musical comedy with a customer a delightful experience and therefore an item of personal consumption, or a painful duty and so chargeable to the cost of producing income? The distinction is subjective. Close questions are likely to be resolved by the taxpayer in his own favor when hunting trips in Canada can so easily become confused with Christmas turkeys for the poor.[16]

Since the value of deductions and exemptions as tax expenditures confer more benefit on high-income individuals than those of lower economic rank, they have been criticized as "upside-down" subsidies. But "so golden is the egg," Philip Stern has written, "most Washington observers believe that the expense-account goose is not likely to perish easily or soon." No less a figure than the present Commissioner of Internal Revenue agrees with Stern. "I don't think," Mr. Donald C. Alexander told a meeting of the Ohio Bar Association, "that tax shelters and tax preferences are going to disappear soon, if at all . . ."

So it appears that the worldly wise and well-endowed will continue to take Caribbean cruises, maintain yachts and hunting lodges, and patronize luxury restaurants, where the waiter captains bow low and the bill will be shared by the U.S. Treasury. The American Management Association has made a list of twenty-eight perquisites — often called "perks" — that have substantial dollar values and are commonly extended by corporations to top executives in lieu of outright compensation. Therefore, says the IRS, they should be added to the gross income of the recipient. A proposal has been drafted that would tighten up on the fringe benefits of the happy few who get million-dollar life insurance policies, all medical expenses paid, salary insurance, private use of company aircraft, country club memberships, chauffeur-driven limousines, and other sweeteners. Whether the effort to curb these selective benefits will succeed or be talked to death is unclear at present writing.[17]

Bills that give special tax breaks to groups, business interests, or individuals who know their way around are often passed in haste toward the end of a session of Congress close to the traditional Christmas time adjournment. The spirit of the holiday season incorporated in these last-minute amendments has given them a special name: "Christmas tree bills." Phrased carefully as amendments to the tax law, such bills are actually private money claims against the government. A particular tax provision — some critics call it a "tax rip-off" — is drafted in language that sounds general but is specific in application. It is not surprising that the legislators often prefer not to identify the beneficiary. Thus, when tax courtesies are extended to very important persons the taxpayer can remain modestly in the background though the change in the law was made just for him. Louis B. Mayer, the late head of the Metro-Goldwyn-Mayer motion picture studios in Hollywood, wanted his claim to future profits under his retirement contract commuted to a lump-sum settlement in one year. Congress kindly removed Mayer's windfall from the tax tables for ordinary income and placed it under the more favorable capital gains provision. This was accomplished under the neutral-sounding heading "Taxability to Employee of Terminal Payments," more technically known as Section 1240 of the IR Code of 1954. The Mayer amendment fitted only one person in the United States, and saved the movie magnate roughly $2 million in taxes. Similar acts of congressional grace have benefited the estate of Charles Edward Merrill, founder of the world's largest firm of stockbrokers, and Mrs. Gerard Swope, widow of the former president of the General Electric Company.

Historically, the tax-writing committees of Congress start out bravely at the beginning of the sessions, waving a banner with a strange device, "Reform." But as the weeks and months pass and the end of the session approaches, it turns out that the revolution is off and the rites of Christmas will be celebrated in the spirit of the season. In November 1975 a very generous Santa Claus, Representative Philip Mitchell Landrum (D.-La.), offered a finger-lickin' goody in the shape of a seemingly routine amendment at a late-night meeting of the weary House Ways and Means Committee. Landrum would permit individuals who had capital losses of over $30,000 to carry them back for three years to offset taxes paid on capital gains in those years. The amendment was a gratuity worth at least $15 million to H. Ross Perot, a colorful

Texas high-roller who, according to the *Wall Street Journal*, made heavy campaign contributions toward the expenses of members of the Ways and Means Committee and the Senate Finance Committee. Perot's legal adviser couldn't have had better connections; he was Sheldon C. Cohen, former Commissioner of Internal Revenue, who got up the bill and kept a tally of who voted how. Cohen gave the bill to someone on the committee, he couldn't recall who, and later acknowledged modestly that it "apparently was used." [18]

All in all, a crude instance of trick or treat. However, when the bill, by that time widely publicized and condemned as the "Perot" amendment, reached the floor of the House it was too hot to handle and so was rejected by a lopsided margin.[19]

Representative Sam M. Gibbons (D.-Fla.) put this whole subject of tax favors in perspective during the debate on the 1975 energy bill, which had many Christmas tree ornaments attached to it. He asked the members of the House to be extremely quiet so that "they can hear the sound of the tiny reindeer hooves as they approach this Merry Christmas season in June . . . We are about to open the Christmas presents. This is the loophole section . . . I feel very terrible in trying to shoot Santa Claus down, but let me remind the Members that for every gift there has to be a giver." The gifts, Gibbons objected, are not subject to the scrutiny of the appropriations process and "will keep going on once we put them in the code . . . and there is no end to it." [20]

Tax shelters are very interesting phenomena for those who are in a position to avail themselves of the opportunities they offer. What are shelters? Here is an incomplete list: oil-well drilling ventures, movie production and distribution, rental real estate, the purchase of works of art or of Scotch whisky in the cask, cattle feeding and breeding, equipment leasing, and the development of orchards and vineyards. Thus a pro-

fessional athlete, a banker, or prosperous doctor can become a part owner of a Boeing 707, a fleet of locomotives, or of cattle he never sees, even something quaintly called "Rent-a-Pig." The idea common to these enterprises is that limited partners advance money for prepaid expenses that would normally be taken in a later year but are bunched in the last days of the current year so that an artificial loss is charged against income from regular sources, such as salaries or fees. Tax shelters are not for people in average circumstances; they appeal to high-bracket earners like surgeons, lawyers, corporation executives, especially Californians, such as movie and television personalities who have large incomes and short working lives. The partner invests in enterprises he knows nothing about, like mink ranches or avocado groves, managed by others who hold forth the lure of immediate "front-end" deductions, tax-sheltered income in the form of long-term capital gains, and depreciation allowances that reflect imaginary decline in the worth of the property. Since the deductions are taken before the money is spent and the sheltered income rises spectacularly, there is strong pressure on the rich who feel poor to repeat the performance, pushing the day of reckoning into the remote future or yielding to the temptation to hide some income on their next tax return.[21]

If the deal goes sour all is not lost. The taxpayer has already had his tax deferral. In some instances he may get an immediate write-off of the loss. If so, it comes off the top; that is, at the highest percentage bracket in which his 1040 falls. Investments in low-cost rental housing provide a very attractive way to lay out money in something that is increasing in value while the investor shows paper losses. The rules permit rapid depreciation and most of the money comes from mortgage financing. This system of making money while appearing to lose it requires, however, a good deal of expertise, and in a study conducted under the aegis of the Brookings Institution a few years ago only half of the high-income respondents surveyed in a nationwide sample had even heard of real estate as a tax deduction and only one-fifth had made or thought of making such investments.

Northern Mexican truck crops, which produce three or four harvests a year, offer a way for the remote partner to take future costs off his current tax return. This shelter is known to connoisseurs of taxmanship as the "Mexican vegetable roll-over," and if the participant keeps on planting and deducting and planting and deducting he can postpone payment of his U.S. income taxes indefinitely. Modifications in the Internal Revenue Code have closed the door on some tax havens, such as orange and almond groves. But other opportunities still exist — wine grapes, walnuts and cashew nuts, and kiwi fruit (*Actinidia chinensis*), a vine native to Asia, bearing fuzzy, edible fruit, popularly known as "Chinese gooseberries." A common criticism heard from those who do not move in tax-shelter circles is that the manipulation of the IR Code provisions relating to farming has distorted our agricultural production, pushing it away from field crops and toward overinvestment in selected tree and fruit crops. Abuses in the murky, multibillion-dollar world of tax shelters have produced a number of major scandals, especially in the areas of cattle-feeding operations and oil and gas exploration, the schemes sold by glittering prospectuses addressed to "Mr. and Mrs. Fortunate Participant," and followed up by glib salesmen who have perfected their skills as "closers" in selling lake-front lots and encyclopedias.[22]

Although it is an article of faith among those disillusioned with the distribution of wealth in this country that the rich always win and the poor always lose, the doctrine does not quite rise to the level of universal truth. (See footnote refer-

ences to the above paragraph.) Those who overreach sometimes get zapped. If the proposed commitment is not a good
investment, quite apart from its tax consequences, the end
of the tale is likely to be one of fiscal wisdom purchased at a
high price.

"Tax shelters are with us because Congress made it that
way," says IRS Commissioner Alexander. "What Congress
has done, Congress can undo, of course, and our tax laws
never reach final design . . . Approach a tax shelter, like a
porcupine, with care . . . Remember the old adage that the
bulls and the bears may do well, but the pigs are certain to
get hurt." [23]

The way Congress has reluctantly met criticism of the
depletion allowance for oil and gas exploration down through
the years is not encouraging to those who favor eliminating
loopholes, for the trend has been rather to extend special
favors to virtually all natural resources. Coal gets preferential treatment though we are supposed to have enough to
last two thousand years. Esoteric deposits extending from
anorthosite to zircon, and ores for antimony to zinc, are all
tenderly cherished as wasting assets. Yet when a group of
fashion models, known as Shy, Inc., cited the section of the
revenue code that deals with the depletion of natural resources to prove that the members too possessed assets that
got used up, and therefore requested "reasonable allowance
for obsolescence," the taxmen gave the models a dusty answer. "American beauty," the tax-collecting agency said,
"never becomes obsolete." [24]

There have been some small gestures in Congress from
time to time, indicating recognition of the possibility that
human resources become depleted just as surely as a piece
of machinery or an old office building, but they have never
attracted serious support. Authors have brought up the prob-

lem of brain depletion. One California attorney sued for a
tax refund for himself and his wife on the ground that their
bodies were just as much entitled to percentage depletion at
ages of seventy-six and seventy-two as an oil well. But an
appellate court said no, their bodies and skills did not qualify
for the subsidy.[25]

It is never out of season to study the code and regulations
in order not to skin oneself and this exercise perhaps has led
some taxpayers to rely more on the special rates for capital
gains than on any other form of tax subsidy. The basic concept is easy to understand and put in practice, provided of
course that one has capital assets that are liquid and have
advanced in value. It was noted in Chapter 9 that the lowered tax on capital gains has existed almost from the beginning of income taxation under the Sixteenth Amendment.
What we have lived with, involving little change since 1942,
represents a compromise between the views of those who
believe such gains should not be taxed at all and those who
think they should be taxed at the same rate as ordinary income. Tax scholars have long pondered this matter. But the
ideal formula for taxing such gains and balancing off losses,
with fairness to the whole community, remains elusive despite all the intellectual labor that has been expended upon
the subject.

The interest received from municipal bonds, like capital
gains, represents the selection of a particular kind of receipt
for a tax subsidy. Since a "round lot" of most bonds is now
generally considered to be 100, with a face value of $100,000,
and investment counselors discourage the purchase of smaller
lots, which cost more and are subject to a price penalty if
the owner decides to sell, this avenue of escape from income
taxation is not equally open to all taxpayers. Indeed, its at-
tractiveness begins only with incomes in the taxable $40,000–

$50,000 range. Numerous studies show that the individuals who hold the obligations of state and local government entities are the same kinds of taxpayers, and often the same taxpayers, who are knowledgeable about offshore personal trusts and other exotic methods of minimizing taxes and who attend workshops to catch up on the latest developments on the tax-shelter scene. And so, though the basic standard of living has risen generally, the distribution pattern of wealth and income in the United States has varied little in the last fifty or sixty years, while the tax exclusions and preferences have shifted the burden more toward the middle- and lower-income earners. The reaction of the middling taxpayer to this tendency is suggested in a bit of doggerel:

> The rain, it raineth all around,
>   Upon the just and unjust fellas,
> But more upon the just because
>   The unjust have the just's umbrellas.[26]

Although there is a good deal of political posturing in Congress over the distribution of the tax burden, those citizens who provide most of the money show little outright hostility to the institutional structure that permits riches and economic classes. There are protests, coalitions, noisy agitation, yes, but no sign of a broad-based demand for sweeping social changes. Perhaps redistribution of incomes turns out to be, as Irving Kristol has phrased it, "so hellishly difficult" because it calls for persuading large numbers of people to risk the loss of such benefits as they now enjoy for putative improvements that might turn out to be as fragile as a politician's promise.[27] Tax subsidies exist for persons at all income levels. This may explain why there is not more hue and cry against special privileges as an abstract principle. Each social group values its own exemptions and exclusions, its perquisites and dispensations, which have been written into the statute or opened up by rulings and regulations for the elderly, the blind, for veterans, and for those drawing sick pay. To some observers the exemptions begin to look like the benefit provisions of a health and accident insurance policy, and they ask why age, for example, should make any difference if the incomes of different age groups being compared are the same? Union membership dues are tax free, as are Social Security checks, interest on consumer credit, unemployment insurance, and workmen's compensation benefits. It is thought by Congress that it is nobler to own a home than to rent one, for rent is classed as personal consumption and is taxable, but the homeowner can deduct property taxes on his castle and the interest on his mortgage.[28]

Hair-splitting distinctions, and rulings not always clearly articulated, often seem to be the work of some puckish humorist as the signal goes up, "Deduction denied." Fees paid to marriage counselors are not subsidized by the Treasury. So one accountant advised his marriage-counselor client to become a "therapist in sexual inadequacy and incompatability." Semantics transformed the cost of counseling services into a deductible expense. And then there is Irving Gross, who became a more interesting person without help from the IRS. Gross sold advertising time for a group of television stations. When he took a course in American civilization at New York University he deducted the cost as a business expense, arguing that his studies contributed to his "unique" qualities. The Tax Court conceded that his scholarly efforts made him a more interesting companion, possibly a better salesman, but could not find a "direct link" between Irving's studies and his job.[29]

Yet many decisions of the tax authorities, on the other hand, strike one as a sensible response to the proposals of taxpayers who are trying to be good to themselves. Examples appear at various points in these pages. A Los Angeles doctor wanted to deduct payments to his children for answering the telephone at home. But the Tax Court said, "Children normally answer the family telephone," and saw nothing special in the fact that the father was a doctor. One man claimed his dog as a dependent. The code does not say that a dependent has to be a human being. However, the IRS said no.

Although there are a goodly number of small loopholes for the man in the street, he finds himself generally at a disadvantage in the struggle among contending interests that seek to relieve themselves of their tax burden. He represents the great unorganized constituency, with no access to Congress or topflight advice on taxmanship. Knowing nothing of the fiscal charms of coal-mining royalty deals or equipment-leasing, of tax-deductible trips to the Côte d'Azur, of dummy corporations in Curaçao or the Channel Islands, of cozy trusts in Lichtenstein, the wage-earners and middle classes dig down and pay what the tax schedule says is due. Tax shelters work only when there is income to shelter. And there is more to it than that. Those whose main source of income arrives in the shape of highly visible salaries and wages must make up the shortfall resulting from subsidies for those who are deft in exploiting them. Picketing IRS offices and writing nasty letters to the commissioner are poorly directed exercises because it is Congress that makes the tax laws. The IRS carries out the intent, difficult though that may be to discern.

Economists, political scientists, and students of financial policy who are not mixed up in the political process condemn all tax favors because they depart from the principle that the rates should be applied equitably, because all subsidies nibble at the tax base and push the rates up, and because tax expenditures — Professor Surrey speaking — "tumble into the law without supporting studies, being propelled instead by clichés, debating points, and scraps of data and tables that are passed off as serious evidence . . ." [30]

What exists is a two-tier system of income taxation by which the wealthy are officially supposed to pay income taxes at levels scaling up to 70 percent and are then quietly provided with abatements that assure that in most instances the rates will not be effective. Clearly, Congress does not believe in the rates it establishes and is trying to persuade the American people that the electorate's preference for progressivism in income taxation is being carried out, but at somebody else's expense. Among economic writers who take a critical view of this disingenuous arrangement are Professors Lester C. Thurow, who calls it a "trick," and Henry C. Simons, who says explicitly, "One senses here a grand scheme of deception . . ." The power of decision probably lies ultimately with middle-income Americans. It is they who must determine whether we want a more or less egalitarian society, greater or less emphasis on consumption, greater or smaller rewards for initiative. Whatever the decision, it will be administered by the agency described in the next chapter as the biggest business in the United States. [31]

14

The Biggest Business
in the United States

A BRONZE STATUE of Alexander Hamilton, the first Secretary of the Treasury, stands at the foot of the south steps of the Treasury building in downtown Washington, with an inscription cut into one of the faces of the pedestal. The words are those of Daniel Webster. They read: "He smote the rock of the national resources and abundant streams of revenue gushed forth. He touched the dead corpse of the public credit and it sprung up on its feet."

Stated more prosaically, without the Websterian organ tones, and coming down to date, the Treasury Department, operating through its collection agency, the 82,266–employee Internal Revenue Service, mails out and receives annually some 125 million tax returns and about 428 million copies of wage and informational documents, over 100 different, specialized tax guides, and about 323 miscellaneous forms concerned with tax matters and aimed at making compliance easier. The IRS subjects every return to some scrutiny by man or machine, and audits in detail about 2.5 million returns deemed most likely to contain errors. Some ten thousand suspected criminal cases are investigated closely. Of this number about twelve hundred are resolved by guilty pleas or by conviction after trial. In carrying out its mandate according to policy determined by Congress, the IRS operates what has been called the world's biggest direct-by-mail operation and in 1975 collected a record high of $293.8 billion, of which $156.4 billion, or more than half, came from individual income tax receipts.

The IRS is organized along highly decentralized lines, heading up to a national office in the Federal Triangle at Washington. The home office building is huge — seven stories of concrete, limestone, and marble, with three impressive arches at the main entrance rising two stories at the architrave. The design was inspired by historic Somerset House in London's Strand. Somerset House is, appropriately enough, the home of the British tax system, the Inland Revenue.[1]

In addition to the employment of a legal staff of 1590, of which 834 are lawyers, thus making the IRS the world's largest specialized law firm, the service requires personnel who have majors in accounting, business administration, finance, economics, criminology, public administration, political science, education, the liberal arts, and other fields. All would indignantly reject, one feels confident in saying, the dictum of Marcus Tullius Cicero, who in ancient times classified tax-gathering as a sordid occupation, along with the tasks of butchers, cooks, sausage-makers, fishmongers, and stage-dancers. On the contrary, the IRS has distinctly the atmosphere of a blue-ribbon organization. Even though much of the work is as dull as it is essential, if one were on the inside looking out it is possible to imagine without too much romancing that there is a deep, satisfying, intellectual pleasure in knowing that millions and millions of fellow citizens annually fill out income tax forms of dazzling complexity with a fair degree of uniformity, producing a copious flow of paper and money over which the IRS presides, exercising control on the basis of technical knowledge and machinery beyond the comprehension of ordinary citizens, reinforced by vast experience and unlimited legal weaponry. Viewing the tax scene from the inside in all its fantastic variety, the evasions, the clumsy arithmetical mistakes, the taxpayer fulminations and quibbles can be viewed tolerantly as "just so many blemishes on a contemplated perfection of huge scope and vast intricacy." [2]

IRS operations are carried on through 900 offices organized into fifty-eight district offices, which are responsible to seven regional commissioners. Tax returns are processed in ten service centers. Each district office has its own auditing and collection staff. Audit and Collection are the largest divisions of the service. The Inspection Division, established after the scandals of the late forties and early fifties, is completely separate from the rest of the IRS, a "line" organization with authority running directly to an assistant commissioner.

Inspection performs two functions through two divisions. Internal Audit watches how the revenue is being collected, including a continuous review of Automatic Data Processing to prevent fraud from creeping into the world's largest computer system. The other branch of Inspection, called Internal Security, investigates the character and background of the revenue agents as well as the integrity of applicants and appointees, including high officials in sensitive positions. Internal Security also handles discrimination-in-employment cases, investigates complaints of improprieties lodged against IRS people, and checks on accountants and tax lawyers who represent taxpayers before the Service. Internal Security inspectors have authority to administer oaths, require and receive testimony, make arrests, serve warrants, and seize property. They are qualified to handle firearms. If a used-car salesman in, say, North Carolina, or a CPA in New Jersey, offers money to "fix" an audit, if an IRS employee works a refund scheme, Internal Security wants to know about it and usually does, sooner or later. Unethical conduct includes anything that would bring disrepute to the service: associating with shady characters, soliciting or accepting a bribe, selling tickets, canvassing, or representing an insurance company as a sideline, which might coerce a taxpayer into buying insurance — protection in more senses than one.[3]

The Audit Division employs 14,265 revenue agents and 4666 audit and tax technicians, who work in offices and are backed up by clerical and management support. Auditors stay at their desks, deal mainly with the simpler returns of lower- and middle-income salaried workers whose income is largely covered by the W-2 (withholding) forms turned in by their employers. The revenue officer, often called an RO or field agent, is a lawyer, an accountant, or both, and handles the more complicated returns at the taxpayer's place of business. He or she is expected, in the words of the *Handbook*, to be "bold, tenacious, inquisitive and imaginative . . . and dedicated to the aims of the Service." The RO generally gets paid more than the office auditors because he needs to know more tax law, must be more skillful in auditing techniques, and is expected to exercise seasoned judgment. For example, revenue agents as well as district conferees can now (since 1974) consider the hazards of litigation and settle disputes involving $2500 or less at the district level, thus saving the small taxpayer time and the costs of travel to appellate-division offices and the services of expert accountants whose time-charges could run to $50 or $75 an hour.

New agents get boot training in the classroom on tax law, report writing, methods of detecting fraud; and after they start to work on their own they are kept on their toes by staff meetings, employee appraisals, and are guided by manuals and stimulated by field visitations from supervisors.

The experienced agent does not ordinarily get into abstract discussions of tax morality during audits, but he has a built-in spotting scope for finding people who get a honk out of putting one over on the IRS or simply feel that they need the money more than the Treasury does. The real "pro," sketched in the IRS's *Techniques Handbook for In-Depth Audit Investigations* as "James A. Gettum," develops a "feel" for situations in which a dependent named "Butch" might be the family pet, or in which cash donations to a church appear to exceed the charitable impulses of the most devout communicant, or in which the taxpayer lives more expensively than his visible means could support.

The Collection Division, with 6919 officers at its disposal, deals with those who say they cannot pay, those who never filed, the inveterate deadbeats, and sometimes with the innocent taxpayer who has suffered a major misfortune. Much of its work is routine — opening envelopes and writing letters to delinquents, or making cool, courteous telephone calls, or paying pastoral visits if necessary. Collection meets up with some slippery characters and its approach contains elements of a police mentality. Collection officers use their powers sparingly. They could destroy a small businessman's credit overnight, for they can, if they choose, seize a bank account, garnishee wages, take a taxpayer's automobile, and padlock his place of business without a court order. If there is reason to suspect the taxpayer of hiding his assets or going over the hill, the agent can issue a jeopardy assessment or close the taxpayer's "taxable year," as was done in the case of Johansson, the boxer, and demand immediate payment. However, the Supreme Court early in 1976 called for modifications because the procedure does not provide safeguards, such as giving the taxpayer a chance to contest the assessment in Tax Court before the IRS seizes his property. If the money really isn't there, Collection acts pragmatically and takes what it can get. In one case, of special interest to those who never tire of observing that some horses can run faster than others, what the government got was a stable of thorough-breds, which raced at Hialeah Park under Uncle Sam's colors until an income tax assessment of $401,088.46 was satisfied, including interest and a 50 percent penalty.[4]

The Intelligence Division, with a staff of 2626 technical employees, is a criminal enforcement agency responsible for applying the criminal statutes that relate to the revenue. When, in the course of an audit, the RO suspects fraud, he discontinues the audit, giving the taxpayer no reason, closes his briefcase, and departs to report. If his report is solid, the investigation becomes a "jacketed case" and the Intelligence Division's man, known as a special agent, swings into action. From this point on the investigation is conducted mainly by the special agent, who develops the facts regarding the suspected fraud. The taxpayer has opportunities during this period for administrative conferences, but if there is a finding of fraud the Justice Department handles the prosecution. The philosophy of the law does not stress punishment but simply the collection of the revenue. However, the punishment does act *in terrorem* on those whose scruples are not sufficient to balance their hopes of defeating the revenue officers.

The work of an intelligence agent is tedious and time-consuming. Completion of a good case in a year is considered a satisfactory performance. Training is intensive, even including at the end participation in a mock income tax trial. The post is classified as hazardous and advancement is rapid. Most special agents reach grade GS-11 in two or three years and go up to GS-13 and on to GS-15 if they demonstrate managerial ability. (The meaning of these salary categories is explained in the footnotes.)[5]

The Intelligence Division encounters "pockets of noncompliance" in all walks of life, but especially in those occupations not subject to withholding. The heaviest caseload arises from organized crime — illegal gambling, loan-sharking, dealing in narcotics, extortion, prostitution, business fraud, murder-for-hire — in short, the "vice industries." Today's leaders in organized crime are not the legendary mobsters of the 1920s. Nor do they resemble purse-snatchers in T-shirts. Rather, they appear to be respectable businessmen in well-cut suits; they drive Cadillacs (bought for cash), often occupy discreet two-family homes furnished with overstuffed furniture and genteel antimacassars on the chair arms. They are kind to their families, faithful to their church after their fashion, and frequently channel illegal funds into such legitimate ventures as restaurants, nightclubs, real estate, trucking, vending machines, sports, and funeral parlors — for which they often furnish the raw material.

The special agents of the IRS are formidable opponents. They are highly skilled in locating hidden assets and unreported sources of income, in identifying false records and fraudulent tax returns. They untangle intricate transactions, obtain corroborating statements, make third-party investigations, conduct raids, arrest, and interrogate. All of this must be done with care, for in criminal proceedings, unlike civil cases, the burden of proof is on the government.

The special agents employ high-technology aids and sophisticated laboratory procedures. This includes typewriter exemplars, the study of documents through infrared light, use of microscopes, ultraviolet light, and spectrophotofluorometry, which can analyze ball-point pen ink and determine if various writings were made with the same ink, and when, and whether they were made by the same hand. Anthracene gives off a brilliant fluorescent light when exposed to ultraviolet light, though invisible otherwise — very useful for marking documents, clothing, and vehicles. Phenolphthalein is an almost colorless powder that turns red in the presence of an alkaline solution. Sprinkle a little on a doorknob or package. Any person touching the object will unknowingly get the powder on his hands. When he washes them his hands turn bright red. Caught red-handed, indeed!

And there are other kinds of equipment that are more familiar — radios, listening and recording devices, two-way mirrors, binoculars and telescopes, cameras, firearms, and handcuffs. IRS guidelines have for some years required the special agent to identify himself at his initial meeting with the noncomplying citizen, describe his function, and advise the suspect of his constitutional rights along the lines laid down by the Supreme Court in 1966 in *Miranda* v. *Arizona*. But in a recent decision the Supreme Court decided that the IRS men need not advise their quarry of his legal right to remain silent prior to questioning, except when the taxpayer has been arrested. The practical effect of the ruling is that the special agent can hold back the warning until he has extracted all the information he can get from the candidate for prosecution.[6]

An Office of International Operations, with a staff of 524 and offices in fourteen countries, investigates and assists the 300,000 U.S. citizens living abroad who are either genuinely confused about their tax obligations or delinquent in paying up. American nationals living in foreign countries are subject to the American income tax with two qualifications:

First, foreign income taxes paid on foreign income may be credited against income taxes due the United States.

Second, an American citizen who is a bona fide resident of a foreign country, or who remains abroad for seventeen out of eighteen months and is not an employee of the U.S. Government, may exclude from U.S. taxation up to $25,000 of his income earned abroad.

The taxpayer service representative stationed abroad, often

described as a "tax administrator in striped trousers," is attached to the U.S. embassy as well as to the Office of International Operations. He usually has command of one or more foreign languages and knows the statutes governing taxation under which foreign governments operate. The duties of the IRS representative overseas are varied. He audits, collects, gives tax assistance at filing time, and rounds up those neglectful of their fiscal duties. Since he has to work with foreign countries often unconcerned with the efficient collection of American taxes, his powers are somewhat circumscribed as compared with those of his U.S. colleagues. Still, there is a scattering of Americans who cannot safely return from Teheran, Kuala Lumpur, or wherever they are.[7]

The ten service centers around the United States monitor the returns of individuals and corporations, receive envelopes stamped and unstamped, returns completed and uncompleted, signed and unsigned, bank checks that clear and some that bounce, unidentified cash including pennies, protests from habitual liars who contend they sent in their returns but didn't. Receipts include promissory notes and Betty Crocker coupons. The senders are not necessarily jokers. Some are earnest and apprehensive and fundamentally good folk simply seeking some way to pay.

Correspondence at the service centers is handled by computer-generated notices comprising short paragraphs typed in by the computer/printer, which has to get the message across clearly and understandably in a few lines "and if possible with a modicum of the amenities." The computer also sends out those preaddressed tax-return packages that come as a post-Christmas gift from the IRS to its clients, processes the refunds, and catches the taxpayers who file multiple claims for refunds. (One blithe spirit filed seventeen different returns, each calling for a government check.) If a taxpayer writes, "Where's my refund?" the letter goes to an IDRS (Integrated Data Retrieval System) operator, who pushes a button, and the computer/printer answers the letter. If the input is incorrect, however, the computer can crank out some remarkable things, as it did when it showed one taxpayer as having ninety-seven dependents. Most other correspondence is handled by form letters with boxes that can be checked. General inquiries usually receive an individually typed answer from the district office.[8]

It has already been pointed out (see Chapter 11) that to many persons who willingly comply scrupulously with the IR Code it is the paperwork that vexes, "and though vexation is not, strictly speaking, expense," says Adam Smith, "it is certainly equivalent to the expense at which every man would be willing to redeem himself from it." For example, the retirement credit (IR Code Sec. 37) is quite difficult for many elderly citizens to fill out, and no less an authority than Dr. Laurence N. Woodworth, chief of staff of the Joint Committee on Internal Revenue Taxation, has estimated that "perhaps as many as half of the elderly who could use the provision, do not because of its present complexity." There is indeed a Grand Canyon that divides government language from standard English. Guess, if you please, what this means: "gain from sale or exchange of property which is neither a capital asset nor property described in Section 1231." The answer: ordinary income.

The anguished cry of the taxpayer for an income tax form that he can understand is as old as the income tax itself. The pea in the shoe has always been the technical jargon and the Byzantine intricacy of the forms, "the dense print and the obscurely worded sentences," which made Edmund Wilson think of "the far-fetched distinctions of medieval theology." The Secretary of the Treasury in the Ford administration,

William E. Simon, told an audience at a National Conference of the Tax Foundation a number of homely truths about the state of our tax system, including this: "I'm not even sure the IRS experts fully understand the system anymore. How can they when they are dealing with a tax code and regulations that now exceed 6,000 pages of fine print?"

E. B. White, long-time essayist for the *New Yorker* magazine and frequent commentator on life's ironies, cites the income tax as a contributing cause of our tightening energy crisis. "The government itself forces a citizen to burn fuel," he has written.

> I sat up most of one night in January, making out W-2 statements for the employees who were in and out of our house at one time or another during 1974. I'm not good at filling out forms . . . Lights blazed, while the furnace plugged away in the cellar to keep me from freezing to death. The very next morning, a letter arrived from the I.R.S. advising me, in a pleasant and chatty fashion, that our returns for 1972 and 1973 were up for audit and would I please have the following documents ready for the inspector's visit. Then followed a list as long as your arm. If I'm to produce all those curios, the lights will burn late enough to satisfy even the insatiable electric company.

It was and is a singularly bleak employment for the pencil-biting citizen not only to have to levy against himself but to wrestle with such brain-teasers as he confronts in completing Schedule A, transferring his total itemized deductions shown on line 40 over to line 52 on page two, entering on line 51 the adjusted gross income previously calculated on line 17 on page one, subtracting line 52, and entering the remainder on line 53. At line 54 he or she subtracts from the figure on line 53 the appropriate number of exemptions, and there it is on line 55, the grand figure of taxable income. Yet it's really child's play, the IRS says, to figure the tax. See instructions.[9]

In 1913 the revenue act had one section divided into fourteen subsections. Today, the last code section is number 8023(c), and the law is supplemented by official regulations that can be measured only in linear feet, mountainous reports of congressional committees, court decisions, handbooks, treatises, legal journals, and cumulative bulletins containing published rulings. And thousands of rulings exist that have never been published. Criticism of this vast corpus of writings comes even from those professionally trained to deal with it. A Senate staff member has been quoted as saying, after he had read a House bill, "Most of it I can't understand and what I can understand I can't believe." A confession from one of the most distinguished American jurists may be consoling to the common, or confused, variety of taxpayer. The late Judge Learned Hand is speaking:

> The words of such an act as the Income Tax . . . merely dance before my eyes in a meaningless procession: cross-reference to cross-reference, exception upon exception . . . at times I cannot help recalling a saying of William James about certain passages of Hegel: that they were, no doubt, written with a passion of rationality; but that one cannot help wondering whether to the reader they have any significance save that the words are strung together with syntactical correctness.[10]

Several years ago the late Senator Arthur V. Watkins (R.-Utah) came upon a 212-word brain-boggling sentence in an income tax instruction booklet. A spokesman for the IRS hastily passed the problem back to Congress because, he said, the section came from the IR Code. The senator read the sentence several times, but all he got out of it, he explained later, was an aggravated thirst. He tried it out on several colleagues, no strangers to windy sentences, but they, too, ended up confused and dehydrated. Whereupon Senator Watkins offered a prize to the public at large, consisting of a book on simplified English and a copy of the Bible, a literary work with a high reputation for lucid prose. The competition was open to any American who could recast the sentence in clear, understandable words. The contest was administered by a distinguished committee drawn from the School of Commerce of New York University. There were hundreds of entries. But — surprise — the committee rejected them all and so in effect awarded the prize to the IRS, or, rather, to the congressional committee that had drafted the sentence. "Brevity," the prize committee concluded, "is not necessarily a virtue in official documents: precision is." Randolph Paul, in a nicely balanced antithesis, summarized what was at stake: "It is not enough to attain a degree of precision that a person reading in good faith can understand; it is necessary to attain a degree of precision which a person reading in bad faith cannot misunderstand." [11]

To some, probably a majority of taxpayers, simplicity continues to mean the use of language that the ordinary man can understand. To others it has to do with fairness. They are giving their time as well as money to the government, they argue, so why does the task have to be so difficult? Unfortunately, in tax matters, what is simple may not be equitable and what is equitable may not be simple. Fairness is applauded by all men in the abstract. But justice becomes hard to discern in the dense thicket of deductions, exemptions, capital gains and losses, depletion allowances, straight-line and accelerated depreciation, and other recondite and attenuated distinctions that presumably got into the code for the noblest of reasons: to make sure that persons with equal incomes pay equal taxes. And even after one understands, or thinks he has mastered, a difficult section of the IR Code, it turns out more often than not that there is a Catch-22. It reads, "except as otherwise provided . . ."

Despite all that can be said of the necessity for absolute, legal precision in language affecting the collection of the public monies, taxpayers continue to have a low boiling point when they face the niceties of the law. "Life is fleeting, and there is work to do; the law treats time as irrelevant . . ." a greatly vexed Henry W. Wriston, former president of Brown University, told the *Wall Street Journal*. And he suggested that the income tax statute should be retitled "An Act for the Endowment of Lawyers, Accountants and Bureaucrats in Perpetuity and for the Waste of Time and Energy of the Innocent Citizen." Richard Goode, former Treasury Department economist and director of the Fiscal Affairs Division, International Monetary Fund, concurs. He includes in the economic effects of the progressive income tax the diversion of a large pool of talented accountants and tax lawyers "to the socially unproductive activity of complying with the tax."

There is a form for everything. Form 2333 enables businessmen to request blank income tax forms. Form 4211 is needed to find out the shipping and handling charges for sending Form 2333. Form 4868 gets one an automatic extension of time for filing. No reason need be given. Form 2688 gets one another extension beyond the first one, but this time the taxpayer has to have a reason. Form 2311 is a handy IRS tool, used in making the jeopardy assessment when there is reason to believe the taxpayer is likely to hide his assets or skip the country. Altogether there are some 2300–odd IRS forms in use at the present time. Filling out and filing these forms takes time, thought, and a high IQ, moving the authors of *Effects of Taxation: Investments by*

Individuals to suggest that the energies expended and the time lost from constructive activities in coping with the increasing elaboration of the tax structure might "add up to something like an atomic explosion." [12] Some suggestions that have been made to achieve simplification and the probabilities of their adoption will be considered in Chapter 16.

Meanwhile Form 1040 is required to carry an increasingly heavy load of items not always essential to the administration and enforcement of the tax laws. The Employee Retirement Income Security Act of 1974 and other legislation added four new lines to the 1975 form. Four more were required by the Tax Reduction Act of 1975. Three were squeezed in for revenue-sharing purposes, a total of eleven added in one year. The Tax Reform Act of 1976 adds five new entries to the 1040 return and eight to the 1040A, the "short form," in an edition of 81 million copies. These questions and others that we may expect in the future are designed to make sure the distribution of the tax is equitable, but the inequities, like quicksilver, simply roll around from one group of taxpayers to another, according to the will of a particular Congress, while the difficulties of compliance mount. Though the track record on simplification is disappointing, the reasons for the lack of progress should be understood. The code is not a monolith. It is under almost constant review by Congress, the executive branch, the Internal Revenue Service itself, the tax bar, and the lay public; and adjustments are made annually. It will never be easy to fill out the world's most complicated tax form, but one cannot fault the IRS for lack of trying to clarify and simplify. Within the service there is a continuing study made of schedules and instructions, and notice is taken of what is bothering people. Sometimes writer-editors work under extreme pressure, preparing alternative drafts to meet printing deadlines while Congress argues over new tax provisions. Senator Mark O. Hatfield (R.-Ore.) made an interesting suggestion when he introduced into the Ninety-third Congress a bill that would have reduced tax returns to four lines and saved millions of man-hours of nonproductive work. Hatfield explained his proposal with considerable persuasiveness but it never had a chance, possibly because it would have treated all dollars equally. This, Congress is not about to do now or, probably, ever.[13]

All money bills originate in the powerful Ways and Means Committee, which stands at the top of the committee hierarchy in the House. It opens public hearings on tax legislation early in the new year, after Congress has received the recommendations of the President. His advisers may have been working intensively on the legislation for a year or more. Among those groups that help to shape the proposals in the executive branch are the President's Council of Economic Advisers, the Office of Management and Budget, and the Treasury Department, which maintains an Office of Tax Analysis. It evaluates the problems and prepares alternate solutions. There is also an Office of the Tax Legislative Counsel, which drafts legislation and accompanying regulations. Assistance is solicited from the IRS and from experts drawn from outside the government. The Joint Committee on Internal Revenue Taxation, consisting of ten ranking members of the Ways and Means Committee and the Senate Finance Committee, makes its own tax studies, provides advice from its technical staff of lawyers and accountants. This committee also reviews all refunds of $100,000 or more proposed by the Commissioner of Internal Revenue.

Opening day of tax hearings is often a spectacular occasion. The hearings are held in the Ways and Means Committee room, Room 1102 of the Longworth House Office Building, a large, square, high-ceilinged room with no windows. The members of the committee, which was enlarged in 1975 from twenty-five to thirty-seven, are seated on a dais behind two long, curved desks. Out in front, perhaps 400 to 450 citizens are sitting and standing. Committee members all like to be on hand as the photographers' flashes pop and the television cameras catch the animated scene. Later their attendance drops dramatically. By custom, the lead-off witness is the Secretary of the Treasury, chief financial officer of the United States, who delivers a long, carefully prepared statement presenting the administration's program. Members friendly to the occupant of the White House ask helpful questions; those opposed attempt to trap the Secretary into making statements he will regret later. Tightly organized interests from business, agriculture, labor, trade associations (lobbying expenses deductible) follow the Secretary with oral presentations of their views on the proper distribution of the tax load, which fill thousands of pages of testimony; there are written statements, exhibits, and the text of thousands of letters. At the present time there are more than twenty-eight hundred professionals lobbying on Capitol Hill for their clients. The reasons they advance for this or that change, enlarging on the doctrine of fairness, earnestly solicitous of the good health of the economy, are not necessarily the real reasons. That is to say, those who appear watch over their own interests, presenting information and misinformation both publicly and privately with an eloquence, ingenuity, and assiduity that can only be admired. Often their proposals have merit even though their motives are not purely patriotic. Testimony representing low-income groups and the unorganized general public is sparse.

Working in executive session, the Ways and Means Committee "marks up" the bill, that is, decides on the details of the measure and the correct legal language to be used. A draft of the committee report, which can run to several hundred pages, tells what the bill does and why it should be passed, ending with a technical section. This report is relied on later by the IRS and the courts in their effort to carry out the intention of Congress. Debate before the House, which must accept or reject the entire bill except for amendments acceptable to the Ways and Means Committee, usually lasts only two or three days. It is rare for a major tax bill to be rejected.

The Senate Finance Committee operations are similar to those of the Ways and Means Committee. Its seventeen members sit in a U at the end of a long, narrow room on a raised platform, the chairman at the center, witnesses below him. Again the Secretary of the Treasury leads off, testifying on the House version of the bill. Things move faster now. The arguments have already been heard, tediously and often tendentiously. After the Finance Committee has had its mark-up session and the bill is reported out of committee, the full Senate votes.

Two comments on the voting show how true it is that the committee system is the heart of the legislative system. First, the late Senator Wright Patman (D.-Texas), who once said, "The tax laws are passed with the Members not knowing exactly what they mean. They do not know what these commas and semi-colons and certain phrases mean. We must take the word of the committee." And now Senator Russell B. Long (D.-La.), chairman of the Finance Committee: when members of his committee protested, during the vote on the Tax Reduction Act of 1975, that they were being rushed, Long replied, "If every man insists on knowing what he's voting for before he votes, we're not going to get a bill reported before Monday."

After the two legislative branches have voted, the bill goes to the House–Senate Joint Conference Committee for reconciliation of the two versions unless the House accepts the Senate amendments, making a conference unnecessary. This rarely occurs. The adjustment is accomplished in a small room at the Capitol, House conferees on one side of a table, the Senate members on the other. After both houses approve the conference report, the bill goes to the President. He has ten days after a bill reaches the White House to sign or veto it. Great efforts are made to present a bill acceptable to the President and he usually signs it. But if he neither approves nor disapproves, the bill becomes law without his signature, except if Congress is not in session and the ten-day period has passed without presidential action; then the measure is dead. This is the pocket veto. If the bill becomes law, the IRS issues new tax forms and revises its instructions, based on Treasury regulations. This takes time. Often before the new law is fairly in operation the tax technicians and the secretariat of the Ways and Means Committee are back at work on the next recycling of tax policy. For them, there is no business like tax business.[14]

The maintenance of the federal government's solvency and even the stability of our political institutions require that the general public have confidence in the integrity of the tax-gathering agency. A low point in the history of American tax-collection came in the post–World War II period, when collections soared by 700 percent, the number of taxpayers rose from eight million to fifty-two million, with a correspondingly rapid expansion in the personnel of the Bureau of Internal Revenue. In 1951 came shattering revelations of influence-peddling and irregularities of the most sordid character — payoffs, extortion by revenue agents, embezzlement of government funds, and tax cases suppressed as casually as traffic tickets. Grand juries encountered frequent instances of total amnesia, RO's who claimed to have had extraordinary good fortune at the poker table or the races as explanations of sudden affluence. Revenue officials were caught falsifying their own returns and there were instances of congressmen meddling in pending tax cases.

The most damaging evidence that the tax-collection function was in a dangerous state of disarray came in 1951 in hearings conducted by a subcommittee of the Ways and Means Committee, known as the King Committee after its indefatigable chairman, Representative Clarence R. King (D.-Calif.). The heart of the problem was the patronage system. The IRS was staffed by employees who got their jobs from the local political club. If there were three slots to be filled, the club sent up three men, and that was that. This was especially true of deputy collectors and revenue officers. In one case, an interviewer told an applicant at the end of their conversation that he would let him know. The man replied: "You don't understand. I was sent down here by the club. I've got the job."

The King hearings made headlines for months and the disturbing question arose as to how, or whether, adequate methods could be devised to collect and audit the taxes of millions of relatively low-income citizens. As the first necessary step, there were wholesale dismissals and forced resignations. Some 200 persons walked the plank, including forty high officials, among them an Assistant Attorney-General of the United States and the President's appointments secretary. A Commissioner of Internal Revenue, Joseph D. Nunan, Jr., and the head of the Tax Division of the Justice Department went to prison. In 1953 came the total reorganization of the old Bureau of Internal Revenue into the Internal Revenue Service, as recommended by President Truman and incorporated into legislation by Congress. The new name

might be dismissed as merely a cosmetic touch, but there
were sweeping changes of substance: the abolition of political appointments below the level of commissioner; decen-
tralization through new Regional Commissioners of Internal
Revenue, who replaced the old collectors, each of whom had
become an island of power; the establishment of a career
service; and the installation of the independent internal Inspection Division.

Four years later a critical review of what had been accomplished was made by another subcommittee of the Ways
and Means Committee. The report was generally favorable.
The IRS had recovered its reputation as a blue-ribbon service.[15] Today the IRS is again in the dock. Commissioner
Donald C. Alexander was called on to testify eighteen times
before various congressional committees during FY 1975,
and by January 1976 his appearances, reflecting a period of
national malaise, reached a grand total of thirty-four. Meanwhile the agency was investigated generally by two congressional panels, the Federal Bureau of Investigation, the Treasury Department, and the IRS's own investigatory arm.[16] The
specification of charges was as long as a laundry list. Decen-
tralization had led to, or permitted, a number of cloak-and-
dagger operations — serious, sordid, laughable, expensive,
and nonproductive from any point of view.[17] Independent
tests revealed uneven application of the code and IRS rulings
in different geographical regions, and the service was not
bound by its own tax advice, which was frequently wrong.
The attempt by the Nixon White House to use the IRS to
reward its friends and punish its "enemies" was neither
wholly successful nor wholly unsuccessful. Under political
pressure the agency did not break, but it bent considerably.
A nightmare returns. If the disillusioned taxpayers should
refuse en masse to pay up, there would be nothing the IRS

could do about it though our government might be in peril. Small wonder, then, that Mrs. Alexander gave the commissioner a string of Greek worry beads.[18]

If there is one phase of IRS activity that arouses taxpayer sensitivity more than any other, it is the auditing process. Millions of returns are accepted as filed but every return is examined to make sure it is complete, free of routine errors, such as duplicate deductions or failure to reduce medical deductions by 3 percent of adjusted gross income, and free of mistakes in arithmetic. Returns identified for audit are selected by computers, using from twenty-eight to fifty different criteria; for example, there are norms for the relation between deductions and income, and between charity contributions and income. Formulae developed over the years assign weights to various characteristics that have been shown by statistically sound samples to signal underreporting. The formulae are programmed into the computer, each return getting a composite score that measures the probability of tax error. The higher the score, the greater the likelihood that the taxpayer has been careless or less than candid. The computer is stupid but accurate. Its work is followed up by experienced classifiers, who manually grade the returns selected by the machine's statistical models. Thus the findings of technology are double-checked by human judgment. Some returns are also pulled out at random for use in special research studies designed to keep the selection formulae up to date.

A certain percentage of returns are picked for audit from each income class, the percentage examined becoming greater as the adjusted gross income of the taxpayer rises. These percentages are a closely guarded secret, but it is no secret that more examinations are carried out in the higher latitudes of the income-receivers, which is the way it ought to be, says Commissioner Alexander, "in a country with a graduated income tax that depends . . . upon voluntary compliance."

If highly placed personalities receive special handling, the IRS isn't talking about it, though it is known that there is a classification called "sensitive" cases, meaning important personalities in government, politics, sports, business, entertainment, organized religion, or those whose cases might "result in unfavorable publicity or embarrass the Service," the *Manual* says. So a directive has been issued, stating that the commissioner is to be informed (use Form 4341) when VIP's are about to be audited. Efficiency in the IRS is on the uptick. Because of improved methods of selection, the number of "no change" audits, which represent, of course, a waste of man-hours, has fallen from 43 percent in 1968 to 23 percent in 1975, dropping steadily as selection gets a finer tuning.

The honest taxpayer has nothing to fear, according to IRS Publication 556, *Audit of Returns, Appeal Rights, and Claims for Refund,* which may be obtained free from any local IRS office. The examination in no way suggests suspicion of chicanery or criminal liability, but the reader may observe the iron hand in the velvet glove, for the booklet cautions that if a lien or lawsuit is filed, the case will lose its confidentiality and become a matter of public knowledge. The brochure does not mention that the taxpayer who claims a refund may get an audit too.

Returns remain open for three years, assuming that no fraud is found. As a practical matter, a return that has not been flagged in twenty-six months probably won't be audited. What becomes of old 1040s? This question is often asked. They are kept by the service centers for a year. Then they are "retired" to a General Services Administration Records Center. After six years they are destroyed, with the exception of those that remain open for audit, investigation, or other administrative use.

When the revenue agent is assigned a return for review he first develops a plan of action. He dissects. He constructs a battle plan for the coming interview. The case jacket that contains the return includes the previous examiner's report of his findings if the taxpayer has been audited within the past five years, and the agent should be in possession of all recent "appropriate" information, such as newspaper clippings, informers' letters, Form 917 (information bearing on another return), or Form 918A (shows another district is examining a partnership or fiduciary return). The agent is expected to read the earlier report carefully, looking for recurring issues that may suggest pickups for his coming appointment. He lists all items that should be questioned on Form 3858, the additional items that should be probed, and the ones requiring verification, such as T&E expenses and casualty losses inadequately explained.

Armed with the tools of his trade — the tax code, the regulations, Treasury decisions, IRS rulings, latest court cases, and the published tax services — the RO hits the audit trail. In metropolitan areas initial contact is made with the taxpayer by telephone. If done by letter, the letter must be signed by hand. Time and travel are costly, so the agent is well advised to keep on hand an adequate inventory of cases at all times to fill in the, so to speak, chinks. He immediately takes charge in any encounter. This is of paramount importance. He is courteous, inquisitive, but not vindictive. If he is a new agent, he may be tough because he has to prove himself. If the RO is a woman, she too may feel the need to be tough. But an impartial approach is safest, as it may prevent a reversal of the service on appeal.

The revenue officer is directed to exploit the initial interview to the utmost because it is a splendid opportunity to get information that may not be offered so freely by the taxpayer at a later date. Be chatty, relaxed. Create a spontaneous atmosphere, the *Audit Technique Handbook for Internal Revenue Agents* advises. Get the taxpayer to rattle on about himself, his friends, his business, hobbies, financial history, mode of living, investments. Yet do not make him feel that he is under formal interrogation. Direct questions, such as "Would you ever have cash on hand of $100? When? Why?" are in order only if the Tp (taxpayer) clams up. Among "indicators" that guide the agent are the behavior of the taxpayer, his knowledge of taxes and business practices, inconsistent statements, sloppy record-keeping, lame explanations, overeagerness to accept proposed adjustments and get an immediate closing of his file. The question of fraud does not normally come up. Fraud is a serious charge, which is quite distinct from a mistake, reliance on bad advice, carelessness, or an honest difference of opinion. There is nothing wrong, as has been mentioned before, with a Tp shaping events so long as he does not conceal or misrepresent the facts. "There may be a thin line . . ." the *Manual* remarks.[19]

In another part of the forest, the taxpayers encounter the quota system, or think they do. Obviously, if the efficiency rating of an auditor or RO depends on his production, taxpayers are going to be treated inequitably and hassled for money they may not owe. The sums involved need not be great but the anguish is real. As one agent explained to a Mr. Robert Crissey of West Caldwell, New Jersey: "It's obvious that you aren't trying to cheat us, Mr. Crissey, but it wouldn't look good on my record if I let you go for nothing. So why don't we just pick up a nominal sum and that will be that. I have some shopping to do." Crissey has forgotten exactly what they settled on but says he believes it was under $20.

The IRS categorically denies that tax enforcement results are used to evaluate the men in the field or that there are production goals. Philip Long, a real estate dealer of Bellevue, Washington, and his wife, Susan, who was a graduate student in statistics at the University of Washington, spent three and a half years and more than $15,000 in trying to find out the rules by which the IRS operated. They testified before a Senate appropriations subcommittee that the IRS had target quotas broken down by income brackets and geographical areas. Vincent Connery, a former agent who now heads the National Treasury Employees Union, insists that when agents are under pressure they dig up cases to meet quantitative goals. "They have to get something," Connery says, "even though it isn't a killing."

Not so, says the chief of the Audit Division, though he agrees that individual agents may keep a diary, confer privately, and so do some quota-setting on their own. Four former Commissioners of Internal Revenue have denied that agents were promoted because they could extract additional payments from taxpayers, and a former deputy commissioner, William Smith, has testified that although there was a correlation between retrieving the top dollar and rising in the GS grades there were other factors in the equation and the connection was purely coincidental. Probably the truth lies somewhere between the two positions. Certainly in the past there was a quota system. Back in the 1940s, the IRS district offices displayed openly a blackboard showing the performance records of each agent; and in 1948 the then Commissioner of Internal Revenue reported with satisfaction that the average dollar production of each RO had risen significantly since 1946. The fact is, a formal quota is quite unnecessary. The men know why they are there.[20]

It has been suggested that in the administration of the income tax law the small taxpayer gets handled severely.

Certainly he offers an easy target. Low-income consumers, who do not know what they are paying in finance charges on their mortgage or automobile or television set and have vague ideas as to the nature of a conditional sales contract, are vulnerable when an auditor is seeking quick closings. Few among this class of citizens would know the law or the court cases that might support their contentions. They have to take the word of the tax man on determinations that may be entirely fair and highly professional — or possibly not. Nor can they know whether the agent is serious in his proposals or is simply staking out a negotiating position. In any event, the taxpayer with, let us say, an adjusted gross income of $15,000 or less does not have the time, the money, the knowledge, or the fighting spirit necessary to challenge the audit process. Like a small animal caught in a leg-hold trap, the taxpayer is in agony and wants only to escape, ignorant of the fact that the IRS can, if it so chooses, settle tax obligations in monthly installments, that it is perfectly legal for a taxpayer to propose an "offer in compromise," or that he or she can appeal the examiner's additional assessment to higher levels of authority. Under these circumstances, taxpayers sometimes make pathetically naïve gestures of submission, offering bags of home-grown tomatoes, for instance, an old car, clothing, or proposing that they wash the office windows.[21]

It is encouraging to know that today the revenue service is diligent in informing the taxpayer that he has rights of appeal if he does not agree with the computations made by its representative. The initial letter from the district director announcing that his return is going to be examined points this out. Details are given in various IRS publications and in the speeches of the service's high-level officials when they go on the luncheon circuit.

Following the audit, if there is a deficiency in the opinion of the examiner, he will explain it and prepare a short report, a four-part carbon interleaved snap-out assembly, leaving one copy with the taxpayer. If the Tp agrees with the report, the agent will ask him to sign Form 870, Waiver of Restrictions on Assessment and Collection of Deficiency in Tax and Acceptance of Proposed Overassessment. This last phrase means that if the agent finds a refund is due, the taxpayer, presumably with joy and relief, agrees to its correctness.

But the taxpayer may not accept the revenue agent's findings. In that case he will receive a written report, setting out the government's position. This is known as the thirty-day letter. It gives the taxpayer thirty days to request a conference — an amiable, informal chat. Or the Tp can sign an agreement enclosed with the thirty-day letter, which gives him another chance to reconsider and pay up. This stops the interest charge if he is prompt with his check or money order. The taxpayer may, as an alternative, file a formal protest in writing (not required for sums in dispute under $2500) and request that his case be referred to one of the forty offices of the IRS Appellate Division. Many wealthy individuals prefer to start here since district conferees cannot settle cases running above $2500. The conference in the Appellate Division is still informal.

A lawyer or an accountant may or may not guide or represent the taxpayer at either conference level. But a professional can usually make a sounder judgment than the client as to where to start and how best to present the story, especially if there is a gray-area issue such as "unreasonable compensation."

Conferences are a bit like the mazy figures of a minuet. Here mutual concessions are in order, governed by many delicate nuances — when or whether the Tp should yield,

how to get the government man to make the first move toward agreement, what kind of offer the taxpayer should
make (bearing in mind that an offer sets a minimum). Most
disputed cases, more than 99 percent of them, are settled
without a trial. Were it not so, the courts would be more
clogged with tax litigation than they now are.

If, after the appellate conference, agreement is still elusive,
the taxpayer may then request the IRS to send him what is
called the ninety-day letter (150 days if he lives outside the
United States). This is a statutory Notice of Deficiency. It
states the exact amount demanded and lays the basis for an
appeal for a judicial review if the petitioner files his request
within ninety days of the mailing of the notice.

Once out of the IRS appeals system and into the courts,
alternative choices are open to the taxpayer. He may take
his case to a U.S. District Court (jury trial optional) or the
Court of Claims. But if he takes this route he must first pay
the deficiency as claimed and later sue for a refund. Getting
a refund resembles the old recipe for making rabbit pie. First
one must catch the rabbit. The choice of courts is up to the
taxpayer. If he cannot pay, the U.S. Tax Court (filing fee,
$10), not connected in any way with the IRS, is his only
recourse. Lawyers, as a matter of fact, may well prefer the
Tax Court because there is a psychological advantage in not
paying, and in the Tax Court the government claim is stayed
until the court announces its decision. Cases are heard by
single judges. Either party can take the decisions of the
lower courts to the U.S. Court of Appeals. In rare instances
the Supreme Court will accept a tax case. According to tax
folklore, the Court, which receives about twenty-five hundred tax petitions annually, has an informal quota of cases
accepted — six each year.

When the taxpayer chooses to go to the Tax Court and the

amount at issue is $1500 or less, he can elect a shorthand procedure, but there is no appeal from the decision. Should the taxpayer lose in a Tax Court case, he must pay interest on the shortage.[22]

In any court proceeding except in criminal cases the burden of proof rests on the taxpayer, not the Commissioner of Internal Revenue, whose determinations of added tax due enjoy the presumption of correctness. The indignant taxpayer tends to argue from what he perceives to be the equity of the situation. It is difficult for the lay mind to grasp, but equity is irrelevant. The issue turns on the letter of the law — strict legality. Usually it is better to settle somewhere along the line rather than to go for all-or-nothing. The IRS, backed by computer technology, expert knowledge of case law, and enormous experience in judging the risks of litigation, wins most of the court cases. Fortunately for the beleaguered petitioner the IRS would often — but not invariably — rather settle than accumulate unresolved cases. So the pressure is on both parties to achieve a meeting of minds, and the higher the taxpayer goes in the appeals system before making or accepting an offer in compromise, the greater the likelihood of a favorable conclusion. But the Tp can never be sure. He does not know the intentions of his adversary, and the IRS does not wear its heart on its sleeve.[23]

Since the IRS is an organ of government devised by human beings, one might reasonably expect that the service would occasionally indulge in a human gesture, and we find that this is so. To a taxpayer who credited himself with a casualty loss because he had had a skunk in his cellar and could not evict it for a week, a sympathetic district director wrote that the episode was evidently sudden, unexpected, the animal clearly not an invitee, all circumstances that met the criteria for an allowable loss. The government's generosity to householders does not extend, however, to termites. Termite damage is strictly on the homeowner, the IRS says, although courts have disagreed:

In Philadelphia the district director for eastern Pennsylvania, hard-nosed about taxes but an easy mark for little girls, was touched when Marcia Kessler, aged ten, a pretty fifth-grader at Rydal Elementary School, wrote to the IRS, begging the tax-gatherers to stop deducting from her father's paycheck for a week so that he could buy her a pony. The office could not grant the request, but the staff clubbed together to present an enraptured Marcia with a beautiful white Welsh pony named Cotton. The district director warned that Marcia's pony loophole was setting no precedent: "We're not at the mink stole or sports car stage yet," he wrote. "Just at the pony stage." [24]

Few of our millions of income-tax payers have ever actually visited a service center during the heavy filing season and seen the big semitrailers backing up to the loading docks to unload mountains of mailbags stuffed with tax returns, checks attached. Like Niagara Falls, it is a sight not easily forgotten, and is apt to inspire reflection on the awesome powers that surge through the political as well as the natural world. Touching life at its most sensitive points, endowed by Congress with authority that can be and has been abused, the IRS should quite properly be held accountable for its performance and scrutinized as it scrutinizes others. On the whole it gets good marks for carrying out a task of enormous complexity, despite the tales of tax hardships, not necessarily true or untrue, that circulate at cocktail parties and among hard-core tax-resisters.

15

Grin and Bear It

In ancient Egypt the taxpayers kneeled when they paid their taxes to the tax-receiver for the treasury. We are not required by the Internal Revenue Code or Treasury regulations to make such genuflections, nor are the blood sanctions of ruder times invoked by the IRS against tax delinquents. Yet there is an air of hysteria, of tension, sometimes of gallows humor in the letters taxpayers write to the IRS, which betray their fears and anxieties, sometimes accompanied by accounts of intractable personal problems that remind one of the agonies in the "Dear Abby" columns. As Justice Felix Frankfurter noted, "There is a torture of mind as well as body; the will is as much affected by fear as by force." Thus one taxpayer sent the commissioner an angry scribble accompanied by a heavy rock. Another began his letter, scorning all honorific forms of address, with "You bastard . . ."¹

"For the sake of Peace in my house," wrote another client of the IRS, "please send my refund as soon as possible and get my nagging wife off my back." A casualty loss was accompanied by this explanation: "My wife rolled off the road into a ditch with my Ford. Salvage value $75." An undertaker whose business was slow wrote, "I wish you would drop dead." When a district director of the revenue service, following up a taxpayer who had failed to file, sent him an information form to complete and sign, it came back with the message, scrawled across its face, "I have been dead for almost a year."

Some taxpayers have as much difficulty with syntax as income tax. A woman who wrote inquiring about her refund explained that she needed the money "as soon as possible I have been in bed with the doctor for two weeks and he doesn't seem able to do me any good. If things don't improve I will have to send for another doctor." Another woman with communications problems informed the national office of the IRS: "I have been cohabiting with several at headquarters but with no results."

Refunds, so often the cause of trauma, sometimes have a happy ending. A woman in Pleasant Hill, California, wrote: "Uncle Sam, you sweet, generous thing. Imagine your sending us two refund checks each for $114.16 . . . Let us know what you would like us to do with the check." The complimentary closing was "Your loving niece and nephew." Careful handling of mail can pay off in an unexpected way. When Ray Kiefer of Osceola, Missouri, was leafing through some old mail and throwing it into a wastebasket he found an unopened envelope that contained a United States Treasury check for $1700, a refund on his income tax. Equally happy must have been the father of twins at Chanute, Kansas, who asked the tax man if his two bundles of joy born on New Year's Eve would have any effect upon his income tax.

"What time New Year's Eve were they born?" asked the deputy collector, who had estimated that the Tp owed $40.

"At twenty minutes to 12," was the reply. The revenue officers refigured, adding two exemptions, and found that the government owed the young father a $120 refund.

The revenue agency has heard many ingenious excuses for

late filing but possibly none more convincing than the explanation offered by a woman who ran a nursing home at Stoughton, Wisconsin. She related that her paper would have been filed on time, "but the help got sick and left me with five bushels of stuff to be canned at once; two more patients came in and my son came down with the mumps . . . The painter calls me every few minutes to tell me the roof needs repairing and new boards must replace ones rotted out. The furnace got balky and oil spread all over the basement, ruining the potatoes . . . I'm so busy I'm dizzy."

Extracting what amusement they could from the annual filing date for their 1040s, some of the menfolk of Scarsdale, New York, a prosperous suburban community near New York City, held an admission-free "Income Tax Bawl," to which they brought their "exemptions" — wives and children. The taxpayers wore barrels, pajamas, overalls, and other unaccustomed garb, and Eddie Dunn, star of radio and television, acted as master of ceremonies, wearing the striped uniform of a prisoner, on which was pinned the sign "I didn't file last year." One woman came in a laundry bag with a placard explaining, "Just back from the cleaner." All guests received free paper towels for wiping away their tax tears.[2]

A partner in the Chicago office of the big accounting firm Price Waterhouse & Co., with a whimsical turn of mind, has commented that "tax writers and speakers regularly point out traps for the 'unwary,' [who] wind up paying more tax than the wary." His suggestion: "Congress should . . . include a few more traps for the wary." More down-to-earth was the sign a Cincinnati tax-preparer placed in his window: "Let us prepare your tax return and save you time — maybe 20 years." The IRS itself has a taxpayer-assistance program, which has drawn mixed reviews. Taxpayers who telephoned the Manhattan district office in the spring of 1975 for help with their tax problems were startled when they heard a background of recorded music while they waited until an auditor was free. The tune was an old favorite, "Anything Goes."[3]

Although the IRS maintains that it is a service agency (hence its name), taxpayers remain suspicious. Larry Hermone of San Jose, California, fell behind in his tax payments and asked if he could pay his balance due in monthly installments, a perfectly proper request. But the IRS refused to grant any latitude in Hermone's case, so he paid up his back taxes of $2500 by obtaining 250,000 pennies through the Federal Reserve Bank in San Francisco. Two hundred and fifty thousand pennies weigh a ton. They had to be moved by truck to the local IRS office, where an astonished revenue officer received the bulky remittance.

A favorite topic for tax satire is the business deduction, though it is sometimes difficult to determine whether the shafts are directed at the law, the IRS, or the taxpayer. One facetious correspondent suggested to Senator Russell B. Long that the deduction for intangible drilling costs allowed the oil industry be extended to woodpeckers, pointing out that they, like the oil companies, often drilled unproductive holes. Dan Greenburg, author and playwright, explained a business deduction claimed in 1972 in pursuit of his arduous occupation in these words: "The bills totalling $246.37 for Kitty Litter and 9 Lives Kittyburgers are expenses incurred in the maintenance of Bernie, Ollie, and Maurice, who [sic] I employ as watch-cats to protect my office equipment and manuscripts. The above figure is a clear saving of at least $350 over the Holmes Protection Agency's estimate for similar services, provided mechanically, per annum." In conclusion the author explained, "I should be sending you my completed 1973 return as soon as I am able to replace the original, which, as I mentioned in a previous letter, was eaten by my cats."

Russell Baker doesn't have cat problems, but as a regular columnist for the *New York Times* he has complained of running out of ideas and has advanced eloquently his claim for brain depletion. His petition has been conspicuously ignored by the Ways and Means Committee, the Senate Finance Committee, the White House, and the Internal Revenue Service. "Surely the human body . . ." Baker has written, "depreciates just as inexorably as office space . . . I know people who cruise the Caribbean every February on money the Government grants them for owning large, ugly buildings that do nothing more interesting than get a year older every year."

Art Buchwald, syndicated columnist, playwright, commencement speaker, and 1959 Cigar Man of the Year, has illustrated the art of inflating business expenses in this fashion: "Went to Burning Tree to play golf with brother-in-law who wanted to buy my old television set. Green fees and yearly dues, $1,256.40.

"Deal consummated at 17th hole. Dinner and drinks to celebrate sale at Paul Young's Restaurant . . . $30.56." [4]

According to the late Frank Sullivan, long-time contributor to the *New Yorker* magazine and acknowledged sage of Saratoga Springs, New York, filling out Form 1040 is a creative act, like writing a poem. "Officials of the Internal Revenue Department," Sullivan wrote, "who have been kind enough to compliment me on the little income tax returns I file with them annually have sometimes asked me about my method of constructing an income tax return. Do they come to me in a flash, a sudden burst of inspiration? Or do I plan them carefully? Are they 'dashed off,' or are they written only with that 'infinite capacity for taking pains' which someone has aptly defined as genius?"

Sullivan answers that making out a return, alas, is neither a spontaneous nor a joyous expression but "a matter of good, old-fashioned elbow grease . . ." His procedure, he said, was to get an idea, mull it over, collect his deductions, exemptions, salaries, wages, commissions, fees, etc., getting everything in order, "preferably in apple pie order." Equipped with plenty of paper and pencils (for chewing), he addressed the task with an adequate supply of blank 1040 forms: "About 500 usually does the trick." When everything was in a jumble and the author thoroughly confused, he simply ran to his bank and said, "Will you give me a hand with this damn tax return . . . I'm going nuts."[5]

A sharper comment came from Will Rogers, usually genial but speaking in this instance with a cutting edge: "Don't feel discouraged if a lot of our well-known men were not as wealthy according to their tax as you thought they ought to be. They are just as rich as you thought. This publication of amounts had nothing to do with their wealth. It was only a test of their honesty . . ."

High taxes offer a theme that is never exhausted. We can go back to the early years of the century, when Finley Peter Dunne had Mr. Dooley comment: "Thank hivvins we don't git as much gov'ment as we pay for." Or we can understand Arthur Godfrey, who, in the idiom of today's humor, remarked: "I'm proud to pay taxes in the United States. Only thing is — I could be just as proud for half the money." One investment counselor advised, "Put all your money in taxes. That's the only thing that's going up." And Errol Flynn confessed, "My main problem is reconciling my gross habits with my net income." Such good-natured whimsy vanishes, however, in the acerbic mockery of H. L. Mencken: "The intelligent man, when he pays taxes, certainly does not believe that he is making a prudent and productive investment of his money; on the contrary, he feels that he is being mulcted of an excessive amount for services that, in the main, are useless to him, and that, in substantial part, are downright inimical to him." [6]

The provisions of the IR Code and the operations of the IRS in carrying them out have been of inestimable value to one small class of American citizens, especially in springtime — the cartoonists. One artist has depicted a convict asking a prison guard, "Filed your income tax yet?" Another showed an office auditor of the IRS asking a taxpayer, "Mind if I show your deductions to the other fellows in the office? We like to share our laughs." Another caption conveys the innocent remark of a secretary carrying an armload of ledgers to her employer, who is being audited by a revenue agent. The caption: "This set of books, Mr. Cartwell, or the set you keep in the broom closet?"

Sometimes the public relations efforts of the IRS have drawn a mordacious response. One Tp wrote to the head office that he had just heard on the radio that we had a voluntary system of self-assessment in this country. Previously he had thought he had no choice, but now that he understood how the matter lay he wasn't going to volunteer anymore. When Mortimer M. Caplin was Commissioner of the Internal Revenue Service, he composed a message to his millions of constituents in which he quoted Justice Oliver Wendell Holmes's celebrated sentiment, noticed in an earlier chapter: "Taxes are what we pay for civilized society." Some of the replies ran as follows:

"You have presumed to tell me how I should feel about taxes," wrote a man from St. Louis. "In turn, I would advise you to apply yourself to your unpleasant occupation and let the taxpayer form his own opinions."

A Berkeley, California, correspondent pointed out that

Holmes had declared his views in 1935, long before the income tax had become confiscatory, and ventured the opinion, therefore, that "if he had lived to see the Government spend our tax money on plans to send men to the moon and other equally worthless projects he would not have liked to paid [sic] taxes either."

A Kansas City skeptic didn't think Justice Holmes paid any income tax at all, whereas the Caplin letter "leads the average person to believe that he did. There are very few people in this part of these United States who will even bother to find out who Mr. Holmes is and fewer who actually have ever heard of him with the exception of a few Harvard graduates."[7]

Theatergoers of a certain age will remember fondly the arrival of the representative of the IRS at the home of Grandpa Martin Vanderhof in Moss Hart and George Kaufman's comedy *You Can't Take It With You*. But first, to set the scene. The living room that the agent entered was a zany Liberty Hall, where, the stage directions say, "meals are eaten, plays are written, snakes collected, ballet steps practiced, xylophones played, printing presses operated." Several official-looking letters had come for Grandpa but no one in this household of ebullient activists had paid any attention to them though it was recalled later with casual interest by Essie, as she practiced her ballet steps, that they had been sent by the United States Government. The kittens got one. Another was found in the refrigerator. And so it went.

And then one evening the doorbell rang. The whole family rushed to open the door because they thought it was a suitor for Alice. Instead, a tall, solemn stranger entered and presented his card, which read, "Wilbur C. Henderson, Internal Revenue Department." The agent said, "Well, Mr. Vanderhof, the government wants to talk to you about a little matter of income tax."

HENDERSON: According to our records, Mr. Vanderhof, you have never paid an income tax.

GRANDPA: That's right.

HENDERSON: Why not?

GRANDPA: I don't believe in it.

In the end, everything worked out happily for Grandpa Vanderhof because it was discovered that the IRS was in pursuit of a milkman named Martin Vanderhof who had died eight years before. Shamelessly, Grandpa said that he was Martin Vanderhof, Junior. The government apologized. Much of the pleasure audiences have found in this madcap play is undoubtedly due to feelings of identification with Grandpa's antitax stance and feelings of satisfaction at his undeserved victory over the Establishment.[8]

A Washington figure, "sort of pudgy and nondescript . . . the kind of man you often meet but never remember meeting," in the words of an admirer, is James H. Boren, himself a former successful bureaucrat, who repented and founded the International Association of Professional Bureaucrats, partly out of frustration with government red tape, partly as a joke. Boren has found that poking fun at the mumblers and fumblers of the federal bureaucracy is a pleasant and profitable way of making a living. He has written two books, and lectures around the country, mumbling in the best bureaucratic style, at $1000 a night. Boren also awards a medal. It is called the Order of the Bird, and was created by the founder himself, under the pseudonym Vago de los Rios.

"You may be interested in knowing," Jim Boren informed a recent inquirer, "that the first Order of the Bird [a potbellied sculpture] of our organization was presented to an IRS official in recognition of a series of memos on long, medium, and short sideburns.

"The IRS is the one bureaucracy that all other bureaucracies view with apprehensive joy and shufflistic respect,"

Boren continues. "The light thrumming of an IRS bureaucrat can cause a taxpayer's heart to beat with a resounding crescendo of deafening swirility and a simple question can cause gastronomical knotification . . ."

"Accompanied as they are with the Boren flair for maximum publicity," an interviewer wrote recently, "sometimes nominees for the awards will do anything not to get them." [9]

Let us turn now to a subject of perennial interest to all income-tax-paying citizens — tax reform. An illuminating explanation of how this delicate matter is handled appeared in *Roll Call*, the weekly newspaper that circulates on Capitol Hill. The article was written by Dick West, the paper's lighthearted commentator on Washington life and politics. West wrote that reform legislation is prepared by the "slurry method." To explain what he meant, West used this comparison: coal can be transported in lump form by the railroads or can be ground up in "a watery mixture of insoluble matter" and pumped through pipelines. When the widely heralded 1975 tax reforms came before the Ways and Means Committee they were first pulverized, then conveyed to the House floor, where they were watered down into legislative slurry, ready for transport to the Senate. A congressman kindly explained the advantages of the slurry method over reform handled in lump form.

"Before legislation is transported to the Senate," the solon explained, "it must be sifted through a screen of lobbyists." Lumps would be too big to pass through the screen. "But once the reforms have been ground up in committee and watered down on the floor, screening is no problem." [10]

Noting that almost everyone thinks his own taxes are too high and therefore favors the idea of tax reform, Senator Long turned poet during a tax debate to explain what people mean when they call for reform. The poem, which the chairman of the Senate Finance Committee read on the floor of the Senate, explains the subject in two lines:

> Don't tax you, don't tax me,
> Tax the fellow behind the tree.[11]

Few law professors are endowed with the gift of prophecy, but a signal exception is Walter J. Blum, distinguished and witty professor of law at the University of Chicago and a nationally recognized tax expert. Professor Blum has attempted to predict how the rapid changes now taking place in our society may affect our federal income tax system in the future. To prepare himself for interpreting contemporary trends and tendencies, Professor Blum first studied the models other authorities had constructed. He did not find their conclusions very inspiring, and itemized them as follows:

- The law will become more complicated.
- Certainty in applying the law to the facts will increase.
- Certainty in application of the law to the facts will decrease.
- The number of tax forms will increase.
- Tax reform is coming.
- Tax reform won't amount to much.
- Tax advisers will not be eliminated.
- Taxpayers will continue to prefer lower rates rather than high taxes.

So the author decided to go it alone. The pressure for openness in government, Blum believes, will be such that future politicians will be eager to have their Form 1040s audited in order to establish "tax purity." He sees a time coming when all internal conferences and meetings of IRS staff members will be taped and broadcast nationally and catalogued in the *Internal Revenue Cumulative Bulletin.* It will be enlarged, naturally, to accommodate the mass of new material. The information will also be available in cassettes. This will mean that "there no longer would be a need for the Commissioner of Internal Revenue or his assistants to appear in person at tax institutes or conferences and give their usual circuit-riding talks. A tremendous economy in manpower might thus be accomplished."

The attraction of being "cleared" by the IRS will probably be so great that it would be possible for the government to make a charge for the audits, with fees scaled according to the adjusted gross income, or perhaps "the size of the deficiency uncovered by the audit." If the plan is extended to all taxpayers, Professor Blum is ready with a catchy name for the program: "Pay as you owe." Aware that people like to know about the financial affairs of others, the writer speaks enthusiastically of the technology already in existence that could link the IRS computers with the telephone network so that anyone could telephone for anyone else's return. He expects Congress to vote the money for this service as "a national toll-free . . . boost for democracy." In line with the same thought — that an increasing number of citizens are interested in other people's business — informers should be encouraged. This could be accomplished by a more generous deal offered by the IRS, say, a fifty-fifty split, the informer's share to be tax-exempt. Annual prizes would be offered, of course, possibly in the form of a rebate. Another characteristic of the period in history that is our own is the emphasis placed on citizen participation in government. Blum suggests the addition of a new section to Form 1040, perhaps to be called the "Suggestion Box," enclosed prominently with a heavy black band and providing a forum where the common man could make his comments on any aspects of the income tax or IRS administration that interest him. The Midway

prophet also sees the day coming, what with the importance
attached to openness in government, when every taxpayer, no
matter how innocent or how selected, whether by machine,
manually, or at random, will be warned, before his audit
begins, "Beware: we are not necessarily on your side." The
Surgeon General issues warnings; why not the Commissioner
of Internal Revenue?

I have saved Professor Blum's best idea for the last. It
springs from the well-known fact that the taxpayer who is
represented by a skillful professional in the wrestling match
with the IRS comes off better than the defender of the private
purse who goes it alone. Hence, Blum reasons, we need "an
anti-Internal Revenue Service" (AIRS), — an independent,
government-financed department, headed by an anticommis-
sioner. The mission? To keep tax payments down, salary and
promotion of the antiagent to be based on how many tax
dollars he succeeded in keeping from the government. This
will not put the existing tax-preparers out of business, Blum
insists. Competition will be good for both groups and in the
best American tradition of the career open to the talent.

Perhaps here is an idea whose time has come. It addresses
a problem that has been identified and discussed seriously by
the Administrative Conference of the United States, an independent federal agency that has conducted a year-long study
of the Internal Revenue Service and reported its findings in a
thousand pages, reviewing all practices that affect individuals. It finds that settlement procedures have been designed
for the professional tax expert rather than the unrepresented
taxpayer, and has called for the establishment of an independent Taxpayer Assistance Center to provide Tps with
low-cost help.

Equally concerned is Thomas F. Field, a former Treasury
and Justice Department official and founder and executive

director of Taxation With Representation and a companion organization of public service lawyers, Tax Analysts and Advocates. Field has proposed the establishment of a taxpayers' protection agency, separate from the IRS, to act as a taxpayer adviser and adversary of the IRS itself, with power to sue the revenue service for improper rulings or regulations and for the handling of legitimate complaints.

Just what Dr. Blum ordered.[12]

16

Putting It All Together

FROM ITS FIRST APPEARANCE, more than a hundred years ago, the federal personal income tax has been a part of the American political reality, an issue to be reckoned with even during those years when there was no income statute on the books. Bitter clashes of philosophy and heated debate have marked its course. A small hard core of tax purists have rallied around the principle of taxation for revenue only, fighting desperately against two powerful antagonists, also arrayed against each other — the pseudoconservatives, who have always wished to place the tax as an umbrella over favored businesses and industries, and equally determined liberals, who saw the tax, with its inexhaustible resources amply demonstrated in our modern wars, as the means of financing the goals they proposed for achieving social justice, if not for the individual, at least for the mass.

The federal income tax is, then, in the colloquial speech of a hundred years and more, the goose of Aesop's fable, often invoked to make a debating point, often in danger of being eviscerated, yet still today alive and well and producing its fantastic golden eggs in a laying record that is without parallel in poultry history. For this survival and bounty we may be thankful that we are a people who by temperament have found the middle of the road the best route to where we want to go.

Somehow this works, despite the thunder on the left and right. Countervailing forces in our national life have so far blocked the desires of those who would seize the whole treasure at once and in the end kill the generous goose.

Commentators on tax law are generally agreed that our income tax system, though requiring unremitting efforts toward improvement, can bear comparison with that of any other nation in the world that administers a mass income tax, and it is collected with no significant cheating except by fringe elements. But — how high can taxes go before they become self-defeating? Opinions abound and differ, for there is neither a pragmatic nor a precise scientific answer. Almost every major element in the community would like to see government activities curtailed. But not the same ones. For every program of spending there is a constituency. So the downward pressure is dissipated because there are conflicts concerned with values. The outlook is for continuing high income taxes as an accompanying aspect of urbanization, of population growth, of the needs of the "general welfare of the United States," in the language of the Constitution, and of expanding domestic and world responsibilities, which appear destined to grow relatively and absolutely. There is little hard evidence, however, to support the view that income taxation has endangered the wealth-formation process, nor has it measurably curtailed the buying power that our capitalistic society generates.

Far more serious than the citizen's income tax bill in reducing his discretionary ability to command goods and services is the eroding effect of inflation, which often boosts the taxpayer into a higher tax bracket, and the government's policy of creating a soft currency. This has reduced the value of the 1939 dollar to twenty-five cents currently, with no end in sight. There has always been a morbid fear, in certain circles in the United States, of expropriation or a capital levy. We are getting a taste of it now through the back door, so to speak, as cheap dollars push taxpayers up a ladder whose rungs are fixed. The worth of personal exemptions and legitimate deductions shrinks. At the same time the government's real income not only keeps up but actually gains through inflation, which is a hidden tax, imposed, moreover, without legislative action.

The voters, like their counterparts in government, are greedy. They want Medicare, increased Social Security benefits, federal housing assistance, more personal deductions, and a host of other good things — but no increase in taxation. The Federal Reserve Board provides the funds by expanding the money supply. The true cost is concealed, but it is a tax just the same. As Professor Milton Friedman has described our dilemma in a celebrated axiom, "There is no free lunch." However, Professor Joan Robinson, of Cambridge University, England, and a true-believing Keynesian, says of the famous University of Chicago monetarist, "His ideas are absolutely dotty," which shows that our economic augurs do not all read the entrails of the same breed of chicken.[1]

The best protection of wealth is vigorous business activity. Still, the conjecture that income taxes cause the bright and able to withdraw their efforts from the marketplace, and so diminish the supply of brains and risk capital, remains a firmly held though never clearly demonstrated dogma of conservative economic thought.[2] The argument that "men of great enterprise" would relax their efforts because of progressive income taxation appeared as long ago as the House debate on the bill to amend the Revenue Act of 1864. Andrew Mellon in the 1920s wrote a book devoted to the thesis and as Secretary of the Treasury was able to carry thought into action. The spokesman for the Machinery and Allied Products Institute warned the Ways and Means Committee in 1947 that high taxation threatens the very existence of the private enterprise system, and pleaded with the committee not to tamper with the incentives that had made America great. "We must not kill the goose," George Terborgh, the institute's research director, told the committee, invoking once more Aesop's perdurable allegory.

"The question of incentive is essential . . ." Crawford H. Greenewalt, then president of E. I. du Pont de Nemours & Company, said in 1955, when he appeared before the Subcommittee on Tax Policy of the Joint Committee on the Federal Tax Policy for Economic Growth and Stability. "I am afraid that we have not yet reached that state of grace in which people will surely do their best without external motivation." And he enlarged on the thought. The strongest inducement is financial reward, the only reward, incidentally, that can be cut down on a basis of fixed percentages. We do not withhold, for example, 91 percent of an Oscar bestowed on an actress for the best motion picture performance of the year. (The marginal tax bracket in 1955 was 91 percent). The concert violinist, Greenewalt continued, does not have to share his applause with the district director of internal revenue but "we do in fact make the recipient of money rewards, and him alone, give up significant percentages in taxes." The result: men near their top capacity will decide to rest on their oars and young men will opt for an unadventurous life at a modest level of accomplishment.[3]

Studies conducted by the Harvard Graduate School of Business Administration have concluded, on the contrary, that taxes are only one of a complex of influences that shape the behavior of individuals who occupy important positions in business organizations. Diminished effort on the part of the managerial class has been exaggerated, it appears, on the supposition that people do not like to work. In fact, many men work harder under high taxation in order to recapture their absolute incomes and maintain their place in their peer group. The emphasis on taxes as deterrents from economic effort also ignores such intangibles as satisfaction in accomplishment and recognition by society generally. As to whether taxes discourage the rich from providing funds for investment in the industrial plant, a subject of much anxious debate, the rate schedules have very little effect upon their investment programs, according to a study made by University of Michigan economists, which says, in effect, "If you want to become wealthy, work hard and don't worry about taxes."[4]

The top executive enjoys perquisites rich in psychic value — handsome office décor, use of a company automobile and reserved parking space, free medical examinations, first-class air travel, often in a company plane, and the use of boats, chauffeurs, subsidized homes, company-paid resort facilities, and luxurious homes-away-from-home. The American Management Association checked out the special privileges that go with high-level positions in the corporate world and enumerated thirty-four, some of which represented substantial economic benefits and all of which signaled status.

So far reference has been made to the professional managers of large enterprises who carry heavy responsibilities to employees, stockholders, and the public. For American workers on a less elevated level there are just as good reasons for believing that high taxation spurs them on to greater effort as for supposing the opposite. Most people in the labor force have important fixed monetary obligations — mortgage payments, monthly rent, life insurance premiums, contributions to pension funds, to prepaid medical plans, the education of children, maintenance of elderly relatives, installment payments on automobiles and on major household appliances. Such expenses are not easily scaled down. Some workers may no doubt shrug and ask, "What's the use?" but others will try to make the squirrel cage spin faster by moonlighting or becoming partners in two-job families. Age, size of family, personal temperament all enter into the equation. But careful empirical studies offer no convincing evidence that those who are interested in their work are much deterred by even substantial changes in tax rates.

Despite the gloomy gentlemen who inhabit the lounges and bars of such luxurious enclaves as the Duquesne Club (Pittsburgh) or the Metropolitan Clubs (Washington, New York), where they mourn in elegant surroundings the decline and imminent fall of capitalism as a consequence of our modern tax environment, when fact is separated from folklore one finds that taxation has not materially changed the distribution of wealth in the United States over a long period of time nor has it prevented the creation of new wealth. In 1973 *Fortune* magazine described the careers of thirty-nine individuals who had started from scratch and in five years' time amassed more than $50 million, working in such disparate technological fields as birth-control pills, sixty-second cameras, copying machines, computers; and with equal élan and success in more prosaic enterprises, turning out tire retreads, faucets, industrial cleansers, pet foods, ice cream, low-priced drugs, and Florida orange juice.[5]

Only modest results can be claimed for the efforts to reduce the incomes of the very wealthy by taxation. Liberals have not been able to make the income tax significantly more progressive, and conservatives have not been able to make it less so. The caution that Congress has consistently shown in its votes suggests that the national legislature is not out of line with popular feelings and beliefs in resisting any sweeping rearrangement of our economic resources. "That some should be rich," Abraham Lincoln wrote to an association of working men, "shows that others may become rich . . ." And the Supreme Court has said that so long as private property exists some persons will have more than others: "It is from the nature of things," the Court said, "impossible to uphold freedom of contract and the right of private property without at the same time recognizing as legitimate those inequalities of fortune that are the necessary result of the exercise of those rights."

Let a poet who lived close to the American psyche have the last word on this subject:

> "So you want to divide all the money there is
> and give every man his share?"
> "That's it. Put it all in one big pile and split
> it even for everybody."
> "And the land, the gold, silver, oil, copper, you want
> that divided up?"
> "Sure — an even whack for all of us ."
> "Do you mean that to go for horses and cows?"
> "Sure — why not?"
> "And how about pigs?"
> "Oh to hell with you — you know I got a couple of
> pigs."

There is perhaps a slight movement toward redistribution of income in the United States through the income tax system and transfer payments, but it proceeds with glacial speed and it is limited by two realities. First, the growth of our mixed economy has raised the minimum standards of food, clothing, housing, and health, and this keeps down the pressure. Then, those who possess wealth and power, sometimes called collectively the "third house of Congress," are as a class able to buy into the political process in accordance with the biblical injunction, "The prudent man looketh well to his going." [6]

Also to be considered is the expenditure side of the government's books of accounts with its citizens. In the early years of our republic Sydney Smith, English divine and wit, Whiggish writer on secular as well as religious questions, addressed his American cousins in a lively essay alerting them as to what to expect from their government in the area of taxation, pouring his exuberant invective upon the tendencies of all governments to gobble up the material substance of their subjects. "The habit of dealing with large sums will make the government avaricious . . ." Smith warned "and the system itself will infallibly generate . . . political tools and retainers . . . while the prodigious patronage which the collecting of this splendid revenue will throw into the hands of government, will invest it with so vast an influence, and hold out such means and temptations to corruption, as all the virtue and public spirit, even of republicans, will be unable to resist." The eloquence and deep repugnance that Smith brought to the subject of tax collectors may have been due in part to the fact that one of his grandfathers was French.

At about the same time that Smith was writing, a French economist, Jean Baptiste Say, came forward with a seminal idea, that supply creates its own demand, known in the history of public finance as Say's Law, which our contemporary, C. Northcote Parkinson, has updated and rechristened Parkinson's Second Law: "Expenditure rises to meet income." This law throws light on the familiar condition under which, Parkinson says, "The government rarely pauses even to consider what its income is."

These strictures can justly be applied to past U.S. Government policies that have made the expansion of government personnel and bureaus a happy reflex bearing no relation to the revenue that was being collected. "One of the common jokes around Washington," the late Paul H. Douglas wrote when he was Democratic senator from Illinois, "is that an agency will request more than it actually needs, depending on the House to cut the request by 50%, the Senate to restore the amount to 100%, and the conference committee to compromise at 75%, which is the figure wanted by the agency in the first place." [7]

Some Congress-watchers active in the tax field feel that, with the pandemic disease of legislators being an uncontrollable compulsion to spend the public's money, the quest for order and fairness is futile since the emphasis always seems to be on maintaining decent appearances rather than facing up to hard realities. Orators appearing on the floors of the chambers speak highly of equal sacrifice while bending to spending pressures and clinging to the hope that an expanding economy will miraculously produce a "fiscal dividend" to foot the bill. According to Montesquieu, who said he was quoting an old Spanish proverb, when the natives of Louisiana wished to have fruit, they cut the tree down to get it. The proverb is worthy of congressional attention.

But something new and encouraging has happened to modify Congress's old bad habit of passing appropriation bills without reliable information as to where the money was to come from. A law of July 1974 created a new budget process by establishing the nonpartisan Congressional Budget Office to give the House and Senate Budget Committees analytical and background information to match the fiscal expertise the President has at his command in the Office of Management and Budget. The procedure is new in that it sets up for the first time an alternative budget to the one submitted by the President. It is intended to provide an overview of spending that will tie together the taxing decisions and appropriation authority and keep appropriations in line with revenues. So far the victories of the committees have been limited. But they give hope of bigger things to come under the chairmanship in the Senate of Senator Edmund S. Muskie (D.-Maine) and Representative Brock Adams (D.-Washington) in the House, with a respected economist, Dr. Alice M. Rivlin, as director, to provide independent studies that are technically sound. "Many believe," wrote Eileen Shanahan, a *New York Times* Washington correspondent who specializes in economic affairs, "that sounder budget decisions will be the result." The hour is late. The cumulative deficit for the first eight months of FY 1976 rose to $59.17 billion, as compared with $23.3 for the same months of FY 1975. The White House estimate provided by the OMB makes the budget gap for the full year, as calculated in February 1976, $76.9 billion.[8] A warning sounded by geese saved the Capitol at Rome from the barbarians in 390 B.C. It remains to be seen whether Washington's Capitol Hill will be responsive to the hissings and honkings of the A.D. 1970s.

Tax topics that call for urgent attention and that may be brought under the heading of unfinished business include what to do about Social Security, clarification of the role of the IRS, reassessing the complexity of complying with the law, and finally the question of genuine tax reform. Social Security, or the Old-Age, Survivors, and Disability Insurance System, is possibly the government program that has the broadest popular support. It can list among its plusses the breadth of its coverage, the sense of dignity it has given retired workers who believe they provided for their own old age, the human misery it has relieved, and the fact that it is indexed (since 1972) to keep the pay-out in line with the cost of living. Difficulties include the rising age of the total population and the falling birthrate, which signals a relatively smaller work force, and the fact that Social Security coverage is a compulsory purchase from the government though not insurance in the sense of an individually purchased insurance policy. The system is in a deficit position, with future benefits dependent on future revenues. If the enormous liability that has accumulated, now amounting to trillions of dollars, has to be propped up with withdrawals from general funds, that will be done. Scare stories about the imminent collapse of Social Security are just that and no more. But many recipients would be less than happy to know that their benefits came from general funds, since that would signify that the system was a welfare program, the benefits received no longer a right but the largess of the government.

Economists criticize Social Security for being regressive in that the highest and lowest contributors pay at the same rate. Thus the low-income workers put in a larger proportion of their incomes than do those who earn a larger paycheck and who possibly have other untaxed income from investments. And there is a further effect. The Social Security tax tends to defeat the progressive feature of the income, estate, and gift taxes, since many workers now pay more in Social Security taxes than in income taxes. In a development now familiar to Americans, the original Social Security law was thirty-two pages long. Today it contains 500 pages. The outlook is for each generation to pay for the retirement of its predecessors, with the burden growing because of the demographic changes just mentioned. In 1978 the tax will rise to 6 percent, unless it goes up sooner, and it is generally considered that the employee also pays indirectly the employer's share in lowered wages or higher consumer prices. There is

no way to re-establish Social Security on a sound basis other
than to raise taxes or reduce the benefits. Neither is politically appealing. These questions call for painful decisions
and complicated mathematical computations, most likely to
be faced in a nonelection year.[9]

Because of the extraordinary power the IRS exercises over
the lives and fortunes of the American people, its difficulties
make headline news. Only the passage of time and a good
report card can eliminate the wounds inflicted on the service
by the rumors and scandals of the first half of this decade.
Fortunately, the IRS is taking the initiative in cleaning its
own nest, assisted by close congressional oversight. Other
difficulties of the service, in no sense of its own making, arise
from the temptation Congress and the executive department
seem unable to resist, that of using its forces to solve all sorts
of national problems. The IRS has been asked to police compliance with wage and price controls, as it did in 1971–1972,
to detach its agents for special attacks on organized crime
and serve as guards against airplane highjackings. IRS personnel have been taken off tax-collection activities to strengthen
United Nations security arrangements, to defend Washington against May Day demonstrators, and to perform other
miscellaneous chores. Because the service is the government's biggest law enforcement agency, equipped with special powers to investigate, search, and seize, a case can be
made for, or against, using these capabilities in non-tax-
related work. The choices are complex, involving a balancing
of judgments. The current outlook is for strenuous efforts to
make the IRS apolitical and more tightly controlled than in
the immediate past though not foreclosing entirely the possibility of the agency's lending its resources to the Justice Department or other government bureaus, though under strictly
defined conditions.[10]

Reform of the income tax continues to be a rich field for utopian thought. Sentiment for sweeping changes in tax philosophy may be arranged under these six propositions:

- The rich don't pay their fair share.
- Big corporations don't pay their fair share.
- Congress favors business interests rather than individual taxpayers' interests.
- Loopholes make a mockery of the statutory rates and should be closed.
- The tax calls for simplification because it is too complicated for the ordinary taxpayer to understand and is therefore unsuited for a democracy.
- Taxes are too high.

An approach that has impressive support outside political circles is to tax all gains and receipts. The Constitution permits this. "Income is income," the late Vivien Kellems told the House Ways and Means Committee, and Professor Walter J. Blum has endorsed the "strong presumption" that every dollar of income should be treated the same as every other dollar. Whether progression should rise gently, as it does now, or steeply, or whether the tax should be levied at a flat rate, are separate questions. Any of these plans would go far to meet the propositions listed above. There would be spectacular consequences from spreading the burden over a larger proportion of the population and they would make possible tax reduction of a magnitude never seen since the income tax amendment became law. A study by Pechman and Okner has found that the rates could be reduced by 43 percent across the board and still produce the same amount of revenue for the Treasury. Professor Milton Friedman, who calls the current graduated scale "fraudulent," has advanced a plan for taxing all dollars at a flat rate, which, he calculated a few years ago, would produce the same revenue if the tax was set for all at 23.5 percent. In his latest writings he has gotten the figure down even farther, to an appealing 16 percent.

Another economist, Roger A. Freeman, estimates that if all personal income was taxed, the present rates could be halved, ranging from 7 percent to 35 percent. Or a flat tax of 10 percent would produce the same result, which would get us back to the Hebrew tithe and Secretary Mellon's impossible dream. Secretary of the Treasury William Simon advocated what has come to be called the "clean slate" approach. Simon suggested keeping the historic sliding scale but dropping all preferences, deductions, credits, and exclusions from income. This would permit rates of 10 to 12 percent at the low end and 35 to 40 percent at the high end, or a reduction for all taxpayers of about 30 percent. "I am increasingly attracted to the idea," the Secretary said, "because of its simple elegance and its basic equity toward all taxpayers," and he remarked of our current tax code, "If we didn't have it already, nobody would ever invent it." [11]

It is noteworthy that authorities on taxation of widely differing economic and social outlook, the philosophic purists, the monetarists and pragmatists, all brigaded together, some of whom might not feel comfortable sitting with certain others on the same dais, are in agreement on the need for reform. To a surprising degree, considering their natural contentiousness, they even hold similar views on how the reform could be accomplished. What then are the objections to such a rational approach? The National Association of Manufacturers denies that it is rational and labels it an example of emotional argument based on "fuzzy thinking." The catatonic response of the NAM reflects the fear that thoroughgoing reform means a drastic refashioning of society.

Surprisingly, Thomas F. Field, the public service lawyer, who does not often see eye to eye with the manufacturers' association, agrees that the clean slate approach to tax law revision would introduce too risky a revolution into American life. Nor is there any apparent groundswell of support for a completely fresh start from the policeman who moonlights driving a taxicab, the married schoolteacher, the blue collar worker, the retired druggist on Social Security. They too, no less than the privileged classes they sometimes complain about, can be expected to cling to their perquisites, such as the biggest loophole of all, the personal exemption, which is not a part of statutory law but simply an act of congressional grace.

Why so? Because among the public at large there is a widespread suspicion that if present deductions and exemptions were traded off for permanently lower rates, Congress would yield to the temptation to edge up the percentages again or grant subsidies to cover the preferences that had been repealed, ultimately leaving the taxpayer in worse straits than before — rates restored to old levels, "perks" vanished. Henry W. Block encourages this public skepticism. President of H & R Block, Inc., the giant of the tax-preparing industry, whose fifty-seven thousand employees handle more than 10 percent of the individual tax returns filed, Block warns against what he calls "the seductive rhetoric of one tax structure for all."

Actually the question is moot. What Mathias "Paddy" Bauler, the last of the Chicago saloon aldermen, said of his native city, "Chicago ain't ready for reform," can be justly applied to Congress: Congress ain't ready for reform. Since taxation is a political act, our lawgivers are not supporting proposals that could consolidate the opposition of George Meany, Leonard Woodcock, the Mortgage Bankers of America, the Rockefeller bank, the American Petroleum Institute, the working wives, all of Florida and California, and the united baby sitters of America.

For here we are dealing not merely with arithmetic but with social psychology, and who can measure through mathematics the pains and pleasures of life? The quest for tax justice resembles the search for the Holy Grail. The goal is never reached but the effort has a civilizing effect on those who make it. Taxation will remain one of the inner tensions inseparable from the democratic process, resulting always in a delicate compromise between benefit and sacrifice. With all of the IR Code's imperfections, despite the frailties of human nature and the crudities of the political process, most of the adjusted gross income of American taxpayers is reported, and expenses for the collection of "this splendid revenue" are moderate, about 0.5 percent of the amounts collected. So the dogs bark, the caravan passes. The tax *can* be abused through legal chicanery, and pressure groups do bend it to their own benefit; yet the relation of the sliding-scale income tax to American ideas of fairness is generally sensed.[12]

"The United States has a system of taxation by confession," Justice Robert H. Jackson said in one of his decisions. "That a people so numerous, scattered and individualistic annually assesses itself with a tax liability, often in highly burdensome amounts, is a reassuring sign of the stability and vitality of our system of self-government." What surprised Justice Jackson was that the instances of recalcitrance, self-serving mistakes, and outright fraud were so few.

Perhaps the hypothetical monkey who, it is said, could ultimately write *Hamlet* if left alone in a room with a typewriter for a million years could also under the same circumstances write an income tax law that would be universally acclaimed as being not too high, not too low, and eminently fair to all. It is unlikely that the Ways and Means Committee or the Senate Finance Committee will ever do it, despite their occasional exhibition of simian characteristics. We can never be absolutely certain that we are not paying too much and someone else too little, or that the money is not being squandered. That is what makes the cheese so binding. That is why, as Edmund Burke reminded the British Parliament in his famous speech on American taxation, "To tax and to please, no more than to love and be wise, is not given to men." [13]

NOTES

Notes

THE ABBREVIATIONS below appear in the notes that follow. When several references are grouped in one note they appear in sequence as they relate to the subject; if they document the same point they are alphabetized. The first citation in each chapter gives the facts of publication. Subsequent appearances are in short-title form.

ABBREVIATIONS

AH	*American Heritage*
AHR	*American Historical Review*
B.T.A.	Board of Tax Appeals
Cong. Globe	*Congressional Globe*
Cong. Rec.	*Congressional Record*
DAB	*Dictionary of American Biography*
CB	*Internal Revenue Cumulative Bulletin*
J. of L. and Ec.	*Journal of Law and Economics*
LC	Library of Congress
MVHR	*Mississippi Valley Historical Review*
NYT	The *New York Times*
TC	United States Tax Court
TCM	Tax Court Memorandum
Tp	Taxpayer
US Stat.	*United States Statutes at Large*
WSJ	The *Wall Street Journal*
WP	The Washington *Post*

Part One

1. There Ariseth a Little Cloud *(pp. 3–12)*

1 Richard Goode, *The Individual Income Tax* (Washington, D.C.: Brookings Institution, 1964), pp. 3–4; *NYT*, February 25, 1956.

2 Hugh C. Bickford, *Successful Tax Practice* (New York: Prentice-Hall, 1950), p. 1; *The United States Budget in Brief: Fiscal Year 1975* (Washington, D.C., n.d.), chart on second cover.

3 *NYT*, April 2, 1973. Tax returns for 1974, which have just been analyzed, show that 244 persons with incomes above $200,000 paid no federal income taxes that year although the minimum tax established in 1969 was designed to prevent such escape. See *NYT*, May 6, 1976.

4 In 1974 the Treasury received donations, totaling $418,000, for a special fund earmarked to pay off the national debt. Separate and different in character is the "conscience fund," maintained by guilt-stricken taxpayers. This fund was enriched by a check for $139,000 in January 1975. See *WSJ*, February 21, 1975.

5 Roy Blough, *The Federal Taxing Process* (New York: Prentice-Hall, 1952), p. 4; *Taxes* (October 1974), quoted in *WSJ*, October 23, 1974; *Compania general de Tabacos de Filipinas* v. *Collector of Internal Revenue*, 275 U.S. 100 (1927); *Plummer* v. *Coler*, 178 U.S. 115 (1900) at 138.

6 *NYT Magazine*, January 6, (1974): 8; Sheldon S. Cohen, "Morality and the American Tax System," 34 *George Washington Law Review* (June 1966); 844.

7 *Commissioner of Internal Revenue* v. *Newman*, 159 F. 2d 850 at 851 (2d Cir. 1947); *Estate of Reimer*, 12 TC 913 (1949). See also *United States* v. *La Franca*, 282 U.S. 572 (1931); *Tyler* v. *United States*, 281 U.S. 503 (1929); *Nicol* v. *Ames*, 173 U.S. 509 (1898); *Bull* v. *United States*, 295 U.S. 247 (1934) at 259.

8 The IRS Service Centers received nearly 84 million individual tax returns in FY 1975: *Annual Report 1975 of Commissioner of Internal Revenue*, p. 13.

9 *Pollock* v. *Farmers' Loan & Trust Company*, 157 U.S. 506 (1894).

10 *Blatt* v. *Commissioner*, 6 TCM 94 (1947); *NYT*, April 13, 1974; U.S. Treasury Department, *Internal Revenue Cumulative Bulletin* 1939 (2), p. 153; U.S. Treasury Department, Internal Revenue Service, *Handbook for Internal Revenue Agents*, Audit Division, *IRM* 4231, Sec. 731. The word "home" is defined in federal taxland as meaning the post of duty, the place where the job is. See CB 1939 (2), pp. 152–53; and *Barnhill* v. *Commissioner*, 148 F. 2d 913

at 916 (4th Cir. 1945). State troopers in West Virginia do not pay taxes on their meal allowances because a federal court has ruled that they are always on their employer's premises, which constitute the whole state of West Virginia. See *WSJ*, January 28, 1976.

11 IR Code, Sec. 183(d).

12 *NYT*, January 18, 1953; IR Code, Sec. 1251; ibid., Sec. 215; *NYT*, November 27, 1949; IR Code, Sec. 214; *NYT*, March 15, 1950; *WSJ*, June 4, 1975; *NYT*, March 8, 1952.

13 *WSJ*, October 17, 1973.

14 Revenue Ruling 62–210, CB 1962 (2), p. 88; *WSJ*, August 20, 1975; John J. Thoene, 33 TC 62 (1959); *WSJ*, November 20, 1974; *NYT*, September 22, 1961; *Federal Tax Revision: A Summary of the 1969 Act* (New York: Tax Foundation, 1970), p. 20.

15 *NYT*, January 5, 1975; *WP*, January 6, 1974; *NYT*, March 27, 1975; *WSJ*, March 5, 1975; *NYT*, April 18, 1974.

16 Irving Kristol, *On the Democratic Idea in America* (New York: Harper & Row, 1972), pp. ix, 24.

17 *NYT*, March 25, 1952; ibid., May 26, 1961; *Rutkin* v. *United States*, 343 U.S. 130 (1952); George C. Bovington, "Deducting the Expenses of an Illegal Business," 19 *Montana Law Review* (Spring 1958): 140–48; *Commissioner* v. *Tellier*, 383 U.S. 687 (1966).

18 *WSJ*, February 27, 1974; ibid., January 1, 1974; *NYT*, April 9, 1973.

19 *NYT*, June 6, 1914; ibid., March 17, 1921; ibid., August 12, 1955; ibid., April 27, 1921; ibid., May 21, 1946.

20 Professor Boris I. Bittker, Sterling Professor of Law at Yale University, has felicitously described alimony payments as "the belated cost of past pleasures," in "Income Tax Deductions, Credits, and Subsidies for Personal Expenditures," 16 *J. of L. and Ec.* (1973): 211.

21 *NYT*, February 4, 1974; ibid., May 11, 1975.

22 Paul A. Samuelson, *Economics*, 8th ed. (New York: McGraw-Hill, 1970), p. 160; Joseph A. Pechman, *Federal Tax Policy* (New York: W.W. Norton, 1971), pp. 1, 291; *United States Budget in Brief . . . 1975*, chart on second cover.

23 Lester C. Thurow, *The Impact of Taxes on the American Economy* (New York: Praeger, 1971), p. 164; Boris I. Bittker, "Effective Tax Rates: Fact or Fancy?" 122 *University of Pennsylvania Law Review* (1974): 795.

24 *Cyclopaedia of Political Science, Political Economy, and of the Political History of the United States*, "Taxation, Principles of."

2. An Idea With a Long History *(pp. 13–23)*

1 *Encyclopedia of the Social Sciences,* "Income Tax."
2 Ibid., "Taxation"; Edwin R. A. Seligman, *Essays in Taxation,* 10th ed. (New York: Macmillan, 1925), pp. 1–4, 7; Carl C. Plehn, *Introduction to Public Finance* (New York: Macmillan, 1920), pp. 4, 99, 223–24; Randolph E. Paul, *Taxation in the United States* (Boston: Little, Brown, 1954), p. 715; Samuel Kramer, *History Begins at Sumer* (Garden City, N.Y.: Doubleday, Anchor Books, 1959), pp. 45–49.
3 Otto von Kretschmer, trans. Sara C. Forden, "War Because of Taxes — Not Because of Health," *Hannoversche Allegemeine Zeitung,* December 2, 1972; "Unique German Tax Museum," Washington *News,* April 10, 1973; Sherman Leroy Wallace, *Taxation in Egypt from Augustus to Diocletian* (Princeton: Princeton University Press, 1938; reprinted, New York: Greenwood Press, 1969), pp. 191–93, 202–206, 222.
4 A. H. M. Jones, *The Later Roman Empire 284–602: A Social, Economic and Administrative Survey,* 3 vols. (Oxford: Basil Blackwell, 1964), 1:20, 449–67; *Cyclopaedia of Political Science, Political Economy, and of the Political History of the United States,* "Taxation, Principles of."
5 Edwin R. A. Seligman, *The Income Tax: A Study of the History, Theory, and Practice of Income Taxation at Home and Abroad,* 2nd ed. (New York: Macmillan, 1914), pp. 41–43, 50–53; Plehn, *Introduction to Public Finance,* pp. 54–55, 99; Seligman, *Essays,* pp. 7, 333, 694; Alfred G. Buehler, "Ability to Pay," 1 *Tax Law Review* (1946): 245–46; Paul, *Taxation in the United States,* p. 716.
6 Harry Kalven, Jr., and Walter J. Blum, *The Uneasy Case for Progressive Taxation* (Chicago: Law School of the University of Chicago, Reprint and Pamphlet Series, no. 11, n.d.), p. 428; Stanley S. Surrey and William C. Warren, *Federal Income Taxation, Cases and Materials* (Brooklyn: Foundation Press, 1953), p. 3, footnote.
7 Paul, *Taxation in the United States,* p. 718.
8 Davis Rich Dewey, *Financial History of the United States* (New York: Augustus M. Kelley, 1968), pp. 9–12; Paul, *Taxation in the United States,* pp. 3–4; Margaret C. Myers, *A Financial History of the United States* (New York: Columbia University Press, 1970), pp. 15–16.
9 Dewey, *Financial History,* p. 12; Seligman, *Income Tax,* pp. 367–84.
10 Douglas Edward Leach, *Arms for Empire: A Military History of the British Colonies in North America, 1607–1763* (New York: Mac-

millan, 1973), pp. 271–72. A good account of the transition, between 1773 and 1776, from mutually suspicious, separatist provinces to a union of states is Allan Nevins, *The American States During and After the Revolution, 1775–1789* (New York: Macmillan, 1924).

11 Myers, *Financial History*, pp. 31, 51; Nevins, *American States*, pp. 470–72; Roy Blough, *The Federal Taxing Process* (New York: Prentice-Hall, 1952), p. 473; John Locke, *Two Treatises of Government*, Peter Laslett, ed. (New York: New American Library, Mentor Books, 1963), p. 408.

12 Harry Ammon, *James Monroe: The Quest for National Identity* (New York: McGraw-Hill, 1971), p. 68; Charles A. Beard, *An Economic Interpretation of the Constitution of the United States* (New York: Free Press, 1965), pp. 52–63, 170; Daniel J. Boorstin, *The Americans: The National Experience* (New York: Random House, 1966), pp. 405–406, 413; Richard Hofstadter, ed., *Great Issues in American History: From the Revolution to the Civil War, 1765–1865* (New York: Random House, Vintage Books, 1958), pp. 75, 83; *Knowlton* v. *Moore,* 178 U.S. 41 (1899) at 95. Professor Jackson Turner Main has made a favorable reappraisal of the efforts of the states to meet their obligations under difficult circumstances in his recent study, *The Sovereign States* (New York: Franklin Watts, 1973), p. 243; and see his note on Chapter 7.

13 *McCulloch* v. *Maryland,* 4 Wheaton, 316 (1819).

14 Seligman, *Income Tax,* p. 23; Paul, *Taxation in the United States,* p. 5.

15 Hofstadter, *Great Issues,* pp. 81–82; Samuel Eliot Morison and Henry Steele Commager, *The Growth of the American Republic,* 2 vols. (New York: Oxford University Press), 1:330–34; *Marbury* v. *Madison,* 1 Cranch, 137 (1803).

16 Gerald Carson, *The Social History of Bourbon: An Unhurried Account of Our Star-Spangled American Drink* (New York: Dodd, Mead, 1963), pp. 11–23; John C. Chommie, *The Internal Revenue Service* (New York: Praeger, 1970), pp. 4–5, 7; Frederic C. Howe, *Taxation and Taxes in the United States Under the Internal Revenue System, 1791–1895* (New York: Thomas Y. Crowell, 1896), pp. 21–22, 27; *Knowlton* v. *Moore,* 178 US 41 (1899) at 94. The resistant attitude to taxes on consumption is described in *Report of the Commissioner of Internal Revenue for the Year Ended June 30, 1875* (Washington, D.C., 1875), pp. iv–v.

17 1 *US Stat.,* 598, 600–601.

18 Myers, *Financial History,* p. 77; Howe, *Taxation and Taxes,* pp. 39–43, 45; *American State Papers, Documents, Legislative and*

Executive, 13th Cong., 3rd sess., January 17, 1815, 38 vols. (Washington, D.C., 1832), 6:885–87; Seligman, *Income Tax*, p. 433.

19 Raymond Walters, Jr., *Alexander James Dallas: Lawyer — Politician — Financier, 1759–1817* (Philadelphia: University of Pennsylvania Press, 1943), pp. 170, 179, 187, 197, 200.

20 *Annual Report of the Commissioner of Internal Revenue for the Year Ended June 30, 1918* (Washington, D.C., 1919), p. 3; Roy G. Blakey and Gladys C. Blakey, *The Federal Income Tax* (New York: Longmans, Green, 1940), pp. 3–4; Surrey and Warren, *Federal Income Taxation*, p. 3.

3. The First Federal Income Tax *(pp. 24–36)*

1 U.S. Senate, *History of the Committee on Finance* (Washington, D.C.: U.S. Government Printing Office, 1973), p. 37; Frederic C. Howe, *Taxation and Taxes in the United States Under the Internal Revenue System, 1791–1895* (New York: Thomas Y. Crowell, 1896), pp. 53–55; Robert P. Sharkey, *Money, Class, and Party: An Economic Study of Civil War and Reconstruction* (Baltimore: Johns Hopkins University Press, 1959), pp. 16, 19–20, 27, 31, 49–50; *Cyclopedia of Political Science, Political Economy, and of the Political History of the United States*, "United States Notes"; Robert H. Jones, *Disrupted Decades: The Civil War and Reconstruction Years* (New York: Scribner's, 1973), pp. 202–203.

2 Davis Rich Dewey, *Financial History of the United States* (New York: Augustus M. Kelley, 1968), pp. 263–65, 300; Samuel Eliot Morison and Henry S. Commager, *Growth of the American Republic*, 2 vols. (New York: Oxford University Press, 1937), 1:458, 531, 535.

3 Dewey, *Financial History*, pp. 266–67; Louis M. Hacker, *The World of Andrew Carnegie: 1865–1901* (Philadelphia: J.B. Lippincott, 1968), p. 29; *Cong. Globe*, 37th Cong., 2d sess. (March 12, 1862): 1196.

4 Fred Albert Shannon, *Economic History of the People of the United States* (New York: Macmillan, 1934), p. 170; John D. Buenker, "The Western States and the Federal Income Tax Amendment," 4 *Rocky Mountain Review* (November, 1967): 35; Dewey, *Financial History*, pp. 277, 305; Joseph A. Hill, "The Civil War Income Tax," 8 *Quarterly Journal of Economics* (July 1894): 416, 418, 420, 423. The text of the Revenue Act of August 5, 1861 may be found in 12 *US Stat.* 292 cap. 45.

5 Dewey, *Financial History*, p. 301; Myers, *Financial History*, p.

158; Stanley S. Surrey and William C. Warren, *Federal Income Taxation, Cases and Materials* (Brooklyn: Foundation Press, 1953), pp. 3–4; *Report of the Commissioner of Internal Revenue for the Year Ended June 30, 1875* (Washington, D.C., 1875), pp. iv, vi.; J.G. Randall and Richard N. Current, *Lincoln the President: Last Full Measure*, 4 vols. (New York: Dodd, Mead, 1955), 4:178–79.

6 Surrey and Warren, *Federal Income Taxation*, pp. 3–4; John C. Chommie, *The Internal Revenue Service* (New York: Praeger, 1970), p. 10; Sidney Ratner, *Taxation and Democracy in America* (New York: John Wiley, Science Editions, 1967), pp. 74–75; Hill, "The Civil War Income Tax," pp. 421, 423; Washington *Evening Star*, July 3, 1862.

7 Edwin R. A. Seligman, *The Income Tax: A Study of the History, Theory, and Practice of Income Taxation at Home and Abroad*. 2nd ed. (New York: Macmillan, 1914), pp. 434–38; Internal Revenue Service, *Our Federal Tax System* (Washington, D.C., n.d.), no pagination; Lillian Doris, ed., *The American Way in Taxation: Internal Revenue, 1862–1963* (Englewood Cliffs, N.J.: Prentice-Hall, 1963), p. 33; Chommie, *Internal Revenue Service*, p. 10.

8 George S. Boutwell, *A Manual of the Direct and Excise Tax System of the United States; including the Forms and Regulations Established by the Commissioner of Internal Revenue; the Decisions and Rulings of the Commissioner; together with Extracts from the Correspondence of the Office* (Washington: 1863), pp. v, vii, 306, 313, 319; *Report of the Commissioner of Internal Revenue on the Operations of the Internal Revenue System for the Year Ending June 30, 1863* (Washington, D.C., 1864), p. 3.

9 *Internal Revenue Recorder and Customs Journal*, vol. 1, p. 19, and vol. 11, p. 113, quoted in prepared statement of Donald O. Virden, Chief, Disclosure Staff, Internal Revenue Service, *Hearings Before a Subcommittee on Government Operations, House of Representatives*, 93rd Cong., 1st sess. (May 9 and August 3, 1973): 16–17, and statement of Donald C. Alexander, pp. 91–92, 104; Seligman, *Income Tax*, pp. 434–38, 450–51; George D. Webster, "Inspection and Publicity of Federal Tax Returns," 22 *Tennessee Law Review* (June 1952): 452; *Cong. Globe*, 37th Cong., 1st sess. (July 27, 1861): 306; Elmer Ellis, "Public Opinion and the Income Tax, 1860–1900," 27 *MVHR* (September 1940): 225–31; Ratner, *Taxation and Democracy*, p. 85; *Cong. Globe*, 41st Cong., 2d sess. (April 7, 1870): 2486; *Cong. Globe*, 38th Cong., 2d sess. (1865): 837; *Cong. Globe*, 2d sess. (Feb. 27, 1865): 1138–39; *Cong. Globe*, 39th Cong., 2d sess. (February 22, 1867): 1482; *Cong. Globe*, 39th Cong., 1st sess. (May 23, 1866): 2436–37, 2783–84; *Cong. Globe*,

38th Cong., 1st sess. (May 27, 1864): 2515. The flavor of the debates in the House of Representatives during the Civil War may be sampled in *Cong. Globe*, 38th Cong., 1st sess. (April 26 and 28, 1864): 1876–77, 1940; and for the Senate (May 28, 1864): 2511–15.

10 Ratner, *Taxation and Democracy*, pp. 89–90, 96–98; Joseph A. Pechman, *Federal Tax Policy* (New York: W. W. Norton, 1971), p. 247; Dewey, *Financial History*, comparison of tables on pp. 299 and 305.

11 *Cong. Globe*, 38th Cong., 1st sess. (April 26, 1864): 1884; Chommie, *Internal Revenue Service*, pp. 10, 12–13, 102; *Report of the Commissioner of Internal Revenue on the Operation of the Internal Revenue System for the Year Ending June 30, 1865* (Washington, D.C., 1865), pp. 3–4, 8; *Report of the Commissioner of Internal Revenue on the Operation of the Internal Revenue System for the Year Ending June 30, 1864* (Washington, D.C., 1865), p. 5. Intelligence as a separate unit in the BIR was not established until after the passage of the 1913 law.

12 My narrative and the passages quoted are drawn from *Six Hundred Dollars a Year: A Wife's Effort at Low Living, Under High Prices* (Boston: Ticknor and Fields, 1867), a rare volume in the collections of the University of Chicago Library, which courteously allowed me to read the book. Walter Teller, in his *Twelve Works of Naive Genius* (New York: Harcourt Brace Jovanovich, 1972), printed an excerpt from the book but was unable to discover who "Kitty" was, whether naïve genius or possibly a professional writer, but, he concluded, "I gave her the benefit of the doubt."

13 Hill, "The Civil War Income Tax," p. 436.

14 Richard Cecil Todd, *Confederate Finance* (Athens: University of Georgia Press, 1954), p. ix, 123–25, 130ff., 153, 155–56.

15 Quoted and summarized in Paul, *Taxation in the United States*, pp. 19–22.

16 Ratner, *Taxation and Democracy*, p. 111.

4. Taxes, Tariffs, and Revolt *(pp. 37–52)*

1 Randolph E. Paul, *Taxation in the United States* (Boston: Little, Brown, 1954), p. 25.

2 *Cong. Globe*, 39th Cong., 1st sess. (May 7, 1866): 2436–37.

3 Joseph A. Hill, "The Civil War Income Tax," 8 *Quarterly Journal of Economics* (July 1894): 444–48; The *Nation*, March 18, 1869, quoted in Allan Nevins, *Hamilton Fish: The Inner History of the Grant Administration* (New York: Dodd, Mead, 1936), p. 111.

4 This sketch was first published under the title, "The Mysterious Visit," in the Buffalo *Express*, March 19, 1870, collected for book publication in *Sketches, New and Old* (Hartford: American Publishing, 1875), pp. 316–20.

5 New York *Tribune*, February 5, 1869, quoted in Daniel J. Boorstin, *The Americans: The Democratic Experience* (New York: Random House, 1973), p. 207; George Templeton Strong, *The Diary of George Templeton Strong*, Allan Nevins and M.H. Thomas, eds., 4 vols. (New York: Macmillan, 1952), 4:287; for an early exposition of the views of a leading economist sharply critical of the income tax, see David A. Wells, "The Communism of a Discriminating Income Tax," 131 *North American Rev.* (1880): 236–46.

6 Frederic C. Howe, *Taxation and Taxes in the United States Under the Internal Revenue System, 1791–1895* (New York: Thomas Y. Crowell, 1896), pp. 95, 102; John C. Chommie, *The Internal Revenue Service* (New York: Praeger, 1970), p. 14; Hill, "The Civil War Income Tax," pp. 437–45; Nevins, *Hamilton Fish*, p. 600; *Springer v. United States*, 102 U.S. 586 (1880).

7 Stanley S. Surrey and William C. Warren, *Federal Income Taxation, Cases and Materials* (Brooklyn: Foundation Press, 1953), p. 4; Chommie, *Internal Revenue Service*, p. 18; *A National Historical Landmark: Department of the Treasury* (Washington, D.C., 1972), p. 18; *Report of the Commissioner of Internal Revenue for the Year Ending June 30, 1867* (Washington, D.C., 1867), p. xv; Gerald Carson, *The Social History of Bourbon: An Unhurried Account of Our Star-Spangled American Drink* (New York: Dodd, Mead, 1963), pp. 102, 114ff.

8 *Cong. Rec.*, 53rd Cong., 2d sess. (January 29, 1894): 1600; Martin E. Mantell, *Johnson, Grant and the Politics of Reconstruction* (New York: Columbia University Press, 1973), p. 137; Louis M. Hacker, *The World of Andrew Carnegie: 1865–1901* (Philadelphia: J.B. Lippincott, 1968), p. 26; Robert P. Sharkey, *Money, Class, and Party: An Economic Study of Civil War and Reconstruction* (Baltimore: Johns Hopkins University Press, 1959), p. 60. The quoted phrases are those of Professor Sharkey, who suggests that the strongly–held views of Hugh McCulloch, Secretary of the Treasury from 1865 to 1869, regarding the "heresy" of cheap money were of a quasi-religious character. A useful synthesis of the development of the U.S. economy is Robert Higgs, *The Transformation of the American Economy, 1865–1914: An Essay in Interpretation* (New York: John Wiley, 1971).

9 U.S. Senate, *History of the Committee on Finance* (Washington, D.C., 1973), pp. 37, 39; John Braeman, *Albert J. Beveridge:*

American Internationalist (Chicago: University of Chicago Press, 1971), p. 21; Gilbert C. Fite, *The Farmers' Frontier, 1865–1900* (New York: Holt, Rinehart and Winston, 1966), p. 200; Robert V. Hine, *The American West: An Interpretive History* (Boston: Little, Brown, 1973), pp. 129, 166, 170–71.

10 *The Federalist*, no. 21.

11 Roy G. Blakey and Gladys C. Blakey, *The Federal Income Tax* (New York: Longman's, Green, 1940), pp. 8–9.

12 Strong, *Diary*, 4:524; *Cong. Rec.*, 53rd Cong., 2d sess. (1894): 6695. I am indebted to my editor, Robert Cowley, for calling my attention to this typical expression from Strong of the eastern, conservative, creditor point of view. Similar entries occur in the same volume of the *Diary* at pp. 249, 292.

13 *Santa Clara County v. So. Pac. R.R.*, 118 U.S. 394 (1886) at 396.

14 Charles P. Curtis, Jr., *Lions Under the Throne: A Study of the Supreme Court of the United States Addressed Particularly to Those Laymen Who Know More Constitutional Law Than They Think They Do, and to Those Lawyers Who Know Less* (Boston: Houghton Mifflin, 1947), pp. viii, 141–42, 325. Later Justice Oliver Wendell Holmes, speaking at the beginning of the Progressive era, pointed out that "the Fourteenth Amendment does not enact Mr. Herbert Spencer's *Social Statics*," in *Lockner v. New York*, 198 U.S. 45 (1905) at 75.

15 *United States v. Union Pacific R.R. Co.*, 98 U.S. 569 (1878) at 620; Howard Jay Graham, *Everyman's Constitution: Historical Essays on the Fourteenth Amendment, the "Conspiracy Theory," and American Constitutionalism* (Madison: State Historical Society of Wisconsin, 1968), pp. vii, 3, 18; Higgs, *Transformation*, pp. 57, 79.

16 Graham, *Everyman's Constitution*, p. 32.

17 Ibid., p. 491.

18 Mark Sullivan, *Our Times: The United States 1900–1925*, vol. 1, *The Turn of the Century: 1900–1904* (New York: Scribner's, 1926–1935), pp. 137–41; Bernard Schwartz, *From Confederation to Nation: The American Constitution, 1835–1877* (Baltimore: Johns Hopkins University Press, 1973), pp. 23, 218; Willfred Isbell King, *Economics in Rhyme* (Boston: Richard G. Badger, 1928), p. 30.

19 George Martin, *Causes and Conflicts: The Centennial History of the Association of the Bar of the City of New York 1870–1970* (Boston: Houghton Mifflin, 1970), pp. 3, 42; Kirk H. Porter and Donald Bruce Johnson, compilers, *National Party Platforms 1840–1960* (Urbana: University of Illinois Press, 1961), pp. 58–59, 70, 83–84, 91.

20 Porter and Johnson, *Party Platforms*. pp. 47, 54, 61, 72, 80, 93.

Despite the windiness of party manifestos, their evasiveness and
equivocation on vital matters, Porter and Johnson point out that the
party platforms are nevertheless official statements of position.
They reflect political trends, are especially useful in identifying
the weaknesses in the programs of the opposition parties, and furnish a critique of the actual performance of an administration.
See pp. vi–vii.

21 Carl N. Degler, *Out of Our Past: The Forces That Shaped Modern
America* (New York: Harper & Brothers, 1959), p. 330; (Finley
Peter Dunne), *Mr. Dooley in Peace and War* (Boston: Small, May-
nard, 1899), pp. 197, 200; " Populist Party Platform July 4, 1892,"
in *Documents of American History*, 7th ed., Henry Steele Commager, ed. (New York: Appleton-Century-Crofts, 1963), p. 595.

22 *DAB*, "Donnelly, Ignatius"; ibid., "Weaver, James Baird"; Eric F.
Goldman, *Rendezvous With Destiny: A History of Modern Ameri-
can Reform* (New York: Alfred A. Knopf, 1952), pp. 60–62, 68;
Samuel Eliot Morison, *The Oxford History of the American
People* (New York: Oxford University Press, 1965), pp. 790–91;
Augusta (Ga.) *Chronicle*, quoted in *DAB*, "Tillman, Benjamin
Ryan"; John D. Hicks, *The Populist Revolt: A History of the
Farmers' Alliance and the People's Party* (Minneapolis: University
of Minnesota Press, 1931), pp. 404–409. Hicks's book is the
standard scholarly study. For the historiography of the topic and a
revision of the revisionists, see generally the spirited defense of the
Populist movement in Norman Pollack, *The Populist Response to
Industrial America: Midwestern Populist Thought* (Cambridge,
Mass.: Harvard University Press, 1962).

23 *Cong Rec.*, 53rd Cong., 2d sess., 26, pt. 2 (January 27, 1894): 1561
passim; Thomas Beer, *Hanna* (New York: Alfred A. Knopf, 1929),
p. 173.

24 *Cong. Rec.*, 53rd Cong., 2d sess., 26, pt. 2 (January 27, 1894): 1565,
1567–68, 1611ff., 1640, 1644, 1656–58; Dewey, *Financial History,*
pp. 456–57; Richard Jensen, *The Winning of the Midwest: Social
and Political Conflict: 1888–1896* (Chicago: University of Chicago
Press, 1971), p. 217; Samuel Eliot Morison and Henry S. Commager, *Growth of the American Republic,* 2 vols. (New York: Oxford University Press, 1937), 2:253; New York *Tribune,* January 3,
1894, quoted in Blakey and Blakey, *Federal Income Tax,* pp. 15–
17; Elmer Ellis, "Public Opinion and the Income Tax, 1860–1900,"
27 *MVHR* (September 1940): 242.

25 Louis Eisenstein, *The Ideologies of Taxation* (New York: Ronald
Press, 1961), p. iv.

26 Howe, *Taxation and Taxes,* pp. 232–35; Jensen, *Winning of the*

Midwest, p. 217; Seligman, *Income Tax*, p. 500–501, 508. An even-handed treatment of the yeasty controversies of the period, supported by the modern historiography of the rival systems of thought, is John A. Garraty, *The New Commonwealth 1877–1890* (New York: Harper & Row, 1968).

5. The Second Income Tax (*pp. 53–63*)

1 *Report of the Commissioner of Internal Revenue for the Fiscal Year Ended June 30, 1895* (Washington, D.C., 1895), p. 190; Sidney Ratner, *Taxation and Democracy in America* (New York: John Wiley, Science Editions, 1967), summarizes the law's provisions, including some details not enumerated here, and discusses the measure's defects, pp. 191, 192.

2 John C. Chommie, *The Federal Income Tax* (New York: Praeger, 1970), p. 16; *Cong. Rec.*, 53rd Cong., 2d sess. (January 19, 1894): 1599–1600.

3 93rd Cong., 1st sess., *Hearings Before a Subcommittee of the Committee on Government Operations, House of Representatives*, May 9 and August 3, 1973, prepared statement of Donald O. Virden, Chief, Disclosure Staff, Internal Revenue Service, pp. 14–15; Elmer Ellis, "Public Opinion and the Income Tax, 1860–1900," 27 *MVHR* (September 1940): 234.

4 Simeon E. Baldwin to James P. Pigott, January 12, 1894, quoted in Frederick H. Jackson, *Simeon Eben Baldwin: Lawyer, Social Scientist, Statesman* (New York: Columbia University, King's Crown Press, 1955), p. 144.

5 The striking degree to which congressional eloquence rested on the pathetic fallacy — the ascription of human feelings to the natural world — may be observed in this chapter. Within a few pages we find a Republican solon asserting that roosters crow and hens cackle in appreciation of the protective tariff, while a Democratic leader across the aisle predicts an increase in sunshine and more bird song as a result of the lowering of the tariff and the imposition of an income tax. The Democratic representative was David Albaugh De Armond, *Cong. Rec.*, 53rd Cong., 2d sess. (June 30, 1894), pt. 2, appendix: 406.

6 The Virginia Bar Association. *Two Periods in the History of the Supreme Court, delivered by Justice David J. Brewer of the United States Supreme Court at the Eighteenth Annual Meeting Held at Hot Springs of Virginia August 7th, 8th, 9th, 1906* (Richmond, Va., 1906), pp. 11–12. Artemus Ward: pseudonymn of Charles Farrar Browne (1834–1867), humorous writer and lecturer. Presi-

dent Lincoln read and laughed over his "High Handed Outrage in Utica," September 22, 1862, before reading to his restive cabinet the draft of the Emancipation Proclamation.

7 Ratner, *Taxation and Democracy*, p. 187; Louis Eisenstein, *The Ideologies of Taxation* (New York: Ronald Press, 1961), p. 89.

8 Stanley S. Surrey and William C. Warren, *Federal Income Taxation, Cases and Materials* (Brooklyn: Foundation Press, 1953), p. 5; *Pollock v. Farmers' Loan & Trust Co.*, 157 U.S. 429 (1894) at 431; *Springer v. United States*, 102 U.S. 586 (1880); Chommie, *Federal Income Tax*, p. 13; *Cong Rec.*, 61st Cong., 1st sess., Senate (April 28, 1909): 1570.

9 *Knowlton v. Moore*, 178 U.S. 41 (1899) at 96, 98, 108; Charles F. Dunbar, "The Direct Tax of 1861," 3 *Quarterly Journal of Economics* (Boston, 1889): 436–37, 440–41, 444–45, *Veazie Bank v. Fenno*, 8 Wallace 535 (1869) at 536.

10 A detailed account of the case, including the atmosphere in which it was conducted, is Ratner, *Taxation and Democracy*, pp. 193–212.

11 Randolph E. Paul, *Taxation in the United States* (Boston: Little, Brown, 1954), p. 657; Frederic C. Howe, *Taxation and Taxes in United States Under the Internal Revenue System, 1791–1895* (New York: Thomas Y. Crowell, 1896), pp. 11–12.

12 Randolph E. Paul, *Taxation for Prosperity* (Indianapolis: Bobbs-Merrill, 1947), p. 209; Nathaniel Wright Stevenson, *Nelson W. Aldrich* (New York: Scribner's, 1930), pp. 126–27; *Hylon v. United States*, 3 Dallas 171 (1796) at 181–182.

13 Chommie, *Internal Revenue System*, p. 13; "Communism" as it appears here refers to the then vividly remembered horrors of the Paris Commune of 1871. Choate's speech appears in *Pollock v. Farmers' Loan & Trust Co.*, 157 U.S. 429 (1894) at 532–553. It has also often been reprinted in modern collections of documents.

14 *Pollock v. Farmers' Loan and Trust Co.*, 157 U.S. 429 (1894) at 596; *DAB*, "Fuller, Melville W."; *Pollock v. Farmers' Loan & Trust Co.*, 158 U.S. 601 (1895) at 695; Margaret G. Myers, *A Financial History of the United States* (New York: Columbia University Press, 1970), p. 240.

15 The figure for the number of millionaires was published in the New York *Tribune*, June 1892, monthly supplement, quoted in Ratner, *Taxation and Democracy*, p. 220.

16 Myers, *Financial History*, p. 241; Roy Blough, *The Federal Taxing Process* (New York: Prentice-Hall, 1952), p. 386; Samuel Eliot Morison and Henry S. Commager, *Growth of the American Republic*, 2 vols. (New York: Oxford University Press, 1937), 1:253; Ellis, "Public Opinion and the Income Tax," pp. 225–26;

Allan Nevins, *Grover Cleveland: A Study in Courage* (New York: Dodd, Mead, 1932), p. 670; New York *World*, May 21, 1895. In an appendix to the Nevins volume, contributed by Professor Sidney Ratner, the latter wrote, "The income tax decision unquestionably excited more feeling than any action by the Supreme Court since the Dred Scott opinion." See p. 666.

17 *Pollock* v. *Farmers' Loan & Trust Co.*, 157 U.S. 429 (1894) at 553. Choate was alluding to a prediction of Richard Olney, the Attorney General who presented the government's case, that if the income tax was declared unconstitutional, there would be mass meetings of protest, riots, and "the Supreme Court itself perhaps swept away." See D. M. Marshman, Jr., "The Four Ages of Joseph Choate," 26 *AH* (April 1975): 38.

18 Paul, *Taxation in the United States*, pp. 31, 63; *Report of the Commissioner of Internal Revenue for the Fiscal Year Ended June 30, 1895* (Washington, D.C., 1895), pp. 18, 190–91; *Report of the Commissioner of Internal Revenue for the Fiscal Year Ended June 30, 1896* (Washington, D.C., 1896), p. 212. Formal instructions to taxpayers for getting their money back were printed in the *U.S. Revenue Journal and Internal Revenue Record*, October 16, 1895, pp. 424–25. It could be done. But it wasn't easy.

19 Arthur Hope-Jones, *Income Tax in the Napoleonic Wars* (Cambridge: Cambridge University Press, 1939), pp. ix, 1. The general policy of the IRS today is to destroy most old tax returns after six years.

20 Ellis, "Public Opinion and the Income Tax, p. 242.

6. Protecting the Protective Tariff *(pp. 64–75)*

1 Eric F. Goldman, *Rendezvous with Destiny* (New York: Alfred A. Knopf, 1966), p. 45; Henry F. Pringle, *Theodore Roosevelt: A Biography* (New York: Harcourt, Brace, 1931), pp. 160–61; Louis M. Hacker, *The World of Andrew Carnegie: 1865–1901* (Philadelphia: J.B. Lippincott, 1968), p. 167; Richard Jensen, *The Winning of the Midwest: Social and Political Conflict: 1888–1896* (Chicago: University of Chicago Press, 1971), pp. 179, 183, 305; C. H. Jones to Bryan, May 8, 1893, Bryan Papers, LC, giving his views on the income tax as "the most effective weapon against . . . concentration of U.S. wealth . . ." The Jones letter is summarized in Louis W. Koenig, *Bryan: A Political Biography of William Jennings Bryan* (New York: Putnam's, 1971), p. 129; Arthur Wallace Dunn, *From Harrison to Harding: A Personal Narrative, Covering a Third of a Century 1888–1922*, 2 vols. (New York: Putnam's, 1922), 1:197–99.

2 Kirk H. Porter and Donald Bruce Johnson, compilers, *National Party Platforms: 1840–1960* (Urbana: University of Illinois Press, 1961), pp. 98, 105, 110; Dunn, *Harrison to Harding*, 1:196; Thomas Beer, *Hanna* (New York: Alfred A. Knopf, 1929), pp. 151, 157, 160 *passim;* Thomas A. Bailey, *The Man in the Street: The Impact of American Public Opinion on Foreign Policy* (New York: Macmillan, 1948), p. 22; C. Roland Marchand, *The American Peace Movement and Social Reform: 1898–1918* (Princeton: Princeton University Press, 1972), p. 62; Lewis L. Gould, "The Republican Search for a National Majority," in H. Wayne Morgan, ed., *The Gilded Age*, revised and enlarged edition (Syracuse: Syracuse University Press, 1970), p. 187; H. Wayne Morgan, "Populism and the Decline of Agriculture," Morgan, ed., *Gilded Age*, p. 169; Beer, *Hanna*, p. 165; Gilbert C. Fite, "Republican Strategy and the Farm Vote in the Presidential Campaign of 1896," 65 *AHR* (July 1960): 796; H. Wayne Morgan, *Willliam McKinley and His America* (Syracuse: Syracuse University Press, 1963), p. 234; Peter Norbeck to Selma Norbeck, February 15, 1926, Norbeck Papers, University of South Dakota, quoted in Fite, "Republican Strategy," p. 806.

3 Davis Rich Dewey, *Financial History of the United States*, 12th ed. (New York: Augustus M. Kelley, 1968), pp. 463–65; Dunn, *Harrison to Harding*, 1:223; Morgan, *McKinley and His America*, pp. 277–78.

4 *DAB*, "Aldrich, Nelson Wilmarth"; Beer, *Hanna*, p. 236; Horace Samuel Merrill and Marion Galbraith Merrill, *The Republican Command: 1897–1913* (Lexington: University Press of Kentucky, 1971), p. 25; Harold U. Faulkner, *The Decline of Laissez-Faire: 1897–1917* (New York: Rinehart, 1951), pp. 59–61; Margaret Leach, *In the Days of McKinley* (New York: Harper & Row, 1959), pp. 140–41; Dewey, *Financial History*, pp. 464–65.

5 Samuel Eliot Morison, *Oxford History of the American People* (New York: Oxford University Press, 1965), p. 800; H. Wayne Morgan, *America's Road to Empire: The War with Spain and Overseas Expansion* (New York: John Wiley, 1965), pp. 8–9, 41–43; William Henry Harbaugh, *Power and Responsibility: The Life and Times of Theodore Roosevelt* (New York: Farrar, Straus and Cudahy, 1961), p. 101. Former Secretary of State Richard Olney wrote to ex-President Cleveland of de Lôme, whose political career was ended by the letter, "Poor Dupuy must realize how much worse a blunder can be than a crime," quoted in Morgan, *America's Road*, p. 43.

6 Beer, *Hanna*, pp. 171, 194, 198; Nathaniel Wright Stephenson, *Nelson W. Aldrich* (New York: Scribner's, 1930), pp. 151, 153,

155; Theodore A. Dodge, review of Theodore Roosevelt, *The Rough Riders*, 5 *AHR* (January 1900): 380; quoted in I.E. Cadenhead, Jr., *Theodore Roosevelt: The Paradox of Progressivism*, Shapers of History Series (Woodbury, N.Y.: Barron's Educational Series, 1974), pp. 50–51; Theodore Roosevelt, *The Works of Theodore Roosevelt*, Hermann Hagedorn, ed., National edition, 20 vols. (New York: Scribner's, 1926), 2:136, quoted in Cadenhead, *Theodore Roosevelt*, pp. 58–59; Dunn, *Harrison to Harding*, 2:261–62, 264–66, 270; Morgan, *McKinley*, p. 379; Harbaugh, *Power and Responsibility*, pp. 103–106ff.; "Platform of the American Anti-Imperialist League, October 17, 1899," Richard Hofstadter, ed., *Great Issues in American History from Reconstruction to the Present Day, 1864–1969* (New York: Random House, Vintage Books, 1969), pp. 202–204.

7 *Annual Report of the Commissioner of Internal Revenue for the Fiscal Year Ended June 30, 1918* (Washington, D.C., 1919), p. 3; Claude G. Bowers, *Beveridge and the Progressive Era* (Cambridge, Mass.: Houghton Mifflin, 1932), pp. 354ff.

8 Roy G. Blakey and Gladys C. Blakey, *The Federal Income Tax* (New York: Longman's, Green, 1940), p. 20; Sidney Ratner, *Taxation and Democracy in America* (New York: John Wiley, Science Editions, 1967), pp. 231, 237; Stanley S. Surrey and William C. Warren, *Federal Income Taxation: Cases and Materials* (Brooklyn: Foundation Press, 1953), pp. 8–9; *Knowlton v. Moore*, 178 U.S. 41 (1900).

9 Porter and Johnson, *National Party Platforms*, pp. 112–226; Stephenson, *Aldrich*, p. 110.

10 William Allen White, *The Autobiography of William Allen White* (New York: Macmillan, 1946), pp. 335, 337; Morgan, *McKinley*, pp. 489–91; Harbaugh, *Power and Responsibility*, pp. 132–34; Beer, *Hanna*, pp. 224, 236. Dunn, *Harrison to Harding*, 1:335, quotes Hanna on Roosevelt as a possible President in slightly different language, but the pain is the same.

11 White, *Autobiography*, p. 329; Beer, *Hanna*, p. 226; Harbaugh, *Power and Responsibility*, pp. 125, 136; Morgan, *McKinley*, pp. 490, 493–94, 497.

12 Leach, *In the Days of McKinley*, p. 595.

13 Ratner, *Taxation and Democracy*, p. 249.

14 Faulkner, *Decline of Laissez-Faire*, p. 368; Pringle, *Roosevelt*, pp. 359–61.

15 President Roosevelt's 1906 message was read again to the Senate by Senator William H. Borah, Progressive Senator from Idaho, during the debate in the spring of 1909 over the proposal to

amend the Constitution, *Cong. Rec.*, 61st Cong., 1st sess., Senate (May, 4, 1909): 1681, as well as an excerpt from the President's message of 1907, repeating diffidently the same recommendation.

16 John Braeman, *Albert J. Beveridge: American Nationalist* (Chicago: University of Chicago Press, 1971), p. 129; Merrill and Merrill, *Republican Command,* p. 97; Pringle, *Roosevelt,* p. 415, 477; Donald F. Anderson, *William Howard Taft: A Conservative's Conception of the Presidency* (Ithaca: Cornell University Press, 1973), p. 96; Dunn, *Harrison to Harding,* 2:53; *Puck,* October 30, 1907.

7. Clearing the Way for the Sixteenth Amendment
(pp. 76–85)

1 John D. Buenker, "The Western States and the Federal Income Tax," 4 *Rocky Mountain Review* (November 1967): 38; I.E. Cadenhead, Jr., *Theodore Roosevelt: The Paradox of Progressivism,* Shapers of History Series (Woodbury, N.Y.: Barron's Educational Series, 1974), p. 189; Henry F. Pringle, *The Life and Times of William Toward Taft,* 2 vols. (New York: Farrar & Rinehart, 1939), 1:421, 416; Mark Sullivan, *Our Times: The United States 1900–1925,* vol. 4, *The War Begins: 1909–1914* (New York: Scribner's, 1926–35), 4:362–66; Claude G. Bowers, *Beveridge and the Progressive Era* (Cambridge, Mass.: Houghton Mifflin, 1932), pp. 303, 318, 333–34; Horace Samuel Merrill and Marion Galbraith Merrill, *The Republican Command: 1897–1913* (Lexington: University Press of Kentucky, 1971), pp. 283–84; Senator Moses Clapp Memorandum, Box 50, Biographer's Notes, Aldrich Papers, LC, quoted in Merrill and Merrill, *Republican Command,* footnote, p. 27; Arthur Wallace Dunn, *From Harrison to Harding: A Personal Narrative, Covering a Third of a Century 1888–1921,* 2 vols. (New York: Putnam's, 1922), 2:64, 136.

2 Finley Peter Dunne, *Mr. Dooley Says* (New York: Scribner's, 1910), pp. 148–52.

3 Bruce L. Larson, *Lindbergh of Minnesota: A Political Biography* (New York: Harcourt Brace Jovanovich, 1971), p. 79; *Cong. Rec.,* 61st Cong., 1st sess., House (April 2, 1909): 831.

4 Dunn, *Harrison to Harding,* 2:109; "Tariff Cynicism," *Literary Digest,* April 24, 1909.

5 Randolph E. Paul, *Taxation for Prosperity* (Indianapolis: Bobbs-Merrill, 1947), pp. 16–20; *DAB,* "Aldrich, Nelson Wilmarth"; *Cong. Rec.,* 61st Cong., 1st sess. (June 16, 1909): 3344–45; Taft to Horace Taft, June 27, 1909. Taft Papers, LC, summarized in Merrill and Merrill, *Republican Command,* p. 291; Sidney Ratner,

Taxation and Democracy in America (New York: John Wiley, Science Editions, 1967), p. 271.

6 Charles P. Curtis, Jr., *Lions under the Throne: A Study of the Supreme Court of the United States Addressed Particularly to Those Laymen Who Know More Constitutional Law Than They Think They Do, and to Those Lawyers Who Know Less* (Boston: Houghton Mifflin, 1947), pp. 43–45, 56; Davis Rich Dewey, *Financial History of the United States* (New York: Augustus M. Kelley, 1968), p. 486; *Flint* v. *Stone Tracy Co.*, 220 U.S. 107 (1910) at 108 and 110. For a present-day critical estimate of Taft's conduct in the struggle with Congress over the Payne-Aldrich tariff of 1909, see William Henry Harbaugh, *Power and Responsibility: The Life and Times of Theodore Roosevelt* (New York: Farrar, Straus and Cudahy, 1961), pp. 381–82.

7 *Cong. Rec.*, 61st Cong., 1st sess. (June 29, 1909): 3928–29; ibid., Senate (July 3, 1909): 4067, 4109; John Braeman, *Albert J. Beveridge: American Nationalist* (Chicago: University of Chicago Press, 1971), pp. 155–57; John D. Buenker, *Urban Liberalism and Progressive Reform* (New York: Scribner's, 1973), pp. 109–10, 115, 192–95; Richard Hofstader, ed., *Great Issues in American History: From Reconstruction to the Present Day, 1864–1969* (New York: Random House, Vintage Books, 1969), pp. 181–82; Pringle, *Taft,* 1:433–35.

8 *Cong. Rec.*, 61st Cong., 1st sess. (July 12, 1909): 4390.

9 *Evans* v. *Gore*, 253 U.S. 245 (1920) at 260–263; *Brushaber* v. *Union Pacific R.R. Co.*, 240 U.S. 1 (1916). Senator William H. Borah's review of constitutional history and the taxing power during the Senate debate on the amendment includes a summary of what is known and not known regarding the intentions of the Constitutional Convention. See *Cong. Rec.*, 61st Cong., 1st sess. (May 4, 1909): 1696.

10 John D. Baker, "The Character of the Congressional Revolution of 1910," 40 *Journal of American History* (December 1973): 679–91; Harold U. Faulkner, *The Decline of Laissez-Faire 1897–1917* (New York: Rinehart, 1951), pp. 61–63; Pringle, *Taft,* 1:724; Donald F. Anderson, *William Howard Taft: A Conservative's Conception of the Presidency* (Ithaca: Cornell University Press, 1973), pp. 121–22, 135. For an overview of the social forces pressing for tax and other reforms see, as a sampling of a vast literature, Loren P. Beth, *The Development of the American Constitution: 1877–1917* (New York: Harper & Row, 1971); John D. Buenker, "Progressivism in Practice: New York State and the Federal Income Tax Amendment," 52 *New-York Historical Quarterly* (April 1968); Carl N. Degler, *Out of Our Past: The Forces That Shaped Modern*

America (New York: Harper & Brothers, 1959); Louis W. Koenig, *Bryan: A Political Biography of William Jennings Bryan* (New York: Putnam's, 1971); Arthur S. Link, "What Happened to the Progressive Movement in the 1920's?" 64 *AHR* (July 1959); George E. Mowry, *The Progressive Movement 1900–1920: Recent Ideas and New Literature* (Washington, D.C.: American Historical Association, 1958).

11 Porter and Johnson, *National Party Platforms,* pp. 169, 175, 181.
12 Buenker, "Western States and the Federal Income Tax," pp. 47, 52; *NYT Magazine* (March 13, 1938): 6.
13 Richard Goode, *The Individual Income Tax* (Washington, D.C.: Brookings Institution, 1964), p. 1; *NYT Magazine* (March 13, 1938): 6.; Randolph E. Paul, *Taxation in the United States* (Boston: Little, Brown, 1954), pp. 98–99; Walter Lord, *The Good Years: From 1900 to the First World War* (New York: Harper & Brothers, 1960), p. 319.
14 38 *U.S. Stat.,* part I, March 1913 to March 1915, p. 1203; ibid., pp. 114–202.
15 William Allen White, *The Autobiography of William Allen White* (New York: Macmillan, 1946), p. 428.
16 White, *Autobiography,* pp. 345, 350–53; Samuel Eliot Morison, *Oxford History of the American People* (New York: Oxford University Press, 1965), pp. 731, 821; Nathaniel Wright Stephenson, *Nelson W. Aldrich: A Leader in American Politics* (New York: Scribner's, 1930), p. 248.
17 Eric F. Goldman, *Rendezvous With Destiny* (New York: Alfred A. Knopf, 1966), pp. 76, 86, 88.
18 Arthur S. Link, *Wilson: Confusion and Crises, 1915–1916* (Princeton: Princeton University Press, 1964), p. 324; R. Alton Lee, *A History of Regulatory Taxation* (Lexington: University Press of Kentucky, 1973), pp. 2–3; Harry Kalven, Jr., and Walter J. Blum, *The Uneasy Case for Progressive Taxation* (Chicago: Law School of the University of Chicago, Reprint and Pamphlet Series, no. 11, n.d.), pp. 425, 436, 520; *Knowlton* v. *Moore,* 178 U.S. 41 (1899) at 109.

8. The American Taxpayer Faces His First Form 1040
(pp. 86–99)

1 John C. Chommie, *The Federal Income Tax* (New York: Praeger, 1970), p. 16.
2 A quick study of Judge Hull's career up to 1913 and of his political cast of thought appears in Arthur M. Schlesinger, Jr., *The Age of*

Roosevelt, vol. 2, *The Coming of the New Deal* (Cambridge, Mass.: Houghton Mifflin, 1958), p. 189.

3 *NYT*, November 1, 1913; 41 *Trade and Securities Statistics* (New York: Standard and Poor's Corporation, December 1975), p. 79; idem, *Trade and Securities Statistics, Current Statistics,* (July 1976), p. 16; Carl C. Plehn, *Introduction to Public Finance,* 4th ed. (New York: Macmillan, 1920), p. 90; *U.S. Stat.,* vol. 38, part I, October 3, 1913, pp. 166–68, 171, 178, 180; *Annual Report of the Commissioner of Internal Revenue for the Fiscal Year Ended June 30, 1914* (Washington, D.C., 1914), pp. 9, 20.

4 *Annual Report of the Commissioner of Internal Revenue . . . 1914,* p. 20; Arnold Cantor, "The Slippery Road to Tax Justice," *AFL-CIO Federationist* (April 1973), reprint, no pagination; Richard Goode, *The Individual Income Tax* (Washington, D.C.: Brookings Institution, 1964), pp. 3–4; Louis Eisenstein, *The Ideologies of Taxation* (New York: Ronald Press, 1961), pp. 35–36.

5 Willford Isbell King, *The Wealth and Income of the People of the United States* (New York: Macmillan, 1915), pp. 230–35; *Facing the Tax Problem* (New York: Twentieth Century Fund, 1937), table on p. 45; both quoted in Sidney Ratner, *Taxation and Democracy in America* (New York: John Wiley, Science Editions, 1967), pp. 307–308.

6 Ratner, *Taxation,* p. 309; U.S. Congress, House Committee on Ways and Means, *Report No. 5, Act of October 3, 1913,* 63d Cong., 1st sess. (April 22, 1913): 3.

7 Edwin R. A. Seligman, *The Income Tax: A Study of the History, Theory, and Practice of Income Taxation at Home and Abroad,* 2nd ed. (New York: Macmillan, 1914), p. 704; Eric F. Goldman, *Rendezvous With Destiny* (New York: Alfred A. Knopf, 1966), p. 154.

8 Both Gentz and Turgot are quoted in Randolph E. Paul, *Taxation in the United States* (Boston: Little, Brown, 1954), p. 717.

9 Ratner, *Taxation,* p. 179; *NYT*, March 7, 1914; ibid., September 7, 1975; *McCulloch* v. *Maryland,* 4 Wheaton, 316 (1819). Moving abroad and renouncing U.S. citizenship would not provide an escape today from income taxes on U.S. investment income. Congress covered that situation in 1966.

10 *NYT*, June 3, 1914; ibid., May 21, 1917; ibid., February 6, 1919; ibid., February 8, 1919.

11 Eisenstein, *Ideologies,* pp. 63, 67–68.

12 Michael Mulroney to author, July 12, 1976.

13 Davis Rich Dewey, *Financial History of the United States* (New York: Augustus M. Kelley, 1968), p. 491; Roswell Magill, "The

Never Finished Tasks of Federal Tax Revision," 93 *American Philosophical Society Proceedings* (September 1949): 283; *NYT*, February 9, 1915.

14 Eisenstein, *Ideologies*, pp. 75–76.

15 *Brushaber* v. *Union Pacific R.R. Co.*, 240 U.S. 1 (1916); Harry Kalven, Jr., and Walter J. Blum, *The Uneasy Case for Progressive Taxation* (Chicago: Law School of the University of Chicago, Reprint and Pamphlet Series, no. 11, n.d.), pp. 426–28; Stanley S. Surrey and William C. Warren, *Federal Income Taxation, Cases and Materials* (Brooklyn: Foundation Press, 1953), pp. 10–11; *NYT*, February 24, 1914. The origin of the numeration of Form 1040: it was so designated for no particular reason. Various agencies of government were routinely assigned a series of numbers for forms. It fell to the Bureau of Internal Revenue to start income tax forms with 1040.

16 George C. Bovington, "Deducting the Expenses of an Illegal Business," 19 *Montana Law Review* (Spring 1958): 140–48; *NYT*, March 31, 1918; ibid., March 11, 1919; ibid., March 20, 1921; *Commissioner* v. *Tellier*, 383 U.S. (1966) at 687; 366 *United States* v. *James*, 213 (1961).

17 "The Federal Taxing Power and Regulation of Crime," 29 *Indiana Law Review* (Spring 1954): 385; *NYT*, May 17, 1927.

18 *NYT*, July 11, 1923; ibid., March 2, 1921; ibid., January 16, 1921; ibid., December 12, 1915; ibid., December 13, 1915.

9. War, Boom, Bust *(pp. 100–123)*

1 Randolph E. Paul, *Taxation for Prosperity* (Indianapolis: Bobbs-Merrill, 1947), pp. 22–23; *Annual Report of the Commissioner of Internal Revenue for the Fiscal Year Ended June 30, 1918* (Washington, D.C., 1919), p. 2; James L. Potts, "The Relation of the Income Tax to Democracy in the United States," 11 *Western Political Quarterly* (December 1957): 914; Carl C. Plehn, *Introduction to Public Finance* (New York: Macmillan, 1920), p. 421.

2 Clifford B. Hicks, "Tales from the Black Chambers," 24 *AH* (April 1973): 57; Daniel M. Smith, *The Great Departure: The United States and World War I, 1914–1920* (New York: John Wiley, 1965), pp. 77–78; Thomas A. Bailey, *The Man in the Street: The Impact of American Public Opinion on Foreign Policy* (New York: Macmillan, 1948), pp. 108, 154; Mark Sullivan, *Our Times: The United States 1900–1925*, vol. 5, *Over Here: 1914–1918* (New York: Scribner's, 1926–1935), 5:228.

3 Harvey A. DeWeerd, *President Wilson Fights His War: World*

War I and the American Intervention (New York: Macmillan, 1968), pp. 10–11; Arthur Wallace Dunn, *From Harrison to Harding: A Personal Narrative, Covering a Third of a Century 1888–1921*, 2 vols. (New York: Putnam's, 1922), 2:296–98, 300; Arthur S. Link, *Wilson: Confusions and Crises, 1915–1916* (Princeton: Princeton University Press, 1964), pp. 15, 19 *passim,* 37–38, 48–49; Paul, *Taxation for Prosperity,* p. 23.

4 Bruce L. Larson, *Lindbergh of Minnesota: A Political Biography* (New York: Harcourt Brace Jovanovich, 1971), pp. 184, 190; Sidney Ratner, *Taxation and Democracy in America* (New York: John Wiley, Science Editions, 1967), p. 354ff.; Davis Rich Dewey, *Financial History of the United States* (New York: Augustus M. Kelley, 1968), p. 501; Margaret G. Myers, *A Financial History of the United States* (New York: Columbia University Press, 1970), pp. 278–79; Roy G. Blakey and Gladys C. Blakey, *The Federal Income Tax* (New York: Longman's, Green, 1940), pp. 104, 119, 122, 124–25.

5 DeWeerd, *President Wilson Fights,* pp. 15, 20–21; Allen Churchill, *Over Here!: An Informal Re-Creation of the Home Front in World War I* (New York: Dodd, Mead, 1968), pp. 44–45; Abel Green and Joe Laurie, Jr., *Show Biz: From Vaude to Video* (New York: Henry Holt, 1951), p. 126; Smith, *Great Departure,* pp. 3, 10, 70, 79; Edwin R. A. Seligman, *Essays in Taxation* (New York: Macmillan, 1925), p. 694; Paul, *Taxation for Prosperity,* p. 25.

6 *Cong. Rec.,* 65th Cong., 1st sess. (1917): 7594; Blakey and Blakey, *Federal Income Tax,* pp. 150–51; Plehn, *Public Finance,* p. 421.

7 Deweerd, *President Wilson Fights,* pp. 201, 206, 242–43; "War-Work or Fight," *Literary Digest* (June 8, 1918).

8 *Eisner* v. *Macomber,* 252 U.S. 189 (1919) at 219–220.

9 Paul, *Taxation for Prosperity,* p. 28; *NYT,* February 21, 1935; Dewey, *Financial History,* pp. 527–28; George D. Webster, "Inspection and Publicity of Federal Tax Returns," 22 *Tennessee Law Review* (June 1952): 460, 469–70; *NYT,* April 12, 1935; *Encyclopedia of the Social Sciences,* "Income Tax."

10 George Creel, *How We Advertised America: The First Telling of the Amazing Story of the Committee on Public Information that Carried the Gospel of Americanism to Every Corner of the Globe* (New York: Harper & Brothers, 1920), pp. 5–7, 87; "For Higher and Juster Taxes," *Literary Digest* (June 8, 1918); *NYT,* March 12, 1918; James R. Mock and Cedric Larson, *Words that Won the War: The Story of the Committee on Public Information 1917–1919* (Princeton: Princeton University Press, 1939), p. 114; *NYT,* March 7, 1918.

Notes   279

11 *Annual Report of the Commissioner of Internal Revenue . . . 1918,* pp. 3, 37. An early but still useful work on psychological warfare is Harold D. Lasswell, *Propaganda Technique in the World War* (New York: Alfred A. Knopf, 1927).

12 *Annual Report of the Commissioner of Internal Revenue . . . 1918,* p. 10; John C. Chommie, *The Internal Revenue Service* (New York: Praeger, 1970), pp. 19–20; Lillian Doris, ed., *The American Way in Taxation: Internal Revenue 1862–1963* (Englewood Cliffs, N.J.: Prentice-Hall, 1963), pp. 187–88; "The Fight for Integrity: History of the Maintenance of the Integrity of the Internal Revenue Service," mimeographed (Washington, D.C.: Internal Revenue Service, 1965 [?]), p. 1; CB *1939(1) (Part 2),* "Committee Reports on Act of October 3, 1913; Act of October 22, 1914; and Revenue Acts of 1916 to 1938, Inclusive," p. 118; "Intelligence Division's First Fifty Years," mimeographed (Washington, D.C.: Internal Revenue Service, 1969), pp. 1–2.

13 Stanley S. Surrey and William C. Warren, *Federal Income Taxation, Cases and Materials* (Brooklyn: Foundation Press, 1953), p. 12; Kirk H. Porter and Donald Bruce Johnson, compilers, *National Party Platforms: 1840–1960* (Urbana: University of Illinois Press, 1961), pp. 215, 234; *NYT,* March 7, 1920.

14 For an analysis of the falling away of Wilson's political support, see Arthur S. Link, "What Happened to the Progressive Movement in the 1920's?" 64 *AHR* (July 1959): 839, 842. Postwar economic strains, including the effects of high income taxes as an intensifying factor, are traced in Warren N. Persons, "The Crisis of 1920 in the United States," 12 *American Economic Review* (1922): 7–19.

15 Dewey, *Financial History,* pp. 519–22; *Annual Report of the Commissioner of Internal Revenue for the Fiscal Year Ended June 30, 1921* (Washington, D.C., 1921), pp. 9–10.

16 Paul H. Douglas, *Economy in the National Government* (Chicago: University of Chicago, 1952), p. 17; *International Encyclopedia of the Social Sciences,* "Taxation: Personal Income Taxes"; "Tax Justice Act of 1975," mimeographed (Arlington, Va.: Taxation With Representation, n.d.), pp. 2–3, 6.

17 *NYT,* April 5, 1923; Potts, "Relation of the Income Tax to Democracy," pp. 914, 916–17; Surrey and Warren, *Federal Income Taxation,* p. 12.

18 *NYT,* March 19, 1922; Plehn, *Introduction to Public Finance,* pp. 3–4; Jonathan Swift, *The Prose Works of Jonathan Swift, D.D.,* Temple Scott, ed., vol. 6, *The Draper's Letters* (London: George Bell, 1903), p. 145; *Cong. Rec.,* 53rd Cong., 2d sess. (1894), appendix: 464–65; Ratner, *Taxation and Democracy,* pp. 185–86;

Cong. Rec., 63rd Cong., 1st sess. (1913): 3839; Dewey, *Financial History*, p. 528; Andrew W. Mellon, *Taxation: The People's Business* (New York: Macmillan, 1924), p. 81; John Kenneth Galbraith, *The Affluent Society* (Boston: Houghton Mifflin, 1958), pp. 268, 278.

19 Robert K. Murray, *The Politics of Normalcy: Government Theory and Practice in the Harding-Coolidge Era* (New York: W.W. Norton, 1973), p. 31; Arthur Schlesinger, Jr., *The Age of Roosevelt*, vol. 3, *The Crisis of the Old Order 1919–1933* (Boston: Houghton Mifflin, 1957), pp. 61–62; Mellon, *Taxation*, pp. 83, 88, 112; CB, "Committee Reports . . ." p. 245. Secretary Mellon and many wealthy men would have welcomed a federal sales tax if it had been politically possible. See Paul, *Taxation for Prosperity*, p. 26.

20 *DAB*, "Mellon, Andrew William"; Mellon, *Taxation*, pp. 97–99, 103, 133, 135; William Allen White, *The Autobiography of William Allen White* (New York: Macmillan, 1946), p. 616. The Richard Olney mentioned here is not to be confused with the government official of the same name who, as Attorney General, defended the income tax provisions of the Wilson-Gorman Tariff Act before the Supreme Court in 1895.

21 Randolph E. Paul, *Taxation in the United States* (Boston: Little, Brown, 1954), p. 162; Victor L. Alberg, "Hoover: The Presidency in Transition," *Current History* (October 1950): 213–19, quoted in Susan Estabrook Kennedy, *The Banking Crisis of Kentucky* (Lexington: University Press of Kentucky, 1973), pp. 26, 133; Paul, *Taxation in the United States*, p. 165.

22 George A. Steiner, *Government's Role in Economic Life* (New York: McGraw-Hill, 1953), pp. 140–41; John R. Craf, *A Survey of the American Economy 1940–1946* (New York: North River Press, 1947), p. 126; *Annual Report of the Commissioner of Internal Revenue for the Fiscal Year Ending June 30, 1932* (Washington, D.C., 1932), p. 1; *Annual Report of the Commissioner of Internal Revenue for the Fiscal Year Ending June 30, 1933* (Washington, D.C., 1933), p. 1; Chommie, *Internal Revenue Service*, p. 20; *NYT*, March 14, 1938.

23 Potts, "Relation of the Income Tax to Democracy," pp. 917–18; Surrey and Warren, *Federal Income Taxation*, p. 13; CB, "Committee Reports . . ." pp. 457–59; Paul, *Taxation for Prosperity*, p. 43; *Cong. Rec.*, 74 Cong., 1st sess., Senate (June 22, 1935): 9907. An incisive survey of the economic radical demagogues of the 1930s and their impact is Arthur M. Schlesinger, Jr., *The Age of Roosevelt*, vol. 3, *The Politics of Upheaval* (Boston: Houghton Mifflin, 1960), chaps. 2–4.

24 *69th Cong., 1st Sess., Senate Report No. 27*, part 1–3 (1926), part 1, pp. 6–8, part 2, p. 2. The report was based on an "explosive investigation of the Bureau of Internal Revenue," headed by Senator James Couzens of Michigan, unorthodox Republican, who revolted against the Harding and Coolidge tax programs. Coolidge tried unsuccessfully to spindle the investigation. See *DAB*, "Couzens, James." Richard M. Ketchum, *Will Rogers: His Life and Times* (New York: American Heritage Publishing Company, 1973), p. 197; Bureau of Internal Revenue, *Income Tax Brevities for Use by Radio Broadcasting Stations: Suggested Items of Timely Public Interest to fill Gap Between Scheduled Programs* (Washington, D.C., 1931), pp. 1–16; Thomas Meehan, *NYT Magazine* (December 31, 1972): 5.

25 U.S. Senate, Committee on Banking and Currency, "Stock Exchange Practices," *Report 1455 Pursuant to Senate Resolutions 84, 56, and 97*, 73rd Cong., 1st sess., pp. 321–27, 333, 394; Arthur M. Schlesinger, Jr., *The Age of Roosevelt*, vol. 2, *The Coming of the New Deal* (Boston: Houghton Mifflin, 1958), pp. 435–37.

26 Paul, *Taxation and Prosperity*, pp. 57, 201–202, 206, 659; *NYT*, June 8, 1937; ibid., June 10, 1937. The proverb: "Voler l'Etat n'est pas voler . . ." Gabrielle Sanchez-Vahle, "Le Coin du Pédagogue," *France-Amérique*, February 28–March 7, 1974.

27 Blakey and Blakey, *Federal Income Tax*, pp. 538, 429; *NYT*, November 5, 1935; Frederick Lewis Allen, *Only Yesterday: An Informal History of the Nineteen-Twenties* (New York: Harper & Brothers, 1931), p. 265; Fred D. Pasley, *Al Capone: The Biography of a Self-Made Man* (Ives Washburn, 1930), p. 10; *NYT*, July 13, 1932. A convenient summary of Capone's career in crime appears in the *DAB*, "Capone, Alphonse." A more extended treatment is Elmer Lincoln Irey, *The Tax Dodgers: The Story of the T-men's War With America's Political and Underworld Hoodlums . . . As Told to William J. Slocum* (New York: Greenberg, 1948).

28 Paul, *Taxation in the United States*, p. 201; *NYT*, January 8, 1937; *NYT Magazine* (April 1, 1962): 66; Edward Alsworth Ross, *Sin and Society* (Boston: Houghton Mifflin, 1907), pp. 36–37; "Tax Informants," IRS Fact Sheet, June 2, 1971.

29 Paul, *Taxation for Prosperity*, pp. 58–59; Doris, ed. *American Way in Taxation*, p. 7.

30 Myers, *Financial History*, pp. 344–45; Craf, *Survey of the American Economy*, pp. 127, 129; Steiner, *Government's Role*, pp. 192, 199–203.

10. The Class Tax Becomes a Mass Tax *(pp. 124–132)*

1 Randolph E. Paul, *Taxation for Prosperity* (Indianapolis: Bobbs-Merrill, 1947), p. 103; Margaret G. Myers, *A Financial History of the United States* (New York: Columbia University Press, 1970), p. 346; Roy Blough, *The Federal Taxing Power* (New York: Prentice-Hall, 1952), pp. 21, 39; Arnold Cantor, "The Slippery Road to Tax Justice," AFL-CIO *American Federationist* (April 1973), reprint, no pagination; U.S. Department of Commerce, Bureau of the Census, *Historical Statistics of the United States 1789–1945: A Supplement to the Statistical Abstract of the United States* (Washington, D.C., 1949), p. 307; Walter B. Heller, "Limitations of the Federal Individual Income Tax," 7 *Journal of Finance* (May 1952), p. 200.

2 Paul, *Taxation for Prosperity*, pp. 105–106; U.S. Department of Commerce, Bureau of the Census, *Historical Statistics*, p. 307; Stanley S. Surrey and William C. Warren, *Federal Income Taxation: Cases and Materials* (Brooklyn: Foundation Press, 1953), p. 15; John R. Craf, *A Survey of the American Economy 1940–1946* (New York: North River Press, 1947), pp. 131–32.

3 Blough, *Federal Taxing Process*, pp. 261–62; Fuller Brush Company, *The Brush-Off* (January and February 1944); *NYT*, January 26, 1942; Sidney Ratner, *Taxation and Democracy in America* (New York: John Wiley, Science Editions, 1967), pp. 518–19; Paul, *Taxation for Prosperity*, pp. 164–65.

4 Myers, *Financial History*, pp. 346–48, 360–62; Ratner, *Taxation and Democracy*, pp. 519–23.

5 Surrey and Warren, *Federal Taxation*, pp. 30, 32; James L. Potts, "Relation of the Income Tax to Democracy in the United States," 11 *Western Political Quarterly* (December 1957): 919; *Cong. Rec.*, 83rd Cong., 2d sess. (1954): A2397; *Historical Statistics*, table, p. 307; *Cong. Rec.*, 63rd Cong., 1st sess., Senate (1913): 3840; Adam Smith, *An Inquiry into the Nature and Causes of the Wealth of Nations*, 2 vols. (London and New York: Everyman's Library, 1911), 2:368.

6 Myers, *Financial History*. pp. 365–68; Harold G. Vatter, *The U.S. Economy in the 1950's: An Economic History* (New York: W.W. Norton, 1963), pp. 5–6; Bernard Schwartz, *The Law in America* (New York: American Heritage Publishing Co., 1974), pp. 204–205; *Carmichael et al v. Southern Coal & Coke Co.*, 301 U.S. 495 (1937); *Steward Machine Co. v. Davis*, 301 U.S. 548 (1937); Paul A. Samuelson, *Economics, 8th ed.* (New York: McGraw-Hill, 1970), pp. 139–40.

7 Joseph A. Pechman, *Federal Tax Policy* (New York: W.W. Norton,

1971), p. 251; George A. Steiner, *Government's Role in Economic Life* (New York: McGraw-Hill, 1953), pp. 226–27; Myers, *Financial History*, p. 381; U.S. Senate, *History of the Committee on Finance* (Washington, D.C., 1973).

Part Two

11. Protesting the Tax: Rhetoric and Action *(pp. 135–151)*

1 *NYT*, June 6, 1975.
2 *Report of the Commissioner of Internal Revenue for the Year Ended June 30, 1875* (Washington, D.C., 1875), p. iv.
3 A list of nongovernmental citizens' interest groups and associations, located in Washington, which make tax analyses and proposals, and monitor tax reform hearings, appears in the *Washington Information Directory, 1975–1976* (Washington, D.C.: Quadrangle/ The *New York Times* Book Co., 1975), pp. 69–70.
4 Vivien Kellems, *Toil, Taxes and Trouble* (New York: E.P. Dutton, 1952), pp. 9–10, 14, 93–94, 154–56; *NYT*, January 27, 1975; ibid., February 1, 1952; ibid., November 27, 1961; Corinne Griffith, *Taxation With Representation: or, Your Tax Money Went That-a-Way!* (New York: Frederick Fell, 1962), pp. 37, 64, 73. The *Wall Street Journal*, protesting against congressmen making the Grand Tour at the expense of U.S. taxpayers, remarked editorially, under the heading "Congressional Jet Set," "Maybe, as some Congressmen insist, the issue is too minor to bother ruffling any feathers over. But that's easy to say when it's the taxpayer's goose who is being plucked," December 2, 1974. Miss Kellems at 71 got her doctorate at the University of Edinburgh. Her dissertation subject: the Sixteenth (Income Tax) Amendment.
5 Douglas Edward Leach, *Arms for Empire: A Military History of the British Colonies in North America 1607–1763* (New York: Macmillian, 1973), pp. 291–92; William L. Roper, "The Plight of the Plain People," *Liberty* (March–April 1964); Pueblo (Colo.) *Chieftain*, October 15, 1964; *NYT*, July 11, 1965; Youngstown (Ohio) *Vindicator*, July 11, 1965.
6 *NYT*, April 16, 1970; ibid., April 16, 1968; ibid., April 16, 1969; ibid., April 18, 1967; ibid., March 16, 1949; ibid., February 15, 1974; *WSJ*, January 30, 1974; *WP*, March 9, 1975; *NYT*, March 12, 1951; Edmund Wilson, *The Cold War and the Income Tax: A Protest* (New York: Farrar, Straus, 1963), p. 115.
7 *NYT*, May 17, 1961; ibid., August 10, 1956; *National Observer*, February 28, 1976; *NYT*, April 18, 1974; ibid., February 2, 1974;

Los Angeles *Times,* April 15, 1975; *NYT,* August 22, 1970; Stockton (Calif.) *Record,* September 11, 1974; ibid., September 12, 1974.

8 *Cong. Rec.,* 94th Cong., 1st sess. (April 18, 1975): S6220-1; press releases, office of Senator William Proxmire, March 11, 1975; ibid., March 18, 1975; ibid., August 21, 1975, all mimeographs; *WSJ,* March 7, 1975; "Washington Whispers," *U.S. News & World Report* (June 24, 1974); *Roll Call,* February 5, 1976; *WP/*Potomac, March 31, 1974; *NYT,* June 18, 1975.

9 "Those 'Rip-Offs' That Irritate Taxpayers," *U.S. News & World Report,* July 22, 1974; *WSJ,* November 12, 1974; Columbus (Ohio) *Sunday Dispatch,* August 18, 1974.

10 Griffith, *Taxation With Representation,* pp. 75–76; Poughkeepsie (N.Y.) *Journal,* March 17, 1974; Liberty Lobby, *Liberty Letter,* no. 153, January 1974; ibid., no. 158, June 1974; ibid., no. 162, October 1974; "Who's Your Lobbyist in Washington? The Story of Liberty Lobby," folder, n.p.; *NYT,* March 9, 1975; National Justice Foundation, *Program: Annual Convention, H.M.S. "Queen Mary," Long Beach, California, October 12, 1974;* "A Prestigious New Movement on the Scene," *The National Educator* (September 1974), no pagination, reprinted in the convention program.

11 *NYT,* July 30, 1974; *Carmichael* v. *Southern Coal Co.,* 301 U.S. 495 (1936) at 509; St. Paul (Minn.) *Dispatch,* July 26, 1973; *United States* v. *Douglass,* 476 F. 2d 260 (5th Cir. 1973); *WSJ,* January 19, 1972; "In the Matter of Mr. & Mrs. Eugene F. House and Newspaper Ad entitled 'A Police State Here . . . You Betcha,' " IRS Fact Sheet, mimeographed, 1 p., February 1, 1974.

12 Phoenix (Ariz.) *Republic,* May 1, 1973; *NYT,* May 3, 1973; IRS Fact Sheet, "Tax Protesters," n.p.; Salt Lake City *Deseret News,* April 20, 1973; *NYT,* March 1, 1952.

13 *WSJ,* October 27, 1975.

14 John C. Chommie, *The Internal Revenue Service* (New York: Praeger, 1970), p. 17; Louis Eisenstein, *The Ideologies of Taxation* (New York: Ronald Press, 1961), pp. 207–209; B. U. Ratchford, "Practical Limitations to the Net Income Tax — General," 7 *Journal of Finance* (May 1952), 204; "Report of the Special Committee on the Proposed Amendment to the Constitution of the United States Limiting the Power of Congress to Tax Incomes, Inheritances and Gifts," *American Bar Association Annual Report, 1952,* vol. 77 (Chicago, 1953), pp. 578–80, 582, 586; "Report of the Special Committee on Proposed Amendment to the Constitution of the United States Relative to Taxes on Incomes, Inheritances and Gifts," *American Bar Association Report, 1962,* vol. 87 (Chicago, 1963),

pp. 348–49; John P. Manwell to author, September 27, 1974. Other groups that supported the movement for establishing a fixed top on the federal income tax appear extensively in the pages of the *NYT Index* during the 1950s, specifically on February 26, 1953, December 2, 1954, and May 21, 1957. For critical commentary on such a restriction, see William L. Carey, "The Income Tax Amendment: A Straight Jacket for Sound Fiscal Policy," 39 *American Bar Association Journal* (October 1953): 885–88; and Erwin N. Griswold, "Can We Limit Taxes to 25 Per Cent?" 190 *Atlantic Monthly* (August 1952): 76–78.

15 Louis Alan Talley, research assistant, Economics Division, Library of Congress, to Joint Committee on Internal Revenue Taxation, "The Proposed 23rd Amendment to the Constitution to Repeal the Power of Congress to Collect Taxes," mimeographed (Washington, D.C., May 23, 1975), 2 pp.; the Library of Congress, Congressional Research Service, "The Reed-Dirksen Amendment: A Proposal to Repeal Federal Estate and Gift Taxes and to Restrict Income Taxes to a Maximum Rate of 25 Per Cent," mimeographed (Washington, D.C., August 26, 1974), 3 pp.; Frank Chodorov, *The Income Tax: Root of All Evil*, introduction by J. Bracken Lee (New York: Devin-Adair, 1954), p. vi–x.

16 Chodorov, *Income Tax*, pp. vii–viii; *NYT,* April 1, 1961; ibid., March 24, 1957. See generally James L. Potts, "The Relation of the Income Tax to Democracy in the United States, 11 *Western Political Quarterly* (December 1957): 911–25; U.S. Congress, Joint Economic Committee, *The Proposed 23rd Amendment to the Constitution to Repeal the Sixteenth Amendment to the Constitution Which Provides that Congress Shall Have Power to Collect Taxes on Incomes: A Study Made by the Staff of the Joint Committee of the United States Senate and House of Representatives to Determine the Effects of its Adoption,* 87th Cong., 1st sess., S. Doc. no. 5 (Washington, D.C., 1961), pp. 1–3, 5–15; Fred P. Graham, "The Role of the States in Proposing Constitutional Amendments," 49 *American Bar Association Journal* (December 1963): 1176–77.

12. Endless Quest: The Privilege of Paying the Least
(pp. 152–166)

1 *NYT,* March 8, 1970, p. 53; Henry C. Simons, *Personal Income Taxation* (Chicago: University of Chicago Press, 1938), p. 108; Peter Clyne, *How Not to Pay Your Debts: A Handbook for Scoundrels?* (London: Abelard-Schuman, 1973), pp. 87–88; Norris Dar-

rell, "Some Responsibilities of the Tax Adviser in Regard to Tax Minimization Devices," 8 *New York University Institute on Federal Taxation* (1950): 986; Harry Graham Balter, *Tax Fraud and Evasion: A Guide to Civil and Criminal Principles and Practice under Federal Law*, 3rd ed. (New York: Ronald Press, 1973), I-7; *Helvering* v. *Gregory*, 69 F. 2d 809 (2d Cir. 1934); Philip M. Stern, *The Great Treasury Raid* (New York: Random House, 1964), p. x; *NYT*, November 7, 1973.

2 Lane Cooper, trans., *The Rhetoric of Aristotle* (New York: Meredith, 1960), p. 44; Harry Kalven, Jr. and Walter J. Blum, *The Uneasy Case for Progressive Taxation*, Pamphlet Series no. 11. (Chicago: Law School of the University of Chicago: n.d.), p. 517; Lester C. Thurow, *The Impact of Taxes on the American Economy* (New York: Praeger, 1971), p. 22; John C. Chommie, *The Internal Revenue Service* (New York: Praeger, 1970), p. 110.

3 Ward Morehouse, *George M. Cohan: Prince of the Theatre* (Philadelphia: J.B. Lippincott, 1943), pp. 144–45, 159, 543–44; *Cohan* v. *Commissioner of Internal Revenue*, 39 F. 2d 540 (2d Cir. 1930) at 543–44; John T. Koehler to author, December 13, 1973.

4 19 BTA, 518, 533 (1930); Balter, *Tax Fraud and Evasion*, II-6-7, 13.

5 Lillian Doris, ed., *The American Way in Taxation: Internal Revenue, 1862–1963* (Englewood Cliffs, N.J.: Prentice-Hall, 1963), p. 191; R. Alton Lee, *A History of Regulatory Taxation* (Lexington: University Press of Kentucky, 1973), p. 196; *Wiggins* v. *United States*, 64 F. 2d 950 (6th Cir. 1933); *Cleveland Press*, November 29, 1973; *NYT*, July 14, 1974. A number of cases strongly suggest that dentists who keep two sets of books should take especial care to keep on friendly terms with former employees.

6 *NYT*, January 17, 1939; ibid., June 6, 1939; ibid., February 13, 1935; ibid., February 27, 1935; "Joe Louis," IRS Fact Sheet, mimeographed, 1 p., May 15, 1970; *Johansson* v. *U.S.* 336 F. 2d 809 (5th Cir. 1964); U.S. Senate Committee on Banking and Currency, "Stock Exchange Practices," *Report 1455 Pursuant to Senate Resolutions 84, 56, and 97*, 73 Cong., 1st sess., pp. 321–27; Ferdinand Pecora, *Wall Street Under Oath: The Story of Our Modern Money Changers*, reprint of 1939 ed. (New York: Augustus M. Kelley, 1968), pp. 190–91, 199–200; Broadus Mitchell, *Depression Decade: From New Era Through New Deal*, vol. 9, *The Economic History of the United States* (New York: Rinehart, 1947), pp. 155–56. See also *NYT*, May 11, 1937; Susan Estabrook Kennedy, *The Banking Crisis of 1933* (Lexington: University Press of Kentucky, 1973), chap. 5.

7 Randolph E. Paul, *Taxation for Prosperity* (Indianapolis: Bobbs-

Merrill, 1947), p. 288; *NYT*, July 30, 1974; ibid., November 23, 1974; ibid., April 8, 1975; ibid., August 4, 1954; *WSJ*, October 17, 1973; ibid., March 14, 1974; *NYT*, February 10, 1974; entry for September 14, 1876, in T. Harry Williams, ed., *Hayes: The Diary of a President, 1875–1881, Covering the Disputed Election, the End of Reconstruction, and the Beginning of Civil Service* (New York: David McKay, 1964), p. 35.

8 Balter, *Tax Fraud and Evasion*, VI-5; *WSJ*, February 16, 1972; Department of the Treasury, Internal Revenue Service, *Handbook for Special Agents*, Intelligence Division, Internal Revenue Manual, chap. 9900: 10-19-64, reprinted November 15, 1972, exhibit 500-2.

9 *Tax Fraud: Course Materials* (Ann Arbor, Institute of Continuing Legal Education, n.d.), pp. 55–56; S. Ralph Jacobs, "Glamorous Fringe Benefits," 36 *Boston University Law Review* (Spring 1956): 151–52, 155–56; Caryl Rivers, "IRS: They're Usually Honest with Newsmen," *Editor & Publisher*, April 11, 1964; *NYT*, April 3, 1975; Jacobs, "Glamorous Fringe Benefits," p. 164.

10 *Tax Fraud: Course Materials*, pp. 3, 38; Balter, *Tax Fraud and Evasion*, IV-2, III-13, XV-4; *Rock Island Arkansas & Louisiana Railroad Company* v. *United States*, 254 U.S. 141 (1920) at 143; *NYT*, February 23, 1970, p. 43.

11 The decision was appealed but Dr. Clyne forfeited his $20,000 bond and disappeared from sight. The U.S. Attorney in Dallas thought Clyne was in Australia and began researching his extradition: *WSJ*, August 27, 1975; ibid., April 26, 1976; ibid., July 7, 1976.

12 Hugh C. Bickford, *Successful Tax Practice* (New York: Prentice-Hall, 1950), p. 142; *WSJ*, August 20, 1975.

13 *NYT*, May 25, 1975; *WSJ*, August 14, 1974; New York *News*, August 7, 1972; "Scientology Churches Get Rulings," 3 *Tax Notes* (October 27, 1975): 27; Christopher Evans, *Cults of Unreason* (New York: Farrar, Straus and Giroux, 1974), pp. 108–109; "Where Are They Now?" *Newsweek* (August 26, 1968); *WSJ*, May 15, 1974; IR Code, Sec. 7605(c); *NYT*, October 24, 1976; Hudson (N.Y.) *Register-Star*. January 15, 1974. For a detailed, often funny, sometimes frightening, account of Scientology, see generally Evans, *Cults*. The IRS is reputed to be investigating the activities of the Reverend Sun Myong Moon's "Unification Church," as to its non-religious activities and nonreligious sources of income and the validity of its claim to the financial advantages of being classified as a religious movement. See generally the *New York Times Index* for the first six months of 1976, especially the issue of June 2, 1976.

13. Loopholes, Deductions, and All That (pp. 167–191)

1 Boris I. Bittker, "Income Tax 'Loopholes' and Political Rhetoric," 71 *Michigan Law Review* (May 1973): p. 1102; Louis Eisenstein, *The Ideologies of Taxation* (New York: Ronald Press, 1961), pp. 182, 185, 190, 193, 224, 227; Stanley S. Surrey, "The Sheltered Life," *NYT Magazine* (April 13, 1975): 50; Walter B. Hill, "Bar Associations: Address Delivered at Atlanta, Georgia, August 7th, 1888," 5 *Georgia Bar Association Reports* (1888): 51.

2 Bittker, "Income Tax 'Loopholes,'" pp. 1103–08; *Turnipseed* v. *Commissioner*, 27 TC 758 (1957).

3 *WSJ*, November 10, 1975; Stanley S. Surrey, "The Congress and the Tax Lobbyist — How Special Tax Provisions Get Enacted," 70 *Harvard Law Review* (May 1957): 1160, 1162; Bittker, "Income Tax 'Loopholes,'" p. 1099; Harvey E. Brazer, *A Program for Federal Tax Revision* (Ann Arbor, Mich.: Institute of Public Administration, University of Michigan, Michigan pamphlets no. 28, 1960), pp. 1–3.

4 Surrey, "Congress and the Tax Lobbyist," pp. 1148, 1153–54, 1156–57, 1175; *WSJ*, October 23, 1974; Samantha Senger, "Income Taxes: Breaking Up Loopholes," 3 *People & Taxes* (March, 1975): 6; George F. Break and Joseph A. Pechman, *Federal Tax Reform: The Impossible Dream?* (Washington, D.C.: Brookings Institution, 1975), p. 12 and chart on p. 15. Surrey develops his theme more fully in *Pathways to Tax Reform: The Concept of Tax Expenditures* (Cambridge, Mass.: Harvard University Press, 1973).

5 *WSJ*, July 9, 1975; ibid., October 23, 1974; Henry C. Simons, *Personal Income Taxation: The Definition of Income as a Problem of Fiscal Policy* (Chicago: University of Chicago Press, 1938), p. 122, footnote; Thomas F. Field, "Tax Reform Groups Mark Anniversary," 4 *Taxation With Representation Newsletter* (January 1975): 1–4; *Cong. Rec.* Senate (January 23, 1974): S357. Passage of the trona bill inspired a student of Professor Boris I. Bittker of the Yale Law School to write:

> A mining tycoon from Verona
> Said: "I wanna get rich, and I'm gonna.
> If you let me deplete
> I won't have to cheat,
> Just watch me decarbonate trona!"

6 Philip M. Stern, *The Great Treasury Raid* (New York: Random House, 1964), p. 85; IRC, Sec. 631(a); *Meyers* v. *Comr.*, 66 TC no. 24, May 10, 1976; *WSJ*, June 9, 1976; ibid., October 29, 1975;

Blatt v. *Commissioner*, 6 TCM 94 (1947); IRS, rev. ruling, 62-189, 1962-CB, 88; *Ochs* v. *Commissioner*, 195 F. 2d 692 (6th Cir. 1950).

7 S. Ralph Jacobs, "Glamorous Fringe Benefits," 36 *Boston University Law Review* (Spring 1956): 169.

8 Stern, *Great Treasury Raid*, pp. 131, 137, 321–22.

9 Louis Auchincloss, *The Partners* (Boston: Houghton Mifflin, 1974), pp. 29–30, 33; Joseph W. Bishop, Jr., "Lawyers at the Bar," 58 *Commentary* (August 1974): 49.

10 *Cong. Rec.*, 53rd Cong., 2d sess., House (January 30, 1894): vol. 26, appendix, p. 465; Joseph A. Pechman, "The Rich, the Poor, and the Taxes They Pay," *The Public Interest* (Fall 1969), quoted in *Cong. Rec.*, 91st Cong., 1st sess., Senate (October 30, 1969): 32362.

11 U.S. Congress, Joint Economic Committee, *Federal Tax Policy for Economic Growth and Stability. Report of the Joint Committee on the Economic Report to the Congress of the United States*, 84th Cong., 2d Sess. (1956), Senate report 1310, pp. 8, 14; *Cong. Rec.*, 2d Sess., House (March 30, 1972): 11366; *Fausner* v. *Commissioner*, 472 F. 2d 561 (5th Cir., 1973); *WSJ*, September 10, 1975.

12 *NYT*, November 28, 1975; Senator William Proxmire to author, March 30, 1976, and May 13, 1976; *Federal Register*, September 5, 1975, p. 41121.

13 "Junkets," 4 *Dollars and Sense* (November 1975); Dick West, "Lame Ducks Start Migrating," Hudson (N.Y.) *Register-Star* (November 11, 1974); "If I Had a Chance to Go, I'd Go More," 5 *Dollars and Sense* (February 1976).

14 The economic rewards of becoming a "tax farmer" as explained to the audience of doctors at the Fairmount Hotel are clearly if somewhat ironically described by Peter Barnes in "Cattle Breeding and Tax Break Rustling with the AMA," San Francisco Bay *Guardian*, August 3, 1972, quoted in *Cong. Rec.*, 92nd Cong., 1st sess., House (August 14, 1972): 28125–26.

15 *NYT*, October 27, 1974; ibid., March 6, 1974; *WSJ*, September 12, 1975 (advertisement); "Une politique d'expansion dynamique," *France-Amérique*, 20–26 novembre 1975; Timothy Ward, "No Frills, First Class All the Way," 3 *People & Taxes* (September 1975): 11; "Speech of Congressman Charles A. Vanik (Ohio) in the House of Representatives: Third World Tax Havens Conference," February 5, 1975, mimeographed, 2 pp. The Tax Reform Act of 1975 attempts to curtail the deductibility of the costs of convention pleasure trips outside North America. See discussion by Al Ullman, chairman of the Ways and Means Committee, "Tax Policy," 29 *National Tax Journal* (March 1976): 6. The Tax Reform Act of 1976

made a characteristic compromise — the deductions were continued but with restrictions drawn tighter.

16 IR Code, Sec. 274(a); *WSJ*, July 3, 1974; Boris I. Bittker, "Income Tax Deductions, Credits, and Subsidies for Personal Expenditures," 16 *J. of L. and Ec.* (1973): 203–204; Richard Goode, *The Individual Income Tax* (Washington, D.C.: Brookings Institution, 1964), p. 96; *Limerick v. Commissioner*, 9 TCM 465 (1950).

17 Bittker, "Income Tax Deductions, Credits, and Subsidies," p. 212; Stern, *Great Treasury Raid*, p. 125; Donald C. Alexander, "Tax Shelters," 45 *Ohio Bar* (June 12, 1972): 889; *NYT*, November 30, 1975.

18 *NYT*, January 24, 1974; Surrey, "Congress and the Tax Lobbyist," pp. 1176–81; Stern, *Great Treasury Raid*, pp. 44–47; Eisenstein, *Ideology*, pp. 156–57; *WSJ*, November 7, 1975. There is a group of good and earnest members of the House who meet regularly in H-302 to study the Bible. Unfortunately, none is a member of the Ways and Means Committee: *Roll Call*, April 1, 1976.

19 William Pietz, "Some Reform Amendments Pass House," 3 *People & Taxes* (December 1975): 1.

20 *Cong. Rec.*, 94th Cong., 1st sess., House (June 12, 1975): 5393.

21 Alexander, "Tax Shelters," pp. 887–88, 890–91; Edwin S. Cohen, "The Administration's Tax Priorities," in *The Challenge of Tax Reform: Proceedings of Tax Foundation's 24th National Conference* (New York: Tax Foundation, 1973), p. 55; Robert Brandon, "Packaging Shelters to Avoid Taxes," 3 *People & Taxes* (September 1975): 3; *WSJ*, January 5, 1972; Internal Revenue Service, "Remarks by Donald C. Alexander, Commissioner of Internal Revenue, Prepared for Delivery Before the Cleveland Tax Institute, Cleveland, Ohio, November 15, 1973," mimeographed, 8 pp., p. 8.

22 "Making Money by Showing Losses," 3 *People & Taxes* (July 1975): 3; Robin Barlow, Harvey E. Brazer, and James N. Morgan, *Economic Behavior of the Affluent* (Washington, D.C.: Brookings Institution, 1966), p. 6; *NYT*, September 10, 1975; IR Code, Sec. 278; William Lin et al., "Producer Response to Income Taxes: An Empirical Test Within a Risk Framework," 27 *National Tax Journal* (June 1974): 192. One famous debacle was Black Watch Farms, Inc. The story of how the tax-shelter cow concept was promoted in one notorious instance, and the names of glittering celebrities who got hurt, appears in *WSJ*, November 26, 1971; and the troubles of another large cattle-feeding concern, Wheatheart, Inc., are discussed in *WSJ*, October 1, 1975. A similar disaster in oil and gas properties was the Home-Stake Production Co., which cost show-business figures, eminent businessmen, politicians, the U.S. Treasury, and therefore the public generally, perhaps $100 million

dollars. See *WSJ*, December 13, 1974; ibid., March 21, 1975; and *NYT*, August 28, 1975, for the grisly details.

23 Alexander, "Tax Shelters," p. 897; IR Code, Sec. 611(a) and 613(b).

24 *NYT*, October 5, 1952; ibid., November 14, 1952.

25 The technical problems that arise during attempts to deal equitably with capital gains and losses in income tax reporting are summarized and evaluated in Break and Pechman, *Federal Tax Reform*, pp. 44–52; Goode, *Individual Income Tax*, pp. 189–221; Joseph A. Pechman, *Federal Tax Policy* (New York: W.W. Norton, 1971), pp. 96–99; Lowell Ponte, "A Modest Proposal: Depletion Allowances and the Body Politic," *Harper's Weekly* (January 10, 1975).

26 Brazer, *Program for Federal Tax Revision*, p. 11; verse quoted by Senator Edmund S. Muskie, *Cong. Rec.* 93rd Cong., 1st sess. (January 23, 1973): 1848. Gail Harmon has reminded me that the small investor does have the option of investing in tax-exempt securities through mutual bond funds.

27 Robert K. Merton, *Mass Persuasion: The Social Psychology of a War Bond Drive* (Westport, Conn.: Greenwood Press, 1946), pp. 166–69; Irving Kristol, "Of Populism and Taxes," *The Public Interest* (no. 28, Summer 1972): pp. 9–11.

28 *Wealth, Taxation and Fiscal Policy* (New York: National Association of Manufacturers, 1972), p. 15; Boris I. Bittker, "Effective Tax Rates: Fact or Fancy?" 122 *University of Pennsylvania Law Review* (1974): 791; Eisenstein, *Ideology*, pp. 39, 41; Walter B. Heller, "Limitations of the Federal Individual Income Tax," 7 *Journal of Finance* (May 1952): 193–94.

29 *WSJ*, March 13, 1974; ibid., September 3, 1975; ibid., November 8, 1972.

30 Surrey, *Pathways to Tax Reform*, p. 6.

31 Gordon Tullock, "Government Redistribution of Wealth and Income: Who, in *Fact*, Ends up with the Fruits of our Labor," Paper delivered at the Center for Constructive Alternatives, Hillsdale College, Hillsdale, Mich., September 28–October 3, 1975, mimeographed, 33 pp.; Lester C. Thurow, *The Impact of Taxes on the American Economy* (New York: Praeger, 1971), pp. 163, 154, 19; Simons, *Personal Income Taxation*, p. 219.

14. The Biggest Business in the United States
(*pp. 192–222*)

1 *A National Historical Landmark: Department of the Treasury* (Washington, D.C., 1972), p. 4; *Annual Report 1974: Commissioner of Internal Revenue* (Washington, D.C., 1975), pp. 12–13; Francis

I. Geibel, "How Internal Audit Functions at IRS," *The Internal Auditor* (September–October 1972), no pagination. Reprinted as IRS Document 6185 (9-72); U.S. Internal Revenue Service, "Statement of Principles of Internal Revenue Tax Administration," IRB (April 15, 1974), p. 2; John C. Chommie, *The Internal Revenue Service* (New York: Praeger, 1970), pp. 68, 87. The author acknowledges a general indebtedness in this chapter to the late Professor Chommie's exposition of the management functions of the IRS, with Chommie's figures brought up to date by the *Annual Report 1975: Commissioner of Internal Revenue,* supplemented by Terence F. Gastelle, Public Affairs Division, IRS, to author, January 28, 1976.

2 *United States Government Organization Manual 1971/72,* p. 114; John Higginbothan, trans., *Cicero on Moral Obligation,* a new translation of Cicero's *De Officiis* with introduction and notes (Berkeley and Los Angeles: University of California Press, 1967), p. 92. For the idea of millions of tax forms being intellectually pleasing to contemplate, I am indebted to H. Mark Roelofs, *The Language of Modern Politics: An Introduction to the Study of Government* (Homewood, Ill.: Dorsey Press, 1967), pp. 136–37. The classic analysis of bureaucracy is Max Weber, *The Theory of Social and Economic Organization,* A. M. Henderson and Talcott Parsons, trans., edited with an intro. by Talcott Parsons (New York: Free Press, 1947).

3 Geibel, "How Internal Audit Functions . . ."; "History, Organization and Functions of Inspection," Internal Revenue Service Doc. 6119 (9-71); Arthur S. Aubry, Jr., "Inspection in the Internal Revenue Service," *Police* (July–August 1971), pp. 5–11, reprinted as IRS Doc. 6147 (10-71). Rules of employee conduct are meticulously spelled out in *Handbook of Employee Responsibilities and Conduct,* IR Manual 0735, 1-1, November 16, 1973.

4 *Annual Report 1975: Commissioner of Internal Revenue,* table 25, p. 147; Terence F. Gastelle to author, April 26, 1974, and June 3, 1974; *NYT,* January 24, 1974; Internal Revenue Service. *Techniques Handbook for In-Depth Audit Investigations,* IR Manual 4235 (December 13, 1971): Sec. 310; *NYT,* January 24, 1974; ibid., February 7, 1950.

5 "Tax Fraud: Course Materials," mimeographed (Ann Arbor, Mich.: Institute of Continuing Legal Education, n.d.), pp. 37, 40, 45, 47, 56; *Dorsheimer* v. *United States,* 74 U.S. 166 (7 Wallace, 1868) at 173; Chommie, *Internal Revenue Service,* pp. 111–13. For readers unfamiliar with the General Services Administration (GS) classification of salaries, the schedule opposite lists the grades, the rates

SCHEDULE OF ANNUAL SALARY RATES BY GRADE

GENERAL SCHEDULE RATES EFFECTIVE OCTOBER 12, 1975
RATES WITHIN GRADE & MINIMUM WAITING PERIOD FOR NEXT STEP INCREASE

GS GRADE	52 WEEKS			104 WEEKS			156 WEEKS			
	1	2	3	4	5	6	7	8	9	10
1	$5,559	$5,744	$5,929	$6,114	$6,299	$6,484	$6,669	$6,854	$7,039	$7,224
2	6,296	6,506	6,716	6,926	7,136	7,346	7,556	7,766	7,976	8,186
3	7,102	7,339	7,576	7,813	8,050	8,287	8,524	8,761	8,998	9,235
4	7,976	8,242	8,508	8,774	9,040	9,306	9,572	9,838	10,104	10,370
5	8,925	9,223	9,521	9,819	10,117	10,415	10,713	11,011	11,309	11,607
6	9,946	10,278	10,610	10,942	11,274	11.606	11,938	12,270	12,602	12,934
7	11,046	11,414	11,782	12,150	12,518	12,886	13,254	13,622	13,990	14,358
8	12,222	12,629	13,036	13,443	13,850	14,257	14,664	15,071	15,478	15,885
9	13,482	13,931	14,380	14,829	15,278	15,727	16,176	16,625	17,074	17,523
10	14,824	15,318	15,812	16,306	16,800	17,294	17,788	18,282	18,776	19,270
11	16,255	16,797	17,339	17,881	18,423	18,965	19,507	20,049	20,591	21,133
12	19,386	20,032	20,678	21,324	21,970	22,616	23,262	23,908	24,554	25,200
13	22,906	23,670	24,434	25,198	25,962	26,726	27,490	28,254	29,018	29,782
14	26,861	27,756	28,651	29,546	30,441	31,336	32,231	33,126	34,021	34,916
15	31,309	32,353	33,397	34,441	35,485	36,529	37,573	38,617*	39,661*	40,705*
16	36,338	37,549	38,760*	39,971*	41,182*	42,393*	43,604*	44,815*	46,026*	
17	42,066*	43,468*	44,870*	46,272*	47,674*					
18	48,654*									

*The rate of basic pay for employees at these rates is limited by section 5308 of title 5 of the United States Code to the rate for level V of the Executive Schedule (as of the effective date of this salary adjustment, $37,800).

RETIREMENT INFORMATION

GENERAL REQUIREMENTS
(a) A minimum of 5 years of civilian service is required before annuity is payable in any case.
(b) Except for retirement on account of total disability, any employee must have been subject to the Retirement Act for at least 1 out of the last 2 years before the separation on which the retirement is based.
(c) Public Law 769, 83d Congress (68 Stat. 1142) prohibits payment of annuities to persons who have committed certain specified offenses or acts, mainly in connection with their Federal employment. An employee who is barred by this law may not receive an annuity.

HOW TO FIGURE YOUR RETIREMENT
(a) Take: 1½% of the "high-3" average salary and multiply the result by 5 years of service;
(b) Add: 1¾% of the "high-3" average salary multiplied by years of service between 5 and 10;
(c) Add: 2% of the "high-3" average salary multiplied by all service over 10 years.
Instead of using the 1½%, 1¾%, and 2%, there may be substituted 1% of the "high-3" average salary plus $25 for any or all of these percentages if such a substitution will produce a higher annuity.

within grade, and the waiting period for the next step increase.

6 Internal Revenue Service, "IRS Special Agents — Their 50-Year Saga — 1919 to 1969," mimeographed (Washington, D.C., 1969), no pagination; Internal Revenue Service, "Intelligence Division's First Fifty Years," mimeographed (Washington, D.C., 1969), p. 5; Department of the Treasury, Internal Revenue Service, *Handbook for Special Agents: Intelligence Division,* chap. 9900, reprinted November 15, 1972 (Sec. 256.5), (256.6), (Secs. 271.11 to 272.7); "Recording Devices and Two-Way Mirrors Used in Connection with Internal Revenue Investigations," mimeographed IRS Fact Sheet, August 9, 1965; *Miranda* v. *Arizona,* 384 U.S. 436 (1966); *WSJ,* April 22, 1976.

7 Chommie, *Internal Revenue Service,* pp. 118–126; IRC (Sec. 33), (Sec. 901–905), (Sec. 911); *Annual Report, 1974: Commissioner of Internal Revenue,* pp. 34–35.

8 Terence F. Gastelle to author, November 8, 1974; *NYT,* April 28, 1975; Robert L. Jack, "Man v. Machine . . ." 24 *Journal of Taxation* (May 1966): 308–309.

9 *NYT,* March 14, 1953; Adam Smith, *The Wealth of Nations,* 2 vols. (London and New York: Everyman's Library, 1911), 2:309; *The Challenge of Tax Reform: Proceedings of the Tax Foundation's 24th National Conference* (New York: Tax Foundation, 1973), p. 12; *WSJ,* August 21, 1974; Edmund Wilson, *The Cold War and the Income Tax: A Protest* (New York: Farrar, Straus, 1963), p. 33; William E. Simon, "Statement by the Honorable William E. Simon, Secretary of the Treasury, at the Tax Foundation's 27th National Conference, New York City, December 3, 1975," mimeographed, 9 pp.; E. B. White, "Letter from the East," *New Yorker* (February 24, 1975); *NYT,* February 4, 1973, slightly adapted.

10 Randolph E. Paul, *Taxation for Prosperity* (Indianapolis: Bobbs-Merrill, 1947), pp. 167, 393; Richard Goode, *The Individual Income Tax* (Washington, D.C.: Brookings Institution, 1964), p. 9; *Federal Tax Changes for the Future: Tax Foundation's 21st National Conference* (New York: Tax Foundation, 1970), p. 15; Learned Hand, "Thomas Walker Swann," 57 *Yale Law Journal* (December 1947): 169.

11 *NYT,* March 20, 1958; ibid., April 9, 1958; ibid., May 5, 1958; Paul, *Taxation for Prosperity,* p. 407.

12 *WSJ,* February 12, 1975; Goode, *Individual Income Tax,* p. 72; *NYT,* November 4, 1974; J. Keith Butters, Lawrence E. Thompson, and Lynn L. Bollinger, *Effects of Taxation: Investments of Individuals* (Boston: Harvard University Graduate School of Business Administration, 1953), p. 50.

13 "Statement by IRS Commissioner Donald Alexander, July 1, 1976, to Commerce, Consumer, and Monetary Affairs Subcommittee of House Government Operations Committee at Oversight Hearings on Bank Secrecy and Reporting Act of 1970," (Washington, D.C.: Bureau of National Affairs, 1976, Taxation and Finance no. 128, J-2); *Wealth, Taxation and Fiscal Policy* (Washington, D.C.: National Association of Manufacturers, 1972), p. 2; *Cong. Rec.*, 93rd Cong., 2d sess. (April 2, 1974); *WSJ*, October 20, 1976.

14 For the history of the Ways and Means Committee and how it operates today, see generally John F. Manley, *The Politics of Finance: The House Committee on Ways and Means* (Boston: Little, Brown, 1970). My paragraphs on how tax laws are shaped and passed summarize very briefly the detailed discussions in Joseph A. Pechman, *Federal Tax Policy* (New York: W.W. Norton, 1971), pp. 44–51; and Roy Blough, *The Federal Taxing Process* (New York: Prentice-Hall, 1952), both standard works on the subject. See also Stanley S. Surrey, "The Congress and the Tax Lobbyists — How Special Tax Provisions Get Enacted," 70 *Harvard Law Review* (May 1957): 1145–82; and Mabel Newcomer, "Congressional Tax Policies in 1943," 34 *American Economic Review* (1944): 734–55. Though this article is thirty-two years old and discusses a specific act, the late Professor Newcomer's description of the congressional approach to tax legislation is timeless. The comment of Senator Patman appears in *Cong. Rec.*, 85th Cong., 1st sess. (1957): 6356; and of Senator Long in *NYT*, March 14, 1975; Richard A. Baker, Senate historian, to author, January 22, 1976; U.S. Senate, *History of the Committee on Finance* (Washington, D.C., 1973), pp. 3, 6. The figure for the number of lobbyists in Washington is taken from an advertisement for a reference work, *Washington Influence Directory*, published in *Roll Call,* January 22, 1976.

15 Internal Revenue Service, "The Fight for Integrity: History of the Maintenance of Integrity of the Internal Revenue Service," mimeographed (1965): 4, 7–8; *NYT*, November 17, 1951; ibid., June 30, 1954; and see the *New York Times Index* generally for 1950–1952, 1954; *Hearings Before a Subcommittee of the Committee on Ways and Means, House of Representatives, on Administration of the Internal Revenue Laws*, 82 Cong., 1st sess., part I, p. 271 *passim; NYT*, December 26, 1952; *NYT Magazine* (January 6, 1974): 8; Chommie, *Internal Revenue Service*, pp. 30–31, 185. In connection with the IRS corruption issue, President Truman permitted this direct quotation: "Wrongdoers have no house with me, no matter who they are or how big they are," (*NYT*, December 16,

1951), which recalls an interesting presidential parallel. When the "Whiskey Ring" scandals broke in the mid-1870s, involving collusion of internal revenue officials in the distillation of untaxed whiskey, President U. S. Grant penned the order: "Let no guilty man escape." However, he backed off when his personal secretary was inculpated. It was reported in the mid-1970s that John Dean, the then paranoid Nixon loyalist, had never heard of the King Committee or its work, a reminder of the aphorism that those who do not know history are compelled to relive it.

16 *Annual Report 1975: Commissioner of Internal Revenue,* p. 1; *WSJ,* January 8, 1976.

17 A sampling of information that became public during 1975 regarding improper intelligence activities by the IRS, especially the investigations carried out under the code name, "Operation Leprechaun": popular and sensational accounts appeared in the *NYT,* March 15 and March 28, 1975. A balanced appraisal is *WP,* March 13, 1975. See also Louise Brown, "The IRS: A Troubled Agency," 3 *People & Taxes* (April 1975): 7; ibid., "IRS Created Own Intelligence Group . . . Involved in Federal Surveillance Effort," p. 9. An official report is "Operation Leprechaun," 94 Cong., 1st sess., *Hearing Before the Subcommittee on Oversight of the Committee on Ways and Means, House of Representatives,* December 2, 1975.

18 *NYT,* February 22, 1976; "Auditing the IRS," *Business Week* (September 1, 1973); *WSJ,* January 24, 1974.

19 *WP,* February 16, 1974; Department of the Treasury, Internal Revenue Service, *Audit Technique Handbook for Internal Revenue Agents,* Audit Division IRM 4231 (January 13, 1969); *Annual Report 1974: Commissioner of Internal Revenue* (1975): 18; Donald Smith, "The Creature From I.R.S.," *NYT Magazine* (April 15, 1973); *WSJ,* February 5, 1973; ibid., February 5, 1975; John S. Nolan, "Audit Coverage and Private Tax Planning," 27 *National Tax Journal* (September 1974): 425; ibid. Donald C. Alexander, "What Are the Federal Tax Administrators Doing?" pp. 413, 415; *Audit of Returns, Appeal Rights . . . ,* Terence F. Gastelle to author, April 21, 1975.

20 *WSJ,* April 2, 1974; Internal Revenue Service, "Policies of the Internal Revenue Service Handbook," *IR Manual* (December 5, 1973); *Annual Report of the Commissioner of Internal Revenue for the Fiscal Year Ended June 30, 1947,* p. 22; "Taxes: Tales of the IRS," *Time* (March 12, 1973); Louise Brown, "IRS Goals Hurt Small Taxpayers," 2 *People & Taxes* (July 1974): 3.

21 Louise Brown, "IRS: Providing a Fair Shake for All?" 3 *People &*

Taxes (March 1975): 7; ibid., "Installment Tax Plan," 2:11; ibid., "You Don't Owe IRS?," 2:11.

22 *Election of Small Tax Case Procedure and Preparation of Petitions* (Washington, D.C.: USTC, January 1974), 9 pp.; *Audit Technique Handbook*, IRM 4231 (22)30; Chommie, *Internal Revenue Service*, pp. 54–64. A chart of the appeal procedure appears in Chommie on p. 54 and also in IRS Publication 556, *Audit of Returns, Appeal Rights* . . .; Louise Brown, "IRS: Providing a Fair Shake . . ." p. 7; Stanley S. Surrey and William C. Warren, *Federal Income Taxation, Cases and Materials* (Brooklyn: Foundation Press, 1953), pp. 56–60; *WSJ*, December 17, 1975.

23 Ralph S. Rice, "Tax, Fact and Fiction: Presumptions in Tax Cases," 1 *South Dakota Law Review* (1956): 56–82; Louise Brown, "Tax Court: Help for Small Claims," 2 *People & Taxes* (December 1974): 6–7.

24 Doris, ed., *The American Way in Taxation*, pp. 276–77; Philadelphia *Inquirer*, August 16, 1969; Philadelphia *Evening Bulletin*, August 15, 1969.

15. Grin and Bear It *(pp. 223–236)*

1 *Watts* v. *Indiana*, 338 U.S. 49 (1949) at 52; Interview with Donald C. Alexander, April 22, 1974.

2 Bill Adler, compiler and ed., *Dear Internal Revenue* (Garden City, N.Y.: Doubleday, 1966), pp. 33, 29, 24; Internal Revenue Service, a compilation of taxpayers' responses to IRS contacts, mimeographed (n.p.); Lillian Doris, ed., *The American Way in Taxation: Internal Revenue, 1862–1963* (Englewood Cliffs, N.J.: Prentice-Hall, 1963), p. 271; *NYT*, March 24, 1929; ibid., March 3, 1945; ibid., September 23, 1943; ibid., March 15, 1952. Probably the best excuse for late filing shown by the records is that of astronaut John L. Swigert, Jr., who realized on his way to the moon aboard Apollo 13 that he hadn't filed his income tax. Flight Control laughed and laughed when they heard about it but Swigert insisted, "It ain't funny." Obliging IRS officials produced a loophole: any Tp outside the U.S. on April 15 is automatically granted a two-month extension. For the story see *NYT*, April 13, 1970; ibid., April 14, 1970.

3 *NYT*, May 25, 1973; *WSJ*, April 10, 1974; ibid., February 19, 1975.

4 *NYT*, July 16, 1972; *WSJ*, August 6, 1975; *NYT*, April 11, 1975; ibid., April 16, 1974; *WP*, December 11, 1962, quoted in U.S.

Treasury Department, Internal Revenue Service, "Tax Deduction for Travel & Entertainment Expenses: History from 1930–1964," mimeographed 1 (Washington, 1964), p. 663.

5 Frank Sullivan, *A Pearl in Every Oyster* (Boston: Little, Brown, 1938), pp. 97–100.

6 Will Rogers, "Will Rogers' Illiterate Digest Poll Fair," November 2, 1924, mimeographed, courtesy of Will Rogers Memorial, Claremore, Oklahoma; *NYT*, December 24, 1972; ibid., March 1, 1953; *The Challenge of Tax Reform: Proceedings of the Foundation's 24th National Conference* (New York: Tax Foundation, 1973), comment made in the question-and-answer period, p. 22; *NYT*, March 6, 1955; ibid., March 1, 1953.

7 *NYT*, April 7, 1974; Doris, ed., *American Way*, pp. 266–69.

8 Moss Hart and George Kaufman, *You Can't Take It With You*, (New York: Farrar and Rinehart, 1937), pp. 3, 26–27, 36–37, 39, 203–204.

9 *WP/Potomac*, February 23, 1975; St. Louis *Globe-Democrat*, December 28, 1971; James H. Boren to author, November 7, 1975. Boren has proclaimed April as International Taxpayers' Month, a time when, the veteran Washington gadfly says, all bureaucrats should say "thank you" by taking a taxpayer out to dinner.

10 Dick West, "Slurry Without Fringe on Top," *Roll Call*, December 11, 1975. In another area, that of tax shelters, connoisseurs of fictitious losses will appreciate a tongue-in-cheek article by Professor Boris I. Bittker, in which he contributes to the literature of tax avoidance two memorable if not admirable creations of his imagination, Professor Code, a law professor, and his grasping student, Ransom. See Bittker, "Tax Shelters and Tax Capitalization, or Does the Early Bird Get a Free Lunch?" 28 *National Tax Journal* (December 1975): 416–19. The point? "Before every early bird, there is an earlier bird."

11 *WP*, March 15, 1976.

12 Walter J. Blum, "Tax Trends and Tendencies Today," *Taxes* (August 1974): 466–70; New York *Post*, October 22, 1974; Louise Brown, "Report Asks Low-Cost Tax Counsel," 3 *People & Taxes* (December 1975): 4–5; Thomas F. Field to author, January 26, 1976.

16. Putting It All Together *(pp. 237–253)*

1 *International Encyclopedia of the Social Sciences*, "Taxation"; *WSJ*, May 21, 1975; "Value of the Dollar 1939 vs. 1975," typescript chart (Milwaukee, Wis.: Northwestern Mutual Life Insur-

ance Company): calculations made for the author, January 14, 1976; *WSJ*, May 6, 1975; Milton Friedman, *Monetary Correction: A Proposal for Escalator Clauses to Reduce the Costs of Ending Inflation,* occasional paper 41 (London: The Institute of Economic Affairs, 1974), pp. 9, 13; idem, *There's No Such Thing as a Free Lunch* (La Salle, Ill.: Open Court Publishing, 1975), pp. 3–4; *NYT*, March 23, 1976.

2 James L. Potts, "The Relation of the Income Tax to Democracy in the United States," 11 *Western Political Quarterly* (December 1957): 922.

3 *Cong. Globe*, 39th Cong., 1st sess. (May 7, 1866): 2784; Roy Blough, *The Federal Taxing Process* (New York: Prentice-Hall, 1952), p. 370; Crawford H. Greenewalt, E.I. du Pont de Nemours & Co., "The Effect of High Tax Rates on Executive Incentive," U.S. Congress, Joint Economic Committee, *Federal Tax Policy for Economic Growth and Stability: Papers Submitted by Panelists Appearing Before the Subcommittee on Tax Policy, Joint Committee on the Economic Report, November 9, 1955,* 84th Cong., 1st sess. (1955): 186–87.

4 Thomas H. Sanders, *Effects of Taxation on Executives* (Boston: Harvard University Graduate School of Business Administration, 1951), pp. 12–14, 17–18, 22, 25; J. Keith Butters, Lawrence E. Thompson, and Lynn L. Bollinger, *Effects of Taxation: Investments by Individuals* (Boston: Harvard University Graduate School of Business Administration, 1953), p. 49. For the view that the economic man is not the whole man, see Robin Barlow, Harvey E. Brazer, and James N. Morgan, *Economic Behavior of the Affluent* (Washington, D.C.: Brookings Institution, 1966), pp. 130, 150. The findings of these economists as to how the rich make and manage their dollars, reported in the work last cited, are conveniently summarized in "It's a Fact — the Rich Are Different," *Business Week* (November 26, 1966).

5 George F. Break, "The Effects of Taxation on Work Incentives," *Federal Tax Policy for Economic Growth,* pp. 192–99; Arthur M. Louis, "The New Rich of the Seventies," 88 *Fortune* (September 1973): 170 ff.

6 *International Encyclopedia of the Social Sciences,* "Taxation"; John Kenneth Galbraith, *The Affluent Society* (Boston: Houghton Mifflin, 1958), p. 83; Abraham Lincoln, "Reply to the New York Workingmen's Democratic Republican Association, March 21, 1864," *The Collected Works of Abraham Lincoln,* Roy P. Basler, ed. (New Brunswick, N.J.: Rutgers University Press, 1953), 7:259; Carl Sandburg, *The People, Yes* (New York: Harcourt, Brace & World,

1936), p. 72; *Coppage* v. *Kansas*, 236 U.S. 1 (1915) at 17; George A. Steiner, *Government's Role in Economic Life* (New York: McGraw-Hill, 1953), p. 307; Proverbs, 14:15. "America can be described," wrote Herbert J. Gans in his stimulating book, *More Equality*, "as an unequal society that would like to think of itself as egalitarian": (New York: Pantheon, 1973), p. xi. See also generally Goode, *Individual Income Tax;* C. Lowell Harriss, *The American Economy: Principles, Practices, and Policies* (Homewood, Ill.: Richard D. Irwin, 1953); and Paul A. Samuelson, *Economics,* 8th ed. (New York: McGraw-Hill, 1970), pp. 106–107.

7 Sydney Smith, *The Works of the Rev. Sydney Smith,* 3 vols. in one (New York: D. Appleton and Co., 1865), p. 140; Thomas Sowell, *Say's Law: An Historical Analysis* (Princeton: Princeton University Press, 1972), p. 3; C. Northcote Parkinson, *The Law and the Profits* (Boston: Houghton Mifflin, 1960), p. 5; Paul H. Douglas, *Economy in the National Government* (Chicago: University of Chicago Press, 1952), p. 58. Parkinson's first law was "Work expands to fill the time available."

8 Louis Eisenstein, "The Rise and Decline of the Estate Tax," *Federal Tax Policy for Economic Growth and Stability,* p. 838; Charles Louis de Secondat de Montesquieu: "*Quant les sauvages de la Louisiane veulent avoir du fruit, ils coupent l'arbre au pied, et cueillent le fruit.*" *Oeuvres Complètes de Montesquieu* (Paris, 1846), chap. 13, *Idée du despotisme,* p. 219; *NYT,* January 25, 1976; *Roll Call,* November 20, 1975; *NYT,* May 13, 1975; ibid., May 16, 1976; George Gross, "The Congressional Budget and Impoundment Control Act of 1974: A General Explanation," mimeographed (Washington, D.C., 1975), pp. 1–19 and attachments; *NYT,* October 19, 1975; *WSJ,* March 25, 1976.

9 Friedman, *Free Lunch,* pp. 18–20, 26; United States Senate, *History of the Committee on Finance,* 93rd Cong., 1st sess., Senate Doc. no. 93-9, pp. 83–92; *NYT,* August 18, 1975; Joseph A. Pechman, "The Rich, the Poor and the Taxes They Pay," *The Public Interest* (Fall 1969), quoted in *Cong. Rec.,* 91st Cong., 1st sess., Senate (1969): 32363; *WP,* September 2, 1973. The history, current position, and future options in the administration of the Social Security Act are surveyed in James E. Wheeler, "Social Security — its place in our tax and retirement systems," 7 *The Tax Adviser* (March 1976): 150–56.

10 *WSJ,* March 14, 1972; *WP,* April 28, 1975.

11 *The Challenge of Tax Reform: 1. Why Tax Reform?* (New York: Tax Foundation, 1972), p. 3; "Tax Reform Scores of Senators and Representatives," mimeographed (Washington, D.C.: Taxation

With Representation, 1975), p. 6; *NYT*, March 24, 1973; Walter J. Blum, "The Effects of Special Provisions in the Income Tax on Taxpayer Morale," *Federal Tax Policy for Economic Growth*, p. 252; Joseph A. Pechman and Benjamin A. Okner, *Individual Income Tax Erosion by Income Classes* (Washington, D.C.: Brookings Institution, 1972), p. 30, reprint 230 from *The Economics of Federal Subsidy Programs*, a compendium of papers submitted to the Joint Economic Committee, part I, *General Study Papers*, 92 Cong., 2d sess. (1972): 13–40; Milton Friedman, with the assistance of Rose D. Friedman, *Capitalism and Freedom* (Chicago: University of Chicago Press, 1962), pp. 173–75; Roger A. Freeman, "Tax Loopholes: The Legend and the Reality," 4 *Imprimis* (November 1975): 2; William E. Simon, "Statement by the Honorable William E. Simon, Secretary of the Treasury, at the Tax Foundation's 27th National Conference, New York City, December 3, 1975," mimeographed, pp. 6, 8.

12 *Wealth, Taxation and Fiscal Policy* (New York: National Association of Manufacturers, 1972), pp. 2, 5, 11; Washington *Star*, August 6, 1975, reprint; Boris I. Bittker, "Income Tax 'Loopholes' and Political Rhetoric," 71 *Michigan Law Review* (May 1973): 1122–23; *WSJ*, February 11, 1976; *NYT*, November 30, 1975. In 1975 Taxation With Representation compiled a voting scale to show the interest of members of the Ways and Means Committee in tax reform. On a scale running from zero to 100, the average score was 43. Representative Sam Gibbons (D.-Fla.) was the only member to get a perfect score. Low man was J. J. Pickle (D.-Tex.) with 6. See 4 *Taxation With Representation Newsletter* (June 1975): 1, 3; Goode, *Individual Income Tax*, p. 308; Joseph A. Pechman, *Federal Tax Policy* (New York: W.W. Norton, 1971), p. 52.

13 *United States* v. *Kahriger*, 345 U.S. 22 (1953) at 36; Edmund Burke, *Selected Works*, W.J. Bate, ed. (New York: Random House, Modern Library, 1960), p. 96.

INDEX

Index

(Index prepared by Nancy M. Donovan)